T0000999

MOTHERCOIN

MOTHERCOIN

THE STORIES OF IMMIGRANT NANNIES

ELIZABETH CUMMINS MUÑOZ

BEACON PRESS
Boston

BEACON PRESS
Boston, Massachusetts
www.beacon.org

Beacon Press books
are published under the auspices of
the Unitarian Universalist Association of Congregations.

Hardcover ISBN: 978-0-8070-5119-1 | Ebook ISBN: 978-0-8070-5118-4
Library of Congress Control Number 2021054428

25 24 23 22   8 7 6 5 4 3 2 1

This book is printed on acid-free paper that meets the uncoated
paper ANSI/NISO specifications for permanence as revised in 1992.

Text design by Michael Starkman at
Wilsted & Taylor Publishing Services

All names of the nannies, their families,
and the families they work for have been changed.

For Sofía, Lucas, and Amelie.

And in loving memory of Emma Weaver,

who taught me that there is dignity in this work.

In listening
lies wisdom.

LUIS ALBERTO URREA

from the foreword to
Underground America:
Narratives of Undocumented Lives

Contents

Introduction

PARK BENCHES

What is a mother worth?

Lafayette Park is a small playground tucked into a corner of a Houston neighborhood known for its family-friendly spaces and two-story stucco and brick homes. In the center, an oak tree stretches its branches over the play equipment—an old swing set, a sandbox bordered by stacked wooden logs, a playhouse with stairs worn concave by years of sneakers and sandals and bare feet climbing each rung.[1] The live oak hovers over the place. Older than the climbing ladder or the squeaky swings or the quiet city street beside it, it is a protective presence shielding children from the suffocating heat of a Houston summer or the cold wind of a January afternoon. An old iron bench in the shape of a square surrounds the thickest part of the tree's trunk, so that a tired caregiver, weary of the heat and the sun or the work of the day, might lean back against the oak's rough bark and watch the children play.

On a cool January afternoon several years ago, I took a place on this bench next to a woman I call Sara,[2] and I asked her to tell me about her life. At twenty-five, Sara carries her years heavy on her shoulders. As children in El Salvador, she and her younger sisters watched their mother leave to migrate north for work in the private homes of Texas. At fourteen, she herself left her village and schooling and girlhood behind to follow the same path. For over a decade, she has cleaned the homes of this city, looked after its little ones, walked its dogs. She has missed her own children's school celebrations and after-school homework sessions, and spent long summer days chasing after flushed blond cheeks and picking up shorts and bathing suits from bathroom floors, while her own children waited for her in the care of others—a distracted neighbor, an ambivalent aunt. Sara has bought a house and sent her children to good schools. She has supported her grandparents and younger sister back home for years. And she has asked herself if her mother's choice was the right one. She doesn't think so. There's been so much pain. But then . . . the house, the education, the hope.

After about two hours of conversation, my children and hers begin to whine and call for us. Cheeks chapped, cold burrowing in beneath unzipped jackets and discarded sweaters as the sun falls behind a line of wild ligustrum. Sara's son and daughter climb into an old SUV, mine into a worn minivan, and we each go back to our homes and our dishes and our bills and our laundry, and to the hopes and fears and uncertainties that will carry us into the night. For me, one question eclipses the others: How much is a mother worth?

There are deep and complicated truths at the heart of this question. Some of these have to do with the distance between what a society says about its mothers and how it treats them. Others have to do with the way a culture teaches its children that value is disbursed differently among its various groups—the privileged and the poor, the fair and the dark, the masculine and the feminine—and how those children grow to reproduce the same cultural value system. And some part of the truth of a mother's worth lies deep in her own chest, in the place where a society's words and actions, and a culture's value lessons, meet the truths she alone has come to know. At this meeting place of world and woman, a sense of self emerges. Though I did not know it at the time, when I invited Sara to tell me about her life that day in Lafayette Park, the story she told expressed her own sense of self. Sara's narrative painted the portrait of a woman conflicted, weary, proud, and overwhelmed by the limits placed on all her good intentions—as a caring nanny, a selfless mother, and a dignified worker.

It has been over a decade since I began asking women like Sara for their stories. I've heard many and read many more, each as unique as the woman who told it, yet all of them bound up in the complicated question of value as it pertains to motherhood, domestic work, and the ideological minefields of immigration policy. Despite the women's individual differences, the stories they tell reveal common themes. All must choose among limited options and carry the burden of choice alone. As they live out the consequence of their choices, they all encounter the public lessons that dark-skinned women learn about whose needs come first and that immigrants learn about the power of status to deny basic humanity. And within the private space of homes much like the two-story stuccos that surround Lafayette Park, each woman must negotiate culture and language and intimacy and livelihood in the shadows of an unregulated industry defined by the unique vulnerabilities of paid carework. Together, these common themes tell the story of immigrant nannies in this country.

The mothercoin

Women like Sara and her mother are part of a broad phenomenon of international migration for domestic and carework that has been growing since the end of the last century, spurred by widening global inequality and an increased demand for domestic service in the north.[3] As cleaners and caregivers move from poorer regions into wealthier ones, they leave behind a material and emotional absence that is keenly felt by their families in the global south. North of these borders, children of wealthier regions are bathed and diapered and cared for in clean homes with folded laundry and *sopa de arroz* simmering on the stove, while their parents work ever longer hours and often struggle with these daily separations.

Somewhere in between, women like those featured here fashion a life at the crossroads of globalization, immigration, and the judgments we make about good mothers who stay home and bad mothers who leave. The mothercoin has something to do with these judgments. When love is elevated and labor is compensated, mothering for pay becomes a complicated proposition. Because even as the work of mothering has become valuable currency in the shadow economy of a largely invisible industry, for these women and those who employ them, the cultural ideal of motherhood remains rooted in loving presence and divorced from economic self-interest. In our popular imagination, mothers are somehow always present—loving tirelessly, sacrificing constantly, protecting fiercely, and making the work of housekeeping and family nourishment as neat and invisible as the pressed sheets of a freshly made bed.

The role of the immigrant nanny is to facilitate this ideal, but it comes at a cost. The choices she makes are limited by the realities she encounters—regional inequity exacerbated by globalism and the neo-liberal policies meant to manage it, labyrinthine immigration practices that refuse to account for the reality of "the female underside of global-ization,"[4] and maternity and childcare policies in the US that willfully ignore the social and economic value of childrearing. Fed by the ideolog-ical rhetoric of immigration and "women's work," these broken systems are patched together by a steady stream of migrant women who are told they are responsible for the choices they make—for the desperation that pushes them north, the children whose needs they cannot meet, and the emotional entanglements that compromise their service.

The mothercoin inflicts a real moral harm when it frames the in-evitable conflicts it creates as the result of a personal choice—to make a woman believe it is somehow in her power to protect herself and the children she loves from the pain of her limited options, if only she were good enough to choose differently. It took me a long time to understand that the deepest injustice of the mothercoin lies in the threat it poses to a woman's sense of herself. Many years of research and interviews, read-ing and reflecting, and finally learning to hear the stories the women were telling.

Beside the sandbox

I didn't set out to write this book. In the beginning, it was only conversa-tions on a weekday-morning playground. I would arrive with my young children, in a stroller or on a trike, diaper bag or picnic basket in hand, and set up on a park bench beside the sandbox. My oldest two took after their father, and when I reached for them, the contrast of their chestnut hair and dark skin wrapped up in my fair arms must have been striking to the nannies who watched us. Though a native Houstonian of Euro-pean ancestry, I'd studied Spanish for years and I spoke it fluently and always to the children. It would have been hard for the nannies in the park not to wonder about us, the *americana* on the playground speaking Spanish to Hispanic-looking children. Hard not to glance furtively as I lifted one child into a bucket swing and offered the other a shovel, or to resist the impulse to move a bit closer, smile directly, and open a conver-sation. "¿Son suyos?" they began to ask. "Are they yours?"

As the days passed and faces became more familiar, one question followed another and stories unfolded, relationships formed. The women became more comfortable with me, and their complaints and frustrations began to come out more freely.

The señora doesn't want the girl's clothes to get dirty at the park, can you believe it?

They count my hours like a hawk.

She yells if her child falls. I mean, kids fall down sometimes!

Sometimes, more intimate details emerged.

He wants to drop out of school, what can I do?

Yes, my daughter is still in Mexico; it's been seven years since I've seen her.

I always thought I'd go back home, but now I don't know.

Throughout our conversations, always in Spanish, I remained a curiosity, a sympathetic ear to be sure, but never one of them. I became an important link in a referral network for housecleaners and nannies, an important source of information about navigating our complicated public school system, a landing place for complaints and concerns, and a witness who might hold the possibility of reaching farther than the park's vinyl-coated chain-link fence.[5]

In the mornings, the park. In the afternoons and evenings, I taught Spanish classes and attended graduate seminars at a local university. To cover the hours in between, I hired part-time nannies like the women in the park, and in the wee hours I rocked and nursed and read about Latin American and US Hispanic literature. I learned about the histories of the regions these women came from, the cultural traditions that made their way into books and films, and the traces of indigenous and rural voices long silenced. I encountered the tradition of the testimonial in the work of Elena Poniatowska and others, that genre of *arte comprometida* that seeks to amplify the voices of those marginalized by society. I read John Beverley on Rigoberta Menchú. And I read Gayatri Spivak, who assured me that while the subaltern may speak it will never be my place to speak for her.[6]

The mornings in the park continued, and the nannies' stories took up a place in my awareness that informed my experiences—as a mother, as a teacher, and as a witness to a public discourse that misunderstands so much. Politicians on border walls. Feminists on domesticity. Sound-bites and sitcoms on the moral obligations of mothers and migrants. If only they knew these women's stories the way I do, I thought, the conversation might look different. All of us might get closer to the truth. So, I began to venture a question in my conversations with the nannies I met: "¿No le gustaría hablar un poco, con la grabadora?" Would you like to talk a bit, with a recorder? Some said no. Many said yes.

My various relationships with the women in this book complicate the ideal of a disinterested mediator, but the ideal itself is not uncomplicated. It's true that, for the women who work for people I know, I will never be neutral, always a proxy for the employers on whom they depend in a relationship defined by unequal power and tremendous vulnerability. But it would be foolish to believe that the others—those strangers in the park with tender young charges and curious eyes—ever saw me as anything other than a proxy for their own employers, whether I knew them or not. Women like me, with passports and bank accounts and thirty-five-dollar copays at the pediatrician's office. With friends who are lawyers and faces for whom doors open and trust is extended, whose voices reach beyond tree-lined parks and red-bricked thresholds, over borders and over walls. I could never pretend that these women's stories are anything other than the narrative they choose to present to all those I represent, or that the version of them that unfolds in this book is anything other than a reflection of my own understanding of those narratives. Questions of truth unravel as they submit to revision and mediation. At its best, it is a beautiful violence.

A beautiful violence

This collection of stories and observations is in many ways a narrative of violence. The violence of disruption and coercion runs through the stories of migration as women leave and are left, homes are lost, and borders are cast in fearful shadows. The agents of violence are often faceless—the price of beans, the loss of a way of life, the shaming power of small-town gossip, a hurricane, a political promise. At other times the oppressor can be named—a border agent, an angry *patrona*, the gang members on a street where children once played or a social worker with hard eyes and a rubber stamp. Social class, gender, and race slice across relationships like a blade and constrict like chains, mediating the voices of worker and wife, migrant and mother, and restraining the expression of an interviewee whose words carry across a digital recorder even as she directs them to me. After the talk, I'm the one who takes up the blade. Transcription, translation, selection. All the methodological necessities required to present a conversation in the form of a neat, coherent passage amount to a form of violence, enacted for the sake of a certain textual beauty.

Throughout this book, I have done what I can to present these women's stories as faithfully as they were presented to me. While the explanation of the broader context of their experiences is firmly grounded in extensive research, the events that they recount are the product of the teller's expression and my understanding. The bulk of each story is based on one key interview—conducted at a specific time and place that will have shaped the nature of the telling. A park bench is different from a living room sofa, just as the person one is today is different from who she might have been last week, and different with me from how she might be with another. Each conversation has been fully transcribed into Spanish, a task I shared with a trusted colleague. Armed with years of experience in professional and scholarly translation, I personally translated all portions of the conversations that appear in the book. In selecting the elements of each story to include, I favored narrative over explanation and tried always to honor the story as a whole and avoid the trap of presenting pieces of stories as evidence for a predetermined argument.

To gather and present personal histories without prejudice is challenging, and I don't know how well I've succeeded. Along the way, I have learned that the power embedded in mediation is as inevitable as the translator's will and the editor's blade, and that truth is more subtle than verified events, and far more powerful. I've also discovered an unanticipated beauty in the textual and narrative violence that these stories embody: carework is beautiful because it is love, personal narrative is beautiful because it empowers, and listening is beautiful because it can lead to knowing a person in the fullness of her humanity.

Over the length of the book, the stories of three women unfold as each chapter picks up where the previous left off. Sara, the young mother from El Salvador who sat beside me in Lafayette Park. Rosa, a grandmother from a rural town in Mexico, who has spent a lifetime managing a large family on both sides of the US–Mexico border. And Pati, a young woman from El Salvador whose experiences as a left-behind child and immigrant nanny have her searching for a language of love to name the wounds inflicted by the logic of transaction.

In part 1, "A Toss of the Coin," we meet these women in their home countries and follow their lives until their arrival in the US. Part 2, "The Flip Side," recounts their experiences working as nannies and domestics in this country, and the conflicts generated by their own motherhood. The last part, "Value Proposition," traces the contradictions inherent to the mothercoin as they manifest in the women's own understanding. Several chapters include the stories of additional immigrant nannies, together creating a larger story about vastly different women who navigate the same broad landscape of choice and circumstance.

Throughout, I write of motherhood using certain key terms. In referring to the social role of "mother," I mean a woman who carries full parenting responsibilities for a child.[7] By "mothering," I mean a practice or set of actions that responds both to the emotional bonds formed between mother and child, and also to the ideals of motherhood that circulate in culture and society.[8] Within these mothering practices, I refer to the daily labor necessary to care for dependent children as "mothering work." It is this work of mothering that is extracted as a form of paid labor in the case of the immigrant nanny, though the extraction is hardly clean. The lines between love, labor, and the ideals of motherhood are as undefined as the Sonoran border and as thorny as the south Texas thicket.

When writing about migration—emigrants who leave, immigrants who arrive—language is fraught with ideology, and labels trigger trenches and lines in the sand. *Illegal* carries damaging moral connotations; *alien* denies humanity; *clandestine* connotes shadows; *undocumented* is often inaccurate, and *un-*anything cancels and erases. For the women in this book, the choice is clear: "*con o sin papeles*," with or without papers. When their words are unavailable, I will use *unauthorized*—not criminal or alien, but subject to a particular kind of authority.

A final note on the morality of pronouns. Throughout these pages I use the first-person plural—*we, us, our*—to appeal to a reader whose place in this narrative may not at first be evident. In truth, we all have a part to play in this tale, because the mothercoin's story is bigger than any one worker or her employer. It spills out of the bounds of strollers and parks and porch screen doors, sweeping the political up into the personal as it reveals these women's private solutions to broad public problems that are very much *ours*. On the one hand, a global economy fueled by the demands of social structures that ignore the value and substance of childrearing. On the other, ideological rhetoric that appeases anxieties by vilifying the immigrant "other" and elevating an impossible ideal of motherhood.

As long as we tell ourselves that this is someone else's story, immigrant nannies and their children will remain in the shadows, bearing the weight of these unsustainable systems on their backs. You can hear it in the stories they tell.

MOTHERCOIN

PART I

A TOSS
OF THE COIN

All these years, I told her, it's like I've been circling beneath a giant,
my gaze fixed upon its foot resting at the ground. But now,
I said, it's like I'm starting to crane my head upward,
like I'm finally seeing the thing that crushes.

FORMER BORDER PATROL AGENT

FRANCISCO CANTÚ[1]

Prelude

There is a singular thread that connects the unassuming bench at Lafayette Park to the distant villages and neighborhoods of Mexico, Central America, and beyond. It's a fine line stretched taut by need and desperation and regional economies that generate both deprivation and abundance. On one end of the line, poverty and insecurity in the global south. On the other end, busy professionals in the global north, with children to tend and laundry to wash and meals to make. Over time, this thread has been woven into a complicated tapestry of economic, political, and social interactions that spreads out over the space between here and there and defines a landscape of limits and possibilities for women like Sara and her mother. Across miles and generations, the needle weaves and lives unfold, forcing hard choices and dangerous journeys. From the north, a pull. From the south, a push.

In poorer regions of the global south, broad global economic restructuring in the latter half of the twentieth century has exaggerated existing inequality, leaving the most vulnerable populations struggling for material survival.[2] As countries worked to compete in a global economy, they acquired increasing debt and shaped their economic policy ever more narrowly toward export-oriented industries and social austerity. Subsistence and small local farming gave way to large-scale agriculture and rapid industrialization; export processing zones created *maquila* factories with little to no worker protections and broad exemptions from

3

local taxes; and state funds were diverted away from social services—education, housing, healthcare.

As economies strain and infrastructures break down, communities become vulnerable to malice and misfortune. In the context of historically continuous corruption among politicians and law enforcement, transnational criminal organizations have gained strength in Mexico and Central America, ratcheting up violence in the region and empowering local gangs.[3] At the same time, weather events in Central America and the Caribbean have intensified the desperation. Hurricanes and earthquakes have killed thousands and devastated fragile economies. Droughts and flooding have threatened food security, leaving these regions less able to support their populations. Meanwhile, US immigration policies intended to alleviate the strain yield to shifting political will.[4]

These powerful push factors have unfolded within profoundly patriarchal cultures, especially in rural communities, that place many women and girls in danger of abuse and all of them subject to limited power and oppressive shame. Abandonment by husbands has long been common in many of these communities and can be accelerated by migrating fathers whose letters and remittances slowly diminish. Abandoned or not, patriarchy is clear about the place of a woman in society: to nourish, comfort, guide, and serve her family. When men desert their families, when wage-earning work is out of reach and mothers must compensate for the failure of social structures, a woman's options are few. The south squeezes, the north tugs.

In the global north, social and economic shifts have created heightened demand for the kind of work migrant women can provide. In a broad demographic shift of this same late-twentieth-century period, women from middle and upper classes increasingly entered the professional workforce, leaving their homes and children in need of care. At the same time, as globalization widened the gap between wealthy regions and poor ones, a lifestyle developed among the professional classes of newly global cities, supported by robust service sectors that made it possible to hire others to manage personal tasks, from maids and nannies to personal shoppers and dog walkers.[5] For many women from the global south, with shrinking options and increasing responsibility to provide for their families, the pull of good-paying, available work in the north has become a singular face of hope.

In Central America and especially in Mexico, hope has long been fed by stories told by visiting and returning migrants. Wages that those back home could never dream of, safe streets, *comadres* with money in their pockets and power in their step. An aunt in Houston, a friend in LA, a distant cousin in North Carolina, a couch to rest on after the journey. And when the sun comes up to chase away the tug and pull of those you've left behind, a referral network of employers to tap into. Within two weeks you could be sending money home to them all. *Imagínate.* Just one crossing away. For those with connections, cash, and the social capital to open the right doors, the gravity of emigration lies in the future that awaits. For others, it's the crossing itself that looms large, a dangerous journey across hostile borders defined by laws and practices that change as often as the shifting economic and political winds.

A push, a pull, a debt incurred. One last goodbye, and a toss of the coin.

CHAPTER 1

MOTHERLAND

We depended on her.
She was our sustenance.

SARA

Sara

Eight-year-old Sara stood close to her two younger sisters and listened carefully to their mother's announcement: "I'm leaving," she began. "I'm going for three years, just long enough to get us running water." Sara was the oldest and she understood better than the other two what those words meant for their family. It wasn't the first time their parents had gone away in search of work. It had cost them all so dearly before. More than two decades later, Sara would sit beside me on a mild January afternoon, tuck a strand of dark hair behind her ear, and begin her tale with wide eyes and a lilting voice.

"I'm from a very poor place in the department of San Miguel, in the foothills of the Chaparrastique volcano, the biggest volcano in Central America. We were from a very poor family, so poor that we didn't have electricity. Where we're from, cars don't even come, we have to do everything walking. The nearest town is like two and a half hours away, walking."

In the early 1990s, when Sara's parents first left their small *cantón*—a handful of dwellings where Sara spent her childhood—the region still bore the scars of the traumatic decade that came before. A brutal civil war had ravaged the people and the land and left the country with a ruined infrastructure, unresolved political conflicts, and a good chunk of its population self-exiled to the safety and economic promise of the US.

"My dad was a guerrillero. He's handicapped now. He lost a hand in the war. After the war, the whole country, our cantón . . . Well, the war affected us a lot. All this, my mom and dad leaving, that was after the war. But even so, the country was never the same."

Though she may not carry memories of the fighting, the legacy of the Salvadoran civil war is an intimate part of Sara's immigrant story. The violence that raged in the 1980s between her country's US–trained military dictatorship and its Marxist-inspired insurgent guerrilleros produced a large-scale exodus of migrants whose northward flight engendered an ideological maneuver that denied political asylum to the refugees.[1] As a result, a generation of Salvadoran and Guatemalan war refugees became "illegal aliens" and moved into a civic life barred from access to legitimate employment or social support.

From one generation to the next, a certain chain of cause and effect unfolded. Some consequences were unforeseen, like the emergence of the Mara Salvatrucha and Barrio 18 gangs on the streets of LA and the transnational criminal networks their deported brothers in arms would create.[2] Others, like generational poverty and negative health outcomes, were as predictable as the disillusionment of a fourteen-year-old girl who would arrive in *el norte* only to discover that her new home did not want her.

At eight years old, Sara might not have understood the ideologies that fueled her country's war-torn past or the transnational dominoes that fed its violent present, but she sensed a certain connection at work between her father's mangled hand and her own intimate experience of poverty in rural El Salvador.

"Before my mom migrated to this country, we didn't have running water. The water that we used was when it rained. We would put a container out to collect the rainwater. There were times when we'd go a week without bathing, not until it rained again. When we didn't have anything to eat, we'd hunt iguanas. We'd eat those, and rabbits, *gosucos*—they're like little turtles; and sometimes we'd go out to look for corn. Like when other people in a better economic situation would harvest their corn, we would go and gather up whatever fell on the ground. We were very poor, not even a few coins for school clothes. My grandmother, she would take one big skirt and make three little ones out of it.

"My mom saw all that poverty and one day she got an opportunity, so she said, 'I'm going. I'm going to leave my daughters and I'll be back soon. I'll just go long enough to get running water for my mom.' So my mom came here to change her life and ours."

Like hunting iguanas and gathering the leftovers of a neighbor's harvest, migration was a family survival strategy, and Sara's parents called on the strategy more than once.[3] The first migration only got them as far as Guatemala. That was the first goodbye.

Sara's parents found work in Guatemala's manufacturing sector, earning enough to send money regularly to the waiting children and their grandparents. But those six months of separation left an indelible mark on the family that would forever link migration to loss.

"My little sister got sick with a fever that never got better," Sara explains. "When my mom got back, she tried to take her to doctors and everything. They never discovered what it was. A year after she got sick, my little sister died. She died when she was four years old. It was because she was so sad, *de tristeza mi hermana se enfermó*." As she speaks these last words, Sara's voice is muted, her hands as quiet on her lap as those of a six-year-old girl who has just learned that the sadness of separation can be deadly.

Back in their rural cantón, the problems of survival persisted. Food, running water, hope. For Sara's family, providing this sustenance meant separation across the kind of distance that fills a child's heart with sadness. So their father packed his bags again, taking his broken heart and lame hand back north to find work in the US. The family he left behind now included a new baby girl. Three years later, when Sara's father sent for her mother to join him, Sara knew it was her job to protect the young girls at her side. "I was the oldest. I was the one who took care of my two little sisters."

That was the second goodbye.

"Three years," her mother had promised. "Three years, and I'll be back."

When Sara's parents migrated north to try their luck in the informal service economy of the US, she and her sisters joined countless children in countries all over the developing world—from the Philippines to Sri Lanka to Tunisia and Grenada—whose family life is defined by distance. They become left-behind children in transnational families, and their stories reveal the other side of globalization's social transaction: beneath the immaterial networks of free-flowing capital and lightning-fast information, very real bodies work in concrete locales to reproduce community and domestic infrastructure in our globalized world.

This is the underbelly of globalization's vast economic and informational networks. But from the perspective of a child whose parents have migrated for work, such interconnectedness is overwhelmed by distance. Very little that mattered to Sara and her sisters flowed freely from one region to another. For these left-behind sisters, the barriers were as real as the letters they waited for and the far-away deserts they imagined. It all played out in the stories they heard, and those they choose to tell.

It was 1993 when Sara's mother, Ana, made her first trip to the US, and in Sara's story, her mom's journey was arranged by a Salvadoran coyote who promised her she would fly.[4]

"She met a coyote who said she wouldn't walk, she'd come by plane. So she got to Mexico, and when she was going to cross the border at Matamoros, she broke her hand running from immigration. She broke her hand and everybody went running, so the group left her there. She was lost in the desert. She almost died, from dehydration, from no food. Until a man who was in the desert too found her and helped her. He said he would come back for her, and he came back at night and helped her across. She ended up in California."

The whole journey took three months, the way Sara tells it.

But Matamoros isn't really a desert. This urban slice of Tamaulipas, Mexico, part of the large subtropical metropolitan hub it forms with neighboring Brownsville, gives way to a Rio Grande fertile with cultivated land to the north. And Border Patrol agents don't chase would-be immigrants on the southern side of the border, while angels of mercy like Border Angels and Humane Borders give water and medical aid, not help across the border.[5] If this all happened in South Texas, where Sara's mother just might have been, Operation Rio Grande would not yet have gone into effect, pushing hopeful would-be migrants away from fortified urban entry points into a brush thick with thorny limbs and cacti. If it was indeed the desert, she was most likely diverted there by a hired guide who knew well enough to stay away from the newly fortified thoroughfares of El Paso and Nogales, where twenty-four seven surveillance had begun to drive migrants into the desert.[6]

Whether Sara's mother encountered hope and desperation in South

Texas or some point to the west, the details matter less to her left-behind child's tale. Either way, Ana must surely have almost died, and the angel with water must surely have delivered her somehow to safety. In Sara's shared memory of her mother's crossing, what matters are the truths she weaves into her own story of their family's transnational unfolding: Her mom's journey was long and hard and she almost died. Bad people left her behind, good people helped when she needed it the most, and in the end she made it to Texas, like a dream.

Back in the shadows of Chaparrastique, life was not so dreamy for eight-year-old Sara and her sisters, six and two. Cared for by their maternal grandparents, the family lived as best they could with the help of monthly remittances sent from Sara's parents in Texas. Together across borders, they found ways to make ends meet.

"We depended on her," Sara would say to me decades later under a blue Texas sky. "She was our only sustenance."

She, Sara says, *ella.* Though her father must surely have been working by her mother's side, Sara remembers only a feminine sustenance, an extension of Mamá's mothering at home. Even across the landscape of memories and adult understanding, Sara's past continues to be the story of mothers.

"When you don't grow up with a person," she considers, "you love her, but it's not the same as when you're with her. I adored my mom. I wanted to see her. I only saw her in pictures. We didn't talk, either, because at that time telephones weren't so common. It was just letters, *puras cartas.* You had to wait a month before you could hear from a person."

Over a separation that stretched out the length of a girlhood, the sisters' relationship with their mom played out in letters and pictures that arrived weeks after they were written. In transnational families like theirs, relationships and loyalties persist across the distance as letters and visits and phone calls and photos maintain the substance and ideal of family. But roles like "mother" and "daughter" take on new meanings.[7] Where once a mother's work, love, and impulse to protect and provide were bound up together in day-to-day acts of care, now these commitments unravel. For Sara in the early 1990s, with no telephone or blue screens or frozen stills of life in America, the idea of *mamá* and *el norte* was left to the imperfect understanding of a child's imagination, fed by the poverty of words on a sheet of paper—and promises that multiplied.

"I'll only go for three years, *mis hijas*. Just long enough to give *abuela* running water."

"I'll visit next year, I promise."

"Next year for Christmas. I'll be there at Christmas."

"Next year, *m'ija*, next year."

"She never returned again," Sara tells me, her black eyes still and un-yielding, "*ella no volvió otra vez.*" The *no* is strong and high-pitched, the final word sharp on her closed lips. She holds my gaze through her lovely round face and waits for her story's dramatic effect. *This is true*, her pause insists, *feel it before I go on.*

Sara's mother would never live in El Salvador again, and in the many years between Ana's last visit as an absent parent and her first as a nostalgic emigrant, the girls would give up on the dream of a family whole and together. Both Sara and her middle sister would one day make their own lives far to the north of their Salvadoran cantón. By that time, all of them had come to accept that some promises were made to be broken.

There was a lot that the girls didn't understand about the circumstances of their parents' migration—why mom and dad couldn't find work at home with them, and why they had to endure the kind of absence that can make a little girl die of sadness. But the greatest mystery was the nature of the distance that separated them from their mother.

"We never believed that my mom was telling us the truth," Sara tells me. "We thought it was that she didn't want to come. We thought that this place, America, was like in El Salvador, where I would go to the capital and the next day I could come back to my house again. That's what we thought."

For Sara and her sisters, their parents' *viaje* meant a trip, not a voyage. So when Ana's weary voice assured them over the telephone, "Next year for Christmas, girls, I promise," the girls imagined their mother no more than a day's journey away, and they wondered what it would take—if not Christmas, if not them—for her to return.

Many years removed from that history of longing, Sara would come to see this part of her childhood from a different perspective. In a modest apartment in Houston, Texas, in close proximity to her own two children, she would reflect on the poverty she had lived and forgive her mother's painful choices. By the time Sara and I come together one winter morning in 2010, she has learned to judge her mother's choices from both points of view.

Her younger sister, Maribel, has not been so understanding.

"This is what happens when people from countries like El Salvador come to the US and leave their children behind," Sara explains. "They suffer a lot, because there are some children who never forgive."

Rosa

"I don't know if God forgot about us," Rosa sighs. "The hard weather dried up the corn fields, and now there are no fields at all to work." She shakes her head and looks down at a hand laid flat on the table before her, thick knuckles and long fingers stretched thin with copper-colored skin, one circled by a gold band. She sits across from me at my own kitchen table, and we talk during a stolen hour between our morning's work and the rush of after-school pick-up. My three-year-old daughter plays in the next room, her songs and games weaving in and out of the story Rosa tells about four decades of mothering and loving across a divided border.

"My parents were peasants, *campesinos*," she explains. "At that time, there was land, but not anymore. Not even my mom is alive anymore."

Though her parents had spent a lifetime working the fields of Puebla's rich central Mexican valley, their way of life had been erased in the years since Rosa's birth, a casualty of climate and a changing industry—farmers with bigger machines and headquarters far removed from the fertile terrain she'd known.[8] And so, sometime in the 1970s, Rosa found herself making ends meet alone in Puebla with five small children and a husband earning American wages in Los Angeles. Rosa looked around at the barren fields that surrounded her parents' rural rancho, a cluster of modest homes and small farming plots just big enough for subsistence agriculture or for selling at a Sunday market, and she understood that a certain way of life had been lost.

But Rosa was not one to cry over what couldn't be changed, and she never would be. She considered herself lucky to have a man who could be counted on to look out for her and the kids, and she set about doing whatever it took to raise up her brood and enjoy life in the living. Others weren't so fortunate, she knew. Rosa assures me that many a man from her world wasted his chance in the US. She had seen it all too often.

"So many I know come here to drink and chase after women. They end up not making anything of it. Then, there are the ones who abandon their wives. They leave them there alone with the kids, and the women have to look for someone new."

Rosa's husband, Arturo, remained loyal, which was as much as she ever asked. She laughs as she explains herself, her bright green eyes set off by dark-blue eyeliner and a delicate web of thin lines. "Men aren't exactly saintly. You don't have to make a saint out of a man, as long as he doesn't forget about you."

Rosa's man never forgot. When he was able, he sent his remittances and she paid the rent, bought the food, and focused on raising her kids. When he came up short, she found a way. Several months into Arturo's first migration, the money stopped coming for three long months. But Rosa managed, as she always would. She raised chickens on her own small square of rented land and found what work there was to find, taking in laundry from more affluent neighbors.

"I washed and ironed laundry for neighbors. Chietla is a big town where there are engineers who earn money, and I worked for those people. You find a way to survive when you want to. Just saying to yourself, 'I don't have enough food to eat,' you've got to find a way to get out there and find it."

But no matter how hard she worked, there were never enough jobs to really get ahead. And though the family could usually count on beans and tortillas and a roof over their head, they could never earn enough in Mexico to make something of themselves, never enough to eat well, *comer bien*.

"Rosa," I ask her, "before you left to come here, did the children suffer from hunger?"

"Well, they weren't starving, no, because there were always beans to eat, the basics—beans, chiles, and tortillas. But they didn't eat well, *no comían bien*."

I'm reminded of Sara's description of her own childhood poverty, how she spoke of hunger in the same way. "They call it 'eating fried,'" Sara explained. "*Comer frito*, like with oil. Because if you ate fried it meant you had a little money. We had to wait a long time to eat something that had been cooked in oil. My mom left us so that we could eat well."

Though miles and years apart, Sara and Rosa both speak a similar language of hunger and hope. In this story of poverty that Rosa and so many like her tell, to be poor in the sense that Rosa and her children experienced it is not so much to be deprived of basic food and shelter, but to live a poverty of hope. With good health, hard work, and a lot of luck, a person might find a way to scrape by—collect eggs from the hen in the yard, take in a neighbor's wash. But to get ahead, *salir adelante*, means more than just surviving. The hope of making something of yourself requires a world that is safe enough and predictable enough to be able to set a goal and achieve it. It's about education and clean clothes and order in the streets, a child's dreams for the future, and the enduring value of cash stowed away under a mattress.

But hope doesn't put dinner on the table, and for Rosa and the kids there were times when even beans and tortillas were hard to come by. During the three months that she spent without her husband's remittances, she had to work hard just to find a way to keep her children sheltered, clothed, and fed. "When my husband didn't send me anything for three months—well, you find a way to survive if you want it. There are ways, but not many, not many."

And Rosa wasn't alone. An older neighbor lady who sold food and snacks in town took Rosa under her wing. The industrious woman enjoyed a steady income from her sale of burritas at the local market. Even into her sixties, Rosa would recall the taste of the crunchy gorditas the woman made, deep-fried cornmeal and spiced relleno, savory and rich and hot with the kind of oil Sara and her family would wait years to taste.

The burrita-maker looked out for her young neighbor. "Güera," she called out one day to Rosa, green-eyed and fair among her mestizo neighbors, "Come toast this maní." So Rosa entered into a kind of street vendor's apprenticeship, roasting seeds and nuts on hot metal racks by the older woman's side. In return, she received a cut of the sales. And in the evenings, the neighbor would often call again: "Güera! I have leftover burritas. Do you want any?" Rosa holds her hands out in front of her, palms up and curved, "Plates this big, filled with gorditas that she gave me, that my kids would eat."

But Rosa's work with the burrita-vendor took time away from her mothering. The extra washing and ironing and the seed-peddling competed with the cooking and the cleaning at home, so many small bodies to tend to and nourish. In Rosa's world, a mother's work undone became the responsibility of the oldest daughter, so it fell to a child, not yet ten years old, to prepare the beans and wipe the sniffles and weave the braids.

"Why me?" Rosa's daughter would ask. "Why am I the one who has to do it?" Rosa knew the answer, though she couldn't really explain it to the girl. *It's what we do*, she would have had to respond, knowing, in her woman's way, that the work of hearth and home is the work of women. It's what she had always been taught, and she had lived the consequences of this lesson long enough to accept it without questioning. So, when her daughter, yet unschooled in the ways we teach our girls to serve, asked, "Why me?" what answer could Rosa have given if not simply, *Because it's what we do*?

"The oldest ones always suffer the most," Rosa laments, her expression passing from laughter to regret, "in everything, Elizabeth, in everything."

In time, Rosa's husband Arturo found his way back to monthly remittances and regained his footing as family provider. "I don't want you to work anymore," he told Rosa. "Just focus on the kids and I'll send you what you need." Rosa was happy to comply and Arturo came through for her, as he always would. His monthly sums arrived on time, regular and just enough for food and rent—but only ever just enough. When he came back to visit, he didn't bring anything more than the shirt on his back. Not a dime in a bank account or hidden away in his bags.

"When he was over there, he always worked. And he was sending me money. I paid the rent and we ate really well. We didn't go without for anything. He was sweet with the children, with me. I never hurt for money when he was working, but when he'd come home, he never brought any money with him."

Rosa had considered the situation, the man and the family and what it would take for them all to make something of themselves, and it became clear to her that just enough was all her husband would ever provide if he were left to it on his own.

"What did you even bother going for?" she confronted. "I mean, it's true I never went without when you were sending us money, but you don't have anything to show for it!" Her voice is as high and shrill in her reenactment as it must have been thirty years earlier when she stood before Arturo, increasingly resolute, and declared, "That's it. I'm going back with you."

Arturo protested, defending his role as provider, but in the end, Rosa's logic won out. "Raro es el hombre que, solo, haga dinero," she tells me. "A man who can make good money on his own is rare."

As a left-behind wife, Rosa had worked to fulfill what she felt was her mothering role in her large family. She'd kept the family together by physical care and apron strings and all the side hustles she could scrounge, and set them on a path of hope for something better by managing her husband's northern earning potential. Choosing to follow Arturo to Los Angeles was a logical next step, a pragmatic response to the way she approached her family role: it was her job to ensure that they survived and thrived, together. The distance that would now separate her from her children fell into a familiar framework, a culture of migration and divided families born of the long-standing history of Mexico–US migration. For Rosa, and scores of Mexican mothers like her, migration meant an expansion of the geography of family.

Within the year, Rosa set out to meet Arturo in Los Angeles. When she said goodbye, she left behind a trail of children, ages ten, eight, six, four, and two. They would live with Rosa's mother and father on the rancho, a little community set miles from the city where school met once a week or so, and everyone had someone up north throwing them a lifeline. For three years, the children studied little and were loved deeply while they ate beans and tortillas and the fried treats their parents' wages afforded them. For three years, they waited for their parents to return packing Levi's and Nikes and pockets full to bursting with enough American dollars for all of them to make something of themselves, never imagining what else their mother would carry when she made her way back to them for good.

Pati

"My father abandoned us when I was five years old. That's why my mom had to emigrate."

Pati sits across from me on a neutral-colored sofa in her tasteful living room, her words soft and searching. In a voice as graceful as her almond-shaped eyes and auburn hair, pulled loose and low at the nape of her neck, she explains away the logic of every circumstance that wounded her, even as her body tells a different story marked by absence and loss.

"It made sense," she reasons. "You can't live on love. You can't survive on love alone."

At thirty-one years old, Pati is worlds away from that first abandonment, and worlds away from the small town in El Salvador where she grew up. Born in 1980, the same war-torn year in which Archbishop Romero was gunned down at the altar and four churchwomen were raped and murdered by the National Guard, Pati began her life in a society marked by violence and misogyny.[9] For resisters like Romero and the Maryknoll nuns, it meant brutal repression. For a child like Pati, it meant a father's flight and a mother's hard choice.

When Pati's father left, it fell to her mother, María, to support the family alone in a shrinking employment landscape. For a year, she struggled to earn enough for her young family. Her options near home were few. At that time, most of the available work in their small town of Santiago Nonualco was agricultural—yucca, maize, coffee—but small farms were on the decline. The state had turned its economic strategy to export industries, and maquiladora factories had begun to bubble up not too far from Pati's town.

Pushing out toys and clothing made in El Salvador and destined for a North American market, these factories feed on foreign capital, foreign materials, and low-wage locals who assemble, pack, and ship products back out to foreign markets, leaving little economic gain behind other than subsistence wages for a rotating door of workers—mostly young women, often single mothers, who are easily subdued, easy on the eyes, and willing to make 68 percent of their male coworkers' salaries. Routine sexual harassment and regular pregnancy tests keep their bodies and their fertility in check; desperation and an ample supply of replacement workers keep their mouths shut.[10]

Amid these shrinking options, Pati's mother, María, settled on emigration as a family survival strategy. By the time Pati was six years old, she had seen enough to understand two important truths: that she had been born into a place where men leave and women and children suffer in their absence, and that a family of five can't survive on love alone.

"As a little girl, I was very mature for my age. I think I understood. It was necessary, it made sense. There was no father in the family. She was mother and father both for us, the one who provided everything. We needed food, and that's what my mom provided for us. She made us see that. My mother never neglected us."

Pati never doubted her mother's devotion, and despite what she has since come to understand about the afterlife of absence, she insists that she never felt neglected. Every month without fail, María sent the children money and letters, her heartfelt commitment pressed onto the page and slipped between the pale green colones her wire transfers produced at the local *casa de crédito*. This love language reached over miles and borders and a child's confusion to mark Pati's emotions with conflict: she believed in her mother's commitment, but she ached for the affection she missed as she and her siblings passed from one relative's home to another.

"First, I was with an uncle, my mother's brother, and then an aunt. Then, she got married, so we went with another aunt. My aunts, they were young and a little irresponsible, so then we went to live with my grandmother. But nothing was the same." Her voice is heavy with emotion as she repeats, "Nothing was the same."

Even Pati with her six small years of memory could see that nothing would ever be the same again. It wasn't just the hugs and the kisses they were missing; it was real life lessons, like how to manage their mother's hard-earned remittances. "We were responsible for our own spending, and for a little girl of eight or ten, it was hard to be responsible about spending money."

In the end, they got by. Despite their empty pockets at the end of the month, their grandparents' home gave them access to orchard and garden, abundant in those fertile volcanic fields. "We had fruit and everything, what my grandparents grew, so you survive how you can. But no, it wasn't easy. It wasn't easy at all for us. We were three girls and a boy and there was no one responsible to lead the family."

In this and so many other ways, Pati experienced her mother's role in the family in terms of what was missing—the lessons her mother wasn't there to teach, the protective presence she could not provide. All of it, the private consequence of a landscape of choice shaped by global economies, broad cultural forces that define a mother's role, and US approaches to border enforcement that changed with the passing winds of boom, bust, and political orientation.

Each time Pati's mother María came home to visit, the trip back north meant crossing the same clandestine borders that had almost swallowed Sara's mother, Ana. María made four crossings in all: First, when Pati was six; then, when she was eight; then at ten; and the last time, after spending a year at home only to leave again after Pati's quinceañera. By that time, María's son and daughters had grown from small children into young men and women, and the crossings had become more burdensome. It was 1995, in the middle of the 1990s' border fortification period, and already the national divide had acquired miles of military-grade lights and sensors, barbed wire and sheet metal and wire-framed screens scratched out across brush and desert. As the border acquired its muscle and the coyotes' fees increased, María knew that it might not be possible to return again.

When Pati was twenty years old, her mother acknowledged the truth. "I won't be able to come back," she told Pati.

By then, the oldest two siblings had already made the move to join their mother in Houston. For Pati, it would take longer than it had for the others. Her decision to migrate would form over time, as she moved about the streets of Santiago Nonualco with a slow-growing loneliness inside. It was the kind of lonely that seeps into a young woman's heart and takes up residence, waiting for the right sort of caress to brush the pain away. She could not have known that the embrace she waited for would come wrapped up in fair skin, clear eyes, and small American arms.

As Pati and the others look northward, two forces that drive the mothercoin converge: Migration as a particularly feminine survival strategy, and a culture of migration powerful enough to cast the proposition as a singular face of hope. Part of a shift so pronounced in the latter part of the last century that it has been called a "feminization of migration," this broad flow of women moving from south to north reflects a unique value proposition.[11] For global markets, the women bring a softer hand to dust a shelf, to hold an infant, to tuck a child into bed. For sending communities, they carry with them an enduring responsibility for the families they leave behind.

Unlike the fathers, uncles, and grandfathers who went before them, these women carry their family roles deep within—mother, sister, daughter, aunt. Their migration is so often a choice for and of family, to support those left behind and to join those gone before. The move becomes a collective survival strategy that responds to the uniquely feminine burden of reproducing hearth and home in a society that lacks the basic structures to sustain that home.[12]

In heading north, this strategy becomes a leap of faith, part of a culturally curated narrative of promise for a better future that has been fed by generations of those who've gone before: to make something of oneself, to eat well, to lift a family up to hope. For Pati, Sara, Rosa, and others, that promise will carry them over hundreds of miles of roads and rail and shoreline and brush. Along the way, the life they knew at home will recede into the stories they tell about a time before, and the future that awaits them will unfold on the other side of a line drawn long across the land.

CHAPTER 2

CROSSING OVER

I came across three times.
Like the song, "Tres veces mojada."

ROSA

Sara

"I want to go over there, with you."

At fourteen years old in her rural cantón in El Salvador, Sara decided she had lived long enough without the mother who left six years before. It was 1999, and by then the telephone had bridged some of the silence between the two, so she was able to hear her mother's voice when Ana answered, "You're just a girl. The journey is too dangerous."

But in the end her mother agreed, and Sara hung up the phone one step closer to soothing the left-behind wanting that fueled her resolve and filled her head with imagined futures. At fourteen, somewhere between girl and woman, she was still young enough to believe that everything she did could be undone.

Shortly after the phone call, Sara found herself hugging her grandparents and little sisters goodbye and setting out for Texas with her mother's close friend by her side. The pair traveled for a month before they arrived at the US–Mexico border crossing at Brownsville, Texas. In all that time, they were never separated and they never lost sight of the forces that guided them—faith in the promise of migrant hope and trust in the skills of their coyote. For three thousand US dollars each, the women were directed through clandestine pathways familiar to the network of hired guides that led them. At each border, they were passed over to another set of hands—the Salvadoran who took them to Guatemala, the Guatemalan who brought them into Mexico, the Mexican who delivered them across the Rio Grande. At each transition, there was nothing for it but to hope and trust.

Both the hope and the trust were part of a larger story that carried Sara along, as it had done for her mother and countless others before her. Over years of sending members north in search of work and security, communities like Sara's have fashioned a familiar narrative that fuels the faith. Long treks over desert-like terrain, running blindly under cover of dark, the pervasive threat of rape, robbery, death but—always—hope. Overwhelming hope. Because the stories that reach would-be migrants are so often told by the ones who make it, the ones who send money home, who visit with gifts and anecdotes and bags filled with hand-me-downs from a señora's overstuffed closets.

Trust in one's guide is a more complicated affair. Charging a flat fee to lead hopeful migrants across the border and beyond its last checkpoint, the coyote (also known as a *pollero* or *patero* in some places) promises a nuanced understanding of the shifting landscape of criminality and bribery along the migrant trail, and skillful navigation of the unwritten rules along the 1,900-mile-long border. These guides—embedded within migrant communities, and often a relative or family friend of the travelers who hired them—have historically relied on mutual trust and familiarity with their clients, but such trust has been strained by a late-twentieth-century increase in the stakes and the violence of the migrant proposition.[1]

Responding to a marked rise in migration from Mexico, reform efforts of the 1980s and 1990s led to a transformation of the US–Mexico border: High-traffic entry points in Texas, California, and Arizona quadrupled their agents and equipped them with twenty-four-hour high-tech surveillance. The Immigration Reform and Control Act (IRCA) of 1986 increased the funding directed to border security by billions of dollars,[2] enabling a series of "operations" that acted as a virtual wall—from Hold the Line in El Paso, to Gatekeeper in San Diego, Safeguard in Nogales, and Rio Grande in South Texas.[3] As a result, traditional entry points became impassable, and hopeful migrants turned toward more extreme routes through arid lands and hostile terrain, rendering the coyote's services indispensable, and far more costly.

At the same time, growing cartel violence in Mexico and emerging transnational criminal organizations in the region meant a double increase in the coyote's fee in order to cover the necessary bribes and *pisos* to criminal organizations and corrupt law enforcement along the route.[4] This illicit landscape introduced a complicated hierarchy and dangerous criminal element into the coyote–migrant relationship such that by the time Sara found herself living out her mother's story in 1999, faith in the familiar guide had weakened.

"My group left me, too," Sara says, referencing her mother's experience. "I ended up in Immigration's hands. They picked me up and gave me permission to come across to this side for three months, no more. Since I was a minor, and my parents were here, they couldn't toss me back, *no me podían tirar pa'trás.* I had to come live with my parents, so they gave me a three-month permission."

Despite the risks and eroding trust, Sara knew that a child could not be "tossed back," that she must be delivered to the safety of a waiting parent. It would take an ideological sea change to get to the summer of 2018, when children were separated from their parents as a matter of policy and kept in cages and tent cities.[5]

The shift would require a cultural narrative as powerful as migrant hope: the story of the criminal immigrant—illicit, deceitful, morally flawed. Born of decades of rhetoric that paints clandestine crossers with the same dark hue as the traffickers and smugglers that threaten them, the image of the criminal immigrant makes dehumanizing policies like family separation possible.[6] It feeds on the threat of the other, poor and dark and unfamiliar, even as it skips over those whose illegal status in the country is triggered by an expiring date on a visa pasted into their passport.[7] In time Sara would feel its sharp sting, but as she waited to be retrieved from immigration authorities, it was the hope that mattered.

On the other side of her journey, though, the story became confused.

"When I got here, I didn't like it," Sara says plainly and waits a beat with her eyes on me. "I missed my sisters, my grandmother. I thought the trip to the United States was something I could do and go back again. I told my sisters, 'Well, it's a trip!' I never imagined how far it was. I was afraid the same thing would happen that happened to us when my little sister died.

"I missed my *abuela.* I wanted to be with her and I felt bad. I thought, 'I behaved badly.'" She pauses, reflects. Inside her story, she is a young girl coming face to face with choices that can't be undone. "I adored my mother, I wanted to be with her—I had only known her through pictures. But when you don't grow up with someone . . ." She looks away as if searching for the words, then says, "You love her, but it's not the same as when you're with her."

Like the hope and the trust, the idea of mother too became confused in Sara's new life. In time, the longed-for woman who had been photos and money wires and promises made, would become a mentor in the working world of Houston's private domestics and nannies. On the flip side of absence, Sara would come to know the value of a coin in the hand.

Rosa

During the three years that her husband worked in LA, Rosa had developed a certain relationship with the distance that separated them. But when it was time to travel by his side, leaving her five children behind, the nature of the miles between them shifted.

"It's hard," she says in a low voice. "The youngest was two years old."

Hard, but not wrong. Because for Rosa, at that time, to be a mother meant lifting her family up as much as it meant being by their side. So she entrusted the kids to her parents and the rancho with its sometimes-open school house and dried-up fields, and she and Arturo made their way north, then west, toward the city of angels. It was 1980, and at that time, the border Rosa and Arturo faced when they arrived in Matamoros was over a decade away from being the militarized line it would later become. But crossing it successfully still required a kind of cunning and familiarity with the ways of the borderlands that the couple were willing to pay for. For $800, they contracted a coyote who concocted a plan to pass them through undetected.

"My husband and I came in a car, crossing over in the motor of a car."

"The motor? How could you possibly—?"

"Like, lying down," she motions the position with a hasty gesture, almost impatient with my misunderstanding, "with your legs bunched up."

"How long were you like that?"

"About ten minutes. Just while we crossed the bridge."

In those ten minutes, the balance of family shifted for Rosa, and she would learn to carry the idea of wife and mother back and forth with her across the line that divided them for the next twelve years. During that period, she crossed the same border two more times. It would take over a decade and a confluence of amnesties, marriages, persistence, and luck to settle them all on one side. Even then, extended family would continue to call, and dreams of homecoming in old age would keep Rosa southward-yearning. Because where Sara drew from the learned story of immigration as a finite journey toward a better life, Rosa's family knew another kind of migrant tale. The same hope, the same promise of wages and comfort and getting ahead, but played out over a more fluid border for Mexican families like hers.

Over the long history of Mexican migration to the US, borders have alternately opened and closed over again, like a tide rising and falling. After the southern boundary of the US jumped over the land and the backs of Mexicans from Tejas to California in 1848, Mexican labor was openly courted through formal contracting agencies and a World War I guest worker program up through the 1920s. The tide shifted during the Great Depression, when plummeting US employment gave way to large-scale and indiscriminate deportation of Mexicans, and then shifted in favor of migrant labor again during WWII, when American men went missing from factories and farms. In response to this wartime labor shortage, the US government instituted the long-standing Bracero guest worker program, an agreement with the Mexican government that would formalize migrant work for over two decades.

Under the umbrella of the Mexican Farm Labor Agreement between Mexico and the United States, the Bracero Program lasted from 1942 to 1964 and opened the border to millions of Mexican men via guest worker contracts that authorized them to enter the US to pick up seasonal farm work without sanction. The flow often spilled beyond the bounds of legality, occasioning greater numbers than the program called for and affecting an entire generation's perception of the prospect of work in the north. Social processes and relationships grew up around the lives that many bracero workers created here. Expectations formed, desires grew, and the profound power of cultural narratives of migration was fortified with eyewitness accounts of life in the north. New migrants learned the way. When the 1960s saw a drop in demand for farm labor, the braceros were disbanded, but the lives they had made here were not.

In the 1980s, when Rosa and Arturo were crossing and recrossing the line, a booming US economy and intensified Mexican precarity evolved into a relatively porous border that would eventually close up again in the ensuing years.[8] All along, it had been the women who stayed put, tending the hearth and using the wages their men sent or brought home to raise new workers and new hearth-tenders. In a way, these left-behind wives had been serving the US economy for generations—birthing and caring for its revolving-door work force.

It wasn't until later, when the slippery gaps at the border squeezed tighter and the heat and thirst and batons fell heavier, that these families of migrant workers became left-behind families of emigrants—an empty chair at the table, one less player on the bench. For some, the response was to follow their men and relocate the project of family, taking advantage of a growing service economy and the amnesty offered by the 1986 Immigration Reform and Control Act (IRCA), which extended a path to citizenship to 2.6 million unauthorized immigrants, even as it threw up a fortified bulwark against future unauthorized immigration. The result was a large-scale shift in Mexican migration to the US at the end of the twentieth century, trading seasonal migrant male workers for entire families and feminizing the face of Mexican immigration.[9]

In the midst of this changing landscape of policy and practice, Rosa carried the idea of family across the border with her three times. The first, when she followed Arturo to LA. The second, when the couple were once again separated and she traveled north to visit him. And the third, when she and her children crossed for good to lay down their roots in Texas soil. Over these occasions, Rosa acquired a nuanced understanding of the language of the clandestine border and all its unspoken codes of right and wrong, profit and power. On the occasion of her second crossing, she found herself in Matamoros, traveling with her adult nephew. The pair were in good hands, guided by a coyote who knew how to read the border-crossing landscape with its asphalt checkpoints, riverbed low points, and the depths of a corrupt official's pocket.

"Those so-called cops, they're the worst there," Rosa tells me, her face tight with disgust. "A bunch of thieves." She flicks her hand the way you would swat away a dirty pest. "The big shots are the worst crooks."[10]

"Did they mess with you guys?" I ask.

"Yes!"

It happened in the evening, she tells me, just after dinner. The coyote had explained that they would cross a little later from a safer spot. First, he took them to dinner, paid for with the funds already forwarded to him by Arturo on the other side. It was a nice place, Rosa mentions, "really nice and pretty," just the kind of evening out that would throw off suspicions of illicit intentions. As the three companions walked away from the restaurant, they caught the eye of a *judicial*, a local cop.[11]

Rosa falls into her character, narrating the encounter in full dialogue. "What are you all doing here?" he asked.

"Just taking a walk," Rosa responded. "What, are we not allowed to take a walk?" defiance in her raised eyebrows, sass in the lilt of her voice. "We're in *México*," she pronounced the word slowly, clearly, because even in that space of neither here nor there, where a person stands relative to the line is everything. People like Rosa know this well. All of them on that Matamoros street did—both the coyote guide, who made a living off of the hard reality of the line, and the Mexican police officer, who, in his own way, did the same.

"No," the cop said, "you guys are headed to the other side. I can tell."

The guide stepped in at this point, insisting on the truth of their fabricated game: "Look, this is my wife, and my brother. We just had dinner—"

"We're just taking a walk!" Rosa protested.

"You're going to have to go down to the station," the officer insisted.

The coyote kept talking and the cop kept listening, but neither of them was trying to convince the other that what they said was true. The language they were speaking had little to do with the words they exchanged.

So when I ask, "But, wait, the Mexican officials were after migrants?" Rosa flashes a wry smile and crosses her arms at her chest. "Excuse me, Elizabeth," she says, "but they're all a bunch of crooks." She laughs long and hard, stretching out her vowels: "They're baaad, baaad guys."

And the bad guy was the one with the uniform.

"I know what you're after," Rosa told him. "You're looking for money. He says, 'Oh yeah, you do know, don't you.' That's what that old crook said. I told him, 'But you don't have anything on us. We're in Mexico, we're Mexicans! What do you want?'" She waits a beat, her arms still crossed as she leans into a high-backed wooden chair across my kitchen table. "Well," she goes on, "it was money!"

"They took us to a room, *un cuartito*—I'm not lying to you." *Un cuartito*, a little room, is a phrase that connotes the beatings and torture behind closed doors that define police and military corruption in much of the region. Just to be in a *cuartito* is a threat in itself.

"You get it," the *judicial* countered, "*Usted sí sabe*. Now we understand each other."

Just like the talk on the street, all the players in this game knew the unspoken rules of the *cuartito*. It was all about the bribe, and no one was pretending anymore. Rosa's guide had the professional foresight to have hidden the real money safely away, leaving a hundred or so for just this situation. He passed it along, and after the cop received his *mordida*, he changed tactics. "If you all want to cross," he said, "we could get you to the other side."

"No!" I react to this twist in Rosa's story.

"Yes!" she cries. "The very same guys, the very same."

It's a big business, this smuggling world, and the more dangerous the crossing, the more illicit actors like the cop and the coyote stand to gain. Back when Rosa was crossing and recrossing the border, the territory was less complicated than it is now. Small networks of coyotes who knew the way, probably a guy from your town, maybe even your cousin. Rosa trusted her guide that day, so they declined the *judicial*'s offer and moved ahead with the plan. After a few hours in a more secure safe house, they made it across under the multiple covers of darkness, evasion, and redirection. She explains how her nephew rode suspended at the top of a large empty gas tank in a truck they had acquired for just this purpose.

"But isn't that toxic?"

"Yeah," she shrugs and goes on, telling me how she traveled inside a car pretending to be the mother of a baby she carried.

"But where was the mom?"

"She wasn't there, she was sending the baby to her sister on the other side—they knew the coyote, it was a good contact."

Nowadays, Rosa assures me, it wouldn't be so easy. She's seen it in the news. "Just today on the news, they kidnapped a child, the coyotes themselves," she tells me. Rosa knows as well as I do that, since the beginning of the twenty-first century, the meaning of "coyote" has shifted away from a "compadre," with shades of the illicit, to something much more sinister. The fiercer the border, the higher the stakes. These days, very few go it alone, and to cross a child takes capital—the kind that a migrant mother on the other side must spend months earning. "If some-body's having their child brought over, it's because they have money," Rosa adds. "They're paying double." And the coyotes know it.

In the end, Rosa made it across. This time and the others. In the past tense, the ordeals become stories to tell across a kitchen table, dramatic and humorous. "All three times I crossed without any problems, per-fectly fine." She chuckles and waves her hand as if batting a fly. "I came across three times," she declares again, and adds in a husky laugh. "Like the song, 'Tres veces mojada.'"

"Tres veces mojado," translated as "Three Times a Wetback," is a 1998 border ballad by the *norteño* band Los Tigres del Norte. The song takes the classic form of the Mexican corrido—a ballad of the people, as de-fiant in the face of injustice as Rosa's sassy challenge to a dirty cop. In this corrido, Los Tigres sing the story of an immigrant from El Salvador who becomes a "wetback" three times over as he battles the violence and injustice of three separate borders: from El Salvador to Guatemala, Gua-temala to Mexico, and finally into the United States. Like Rosa's telling, the crossings in this ballad carry a spirit of collective resistance familiar to the *norteño* group and its audience, one with a long regional history of imposed borders and divested lands.[12]

Much like the morally ambivalent crossers and smugglers in tradi-tional corridos, the *mojados* and coyotes of contemporary migrant com-munities carry the same affinity with resistance, complicating the moral landscape of the US–Mexico borderlands. For Rosa and Los Tigres, bor-der transgression and the culture of *coyotaje* are products of the same historical cultural development—a set of meanings around illegal immi-gration that has grown up in traditional sending communities in Mex-ico, and later in Central America, in response to changing political and economic landscapes. In this sense, the coyote and migrant are primed to play the hero's role in a narrative of hope that is culturally engrained in sending communities. In the words of Los Tigres del Norte, "What I've suffered, I've recovered in spades / To the wetbacks, I dedicate my song."[13]

So, when Rosa waves away the gravity of the bribes and the car mo-tors and the motherless babies and empty gas tanks with a dismissive chuckle, she draws from a tradition that understands the risk and the morality of illegal migration to be a many-sided question, a far more nu-anced affair than sound-bites and stump speeches admit. In this morally complex border space, a lawbreaker can be a hero, a smuggler can be a trusted compadre, and hope for a family's future is an end to justify any means.

Magdalena

Magdalena is a young Salvadoran woman with dark eyes, high cheekbones, and a story heavy with the moral ambiguity of the borderlands. I met with her in my neighbor's home, where she told me about her life over several baskets of her employer's laundry while my kids ran wild with their playmates, tearing around on freshly vacuumed carpets. In a strong voice, sharp with opinion, Magdalena sketches out a tale steeped in the complexities of power, sexuality, and narrative interpretation.

Like Sara, Magdalena grew up with the shadows of the Chaparrastique volcano at her back. In a cantón she calls San Juan Bosco, in the San Miguel province of El Salvador, Magdalena spent her youth with eyes set firmly on the urban horizon of San Miguel. At nineteen, she worked in a maquiladora near the city, assembling garments full time for thirty-six dollars a week.

"Over there, you can make just enough to buy beans," she tells me, "but there's none left over for a plate of meat, you know? There's no work there. That's the reason why, I'd say, 90 percent of immigrants decide to come here to the US. The other 10 percent, they do it to be with relatives here, but 90 percent do it to work and make a better life for their family back home."

Magdalena had seen enough of her compatriots come and go to know that the US was the place to earn the kind of money that means eating well. So, when she heard that a local coyote, a distant cousin of hers, would be leading a group north the next day, Magdalena went straight to his house and knocked on the door.

"You know what?" she told him, "I want to go."

"Are you sure?"

"Yes, I'm sure."

"Alright then, if you're sure, let's go talk to your dad."

They set off for her place and within two hours the decision had been made.

"I couldn't even pack a change of clothes," she tells me. "I couldn't grab a toothbrush. I couldn't grab anything because I didn't have enough time."

"And can you describe the experience a little?" I ask her, "What was it like to come here?"

"Well," she speaks quickly, hands and body constantly at work. "Others talk about horrible experiences, but mine was very nice, *muy bonita.*" She smiles nervously and a bit of color rises in her cheek. She glances my way and then looks quickly down at the laundry again, where she keeps her eyes as she tells her story.

She recounts the discomfort and challenges of the journey, the uncertainty and fear and the twelve people piled into one sleeping compartment of a bus designed for just a couple of passengers, waiting with held breath at the Guatemala–Mexico border. "It's very tiring. You get so stressed because every time the Mexican soldiers stop the buses, you can't even stretch because it makes noise. The problem would be if they happened to go looking at the sleeping cars that day."

"So, it's a question of luck."

"A question of luck, exactly."

Luck carried Magdalena and her fellow travelers through south and central Mexico all the way north to Hidalgo and across the US–Mexico border into what Magdalena describes as the desert, likely the same arid chapparal crossed by others, where she and her fellow travelers walked silently for four hours before their luck ran short.[14]

"We were hidden as we walked, around two in the afternoon. Immigration goes around all over the desert, with helicopters, cars, horses and all that, and so that's where they saw us. They said, 'Stop! Stop right there and don't run!' And well, you have to stop. Then they pick you up, they put you in the car, and they take you to a *garita*, a kind of booth, where they decide if they're going to send you back to your country or leave you here. If you pay, or if they let you go on with a three-month provisional permit. You're supposed to go to the judge, bring the paper, and the judge decides if you have to go back to your country.

"But a lot of people don't go," Magdalena adds. "They just change their address and they're automatically marked for deportation. But as long as you don't commit a serious crime, there's no problem."

Trusting in the stories she's heard of migrants gone before her, Magdalena put her faith in the odds. This is the mechanism of migrant hope, in which stories of success must outnumber stories of failure.[15] But tales of unsuccessful attempts also have their place in these cultures of migration: they teach the would-be migrant that the price of failure can be grave—as oppressive and violent as a dark river current or the heat of a South Texas summer. Magdalena has heard the stories. So have I.

Like the one about the dead migrants in the desert. Luis Alberto Urrea recounts this tale, a group of twenty-six men from small towns in Mexico's interior set out in May of 2001, moving in faith and hope north into Arizona's Sonora desert under the protection of their *pollero* guides. By the end of that month, over half of them were dead, felled by heat stroke under the unforgiving sun as their disoriented guides sought their northern counterparts in vain. An uncle. A father. His son. Urrea tells the story because dead men can't speak, and devastated men won't.[16]

In Urrea's telling, the guides are both victims and criminals, a product of increasingly complex hierarchies of human smuggling across the US–Mexico border. Since the turn of the century's rise in transnational criminal organizations, turf has been fragmented, pay-offs have multiplied, and the calculation of risk has been swept up by inhuman forces of brutality in excess. Stories about this, too, lurk in the contours of migrant hope.

Like the one about the bodies. In August of 2010, a gruesome discovery was made at an abandoned farmhouse in Tamaulipas, Mexico: the decomposing bodies of seventy-two migrants, beaten and executed at close range. The suspected assassins were members of the deadly Zetas, a criminal organization at war with the Gulf Cartel in a complex game of moves and counter-moves played out over a terrain of cancerous corruption among law enforcement and officials alike. In the aftermath of the discovery, a Mexican human rights commission conducted an investigation that found that about 20,000 migrants are kidnapped every year, the vast majority of them Central Americans passing through Mexico on their way to the US.[17]

It's a question of balance. Enough success to fuel the hope, enough failure to temper the innocence, and just enough horror for a girl to consider herself lucky when she finds herself under the cold blast of a border patrol substation's AC and the ambiguous gaze of an agent with a weakness for a pretty face. In a little room, where there is no doubt where the power lies.

"When Immigration caught me," Magdalena begins, "I met this American—the one who would give me provisional permission to come to this country—and he said that he liked me. So he was very nice to me, and well, he offered to take me to his house so that I could bathe. You know, I was really dirty, coming from the desert."

Magdalena flips a wrinkled T-shirt and folds it along clean lines and sharp corners, her hair falling, her dark eyes intent on her work. What words to give this encounter? The agent's manner and gestures, the deep green of his uniform, and the freedom of his car and home. All along, Magdalena's had been an uncertain trajectory. North, yes, but the only future she carried with her was an old phone number for her father's sister, whom she had met only once. The number might be disconnected. Her aunt might not want to help. Magdalena might be on her own once she made it through the tricky borderlands and into her new life. So many uncertainties. And then, after the thorny brush and the lights and the chase, after the trucks and helicopters and exposed flesh under the summer sun, an offer.

"He offered to take me to buy new clothes. He took me to eat . . ." Her voice trails, she reaches for more to fold.

"Is that all?" I ask.

"Yes," she quickly replies. "After that, he took me to the beach, to the movies, et cetera, et cetera." She smiles, giggles audibly, nervously, and draws out the singsong vowel in the last words, "al ciiiine . . . et cétera, et cétera."

"And you never felt compromised in any way, or uncomfortable . . . ?" Then, to fill her silence, "or just fortunate?"

"I felt fortunate. Because the stories a lot of people tell, dying in the desert, well, I felt like . . . He was very nice to me the whole time. He took me to his house. He said, 'I like you, *tú me caes bien*. I'm going to help you. If you clean my house, I can give you money for a bus ticket.' "

From desert to processing station to the damp towels and tiled shower of this *americano's* home, Magdalena considers herself one of the lucky ones. She's heard the stories about all those lonely desert deaths.

I've heard other stories, about the places where border crossing and sexual coercion collide.

A thirty-five-year-old Nicaraguan woman sits by her patrona's pool and tells me about the coyote who turned on her: "They tried to rape me when they were going to cross me over the river. I got away because I was with another woman who was older, and I was able to get away. But that was a horrible experience."

Rosa tells me about her friend, who was less fortunate, "My friend says the coyotes kept her in a house and wouldn't give her to her family. She says after she crossed, the coyote assaulted her. He raped her. She even had a child from him, from that person."

There are so many stories. Journalists and filmmakers and researchers relay the experiences of women and girls raped by smugglers and guides, sometimes forced into temporary prostitution at stash houses on the US side of the border. Young girls given preemptive birth control by desperate caretakers before sending them north in the company of brothers or cousins, or all alone.[18] In the stories, the violators vary—smugglers, gangsters, fellow migrants, traffickers, agents with uniforms and guns and ACs and private homes with locked doors. In all of them, immigration, sexuality, and gender converge in a border zone marked by imbalanced power and exacerbated vulnerability. At the intersection of woman, migrant, and clandestine crossing, luck can take many forms.

After a few days together, the border patrol agent who had taken Magdalena home drove her to Houston. "It turned out he worked here in Houston as a pilot for the government; he's a border patrol agent and also a pilot. So when he had to come here, to Houston, he gave me a ride. It was two days after I entered this country."

Magdalena stands in my neighbor's living room, kids running around freshly made beds and piles of folded garments, and eases through this narrative passage on her way to the story she's anxious to tell, the one about the indignity of life as an undocumented person in America, about workplace raids and demanding patronas. But my thoughts remain with the unnamed agent, and as I consider the story Magdalena presents and interrogate my own suspicions, I try to place him among images of border patrol agents that others have painted for me.

There are the brutal ones, who beat and rape and sometimes kill. "*Since January 2010, at least 120 people have died as the result of an encounter with U.S. border agents. Many more have been brutalized.*"[19]

There are the cold-hearted ones, who desecrate and urinate and slash and destroy. "*[I]t's true that we slash their bottles and drain their water into the dry earth, that we dump their backpacks and pile their food and clothes to be crushed and pissed on and stepped over, strewn across the desert and set ablaze.*"[20]

There are the institutionalized ones, who reduce human beings to ridiculed types and wield flashlights like swords and SUVs like tanks. *"Illegal aliens, dying of thirst more often than not, are called 'wets' by agents. . . . 'Wets' are also called 'Tonks,' but the Border Patrol tries hard to keep that bon mot from civilians. . . . Only a fellow border cop could appreciate the humor of calling people a name based on the stark sound of a flashlight breaking over a human head.*"[21]

And there are the put-upon ones, old school and misunderstood and defending their humanity in an ugly world. *"You come out here and you end up in vehicle pursuits, and there's days that you get assaulted, you get into fights.*"[22]

I consider the danger and the abuses, the heavy flashlights and cold metal chairs, the dignity and the brutality, and I wonder if something about the badge and the innocence and the harsh meeting place of power and vulnerability might not work a sort of moral alchemy on those who might otherwise be decent. Would-be defenders who may not have stopped to question the bigger picture of sovereignty and autonomy and the relative justice of capital and goods that are free to move but people who are not. I wonder if staring at a set of points moving on a rocky horizon might not move an anxious hand to a hasty draw, or if contemplating a soft face gazing downward might not trigger some more primitive impulse. I ask myself if a uniform that could have been a symbol of right might slip too easily into a shield against the moral ambiguities of power and desire.

In Magdalena's case, all I can do is wonder. Explanations as surprising as a life-changing decision made in the space of a couple of hours, or as ambiguous as *"et cétera et cétera"* are implausible only to me, not to her. In the end, what I know of Magdalena's experience across this borderland is the story she chooses to tell. *"Muy bonita,"* she decides, "quite nice."

Pati

For Pati, the passage from one home to another played out over a more intimate landscape. In the seventeen years that passed between her mother María's departure and her own migration, María returned to their home in El Salvador only four times. From Pati's sixth birthday to her twenty-third, the total time mother and daughter spent together added up to a little over two years. And while Pati and her siblings moved from relative to relative, waiting for letters, mismanaging remittances, and eating fruits from their grandparents' orchard, María's day-to-day became ever more entwined with the lives of the children she cared for and the parents who employed her.

Shortly after María arrived in the US back in 1985, she found a position as a live-in nanny-housekeeper in a family with two young children and a comfortable garage apartment that would become her home for decades. The oldest child was the same age as Pati at the time, six years old. He would have needed his nanny in much the same way María's own children needed her—to soothe skinned knees and rumbling tummies, to gather shoes and socks left out in the rain. María cared for the American children, tending to scrapes and braids and errant laces in exchange for a steady income that became remittances, that became food in Pati's belly and money in her pocket. In one way or another, María had been there for all of the children, for twenty-five years.

"My mom is a hard worker," Pati tells me, "and she does her job well." In Pati's voice, I hear both pride and loss. They are two sides of the same coin, one child's skinned knee and another's jingling pocket.

"The señor died of cancer just a few years after she started working there, and the señora, well, she really depended on my mom. The family needed her. And to make a long story short, she's been with them for twenty-five years. The kids don't live there anymore. Now it's just the señora, but even so, my mom still works for them."

María's dual roles as nurturer to one family and breadwinner for another set Pati on two distinct and simultaneous trajectories—one, a longing to be near her mother after a childhood of separation; the other, access to the cash and connections she would need to make a life for herself in the north. Had María not emigrated, Pati would not be sitting on a comfortable sofa in a nicely furnished apartment in Houston's southwest side, confident that her own children will be educated, fed, safe. And she would not have been able to tap the social capital her mother had built up in her immigrant community and among the network of patronas in which she moved. Shelter after a journey, an interview, a job with good wages and negotiated terms.

But on the flip side, Pati's sighs and whispers and quiet sobs trace a second narrative path that chases her words in body and gesture. It began the day her mother said goodbye and played out up through the afternoon I came to sit beside her as she relived her story in the telling, knowing then all that she hadn't known before. About a nanny's love, for instance, and how it can fill up the empty spaces. And about the permanence of the journey, how, really, there's no going back once the choice is made.

By the time she was eighteen, Pati had finished secondary school, trained as a seamstress, and begun her working life in a low-paying job. She had said goodbye to the first of her siblings to head north, her older brother. Two years later, her oldest sister would follow.

"And then, once I was grown up," Pati sighs, "I became depressed. Because I missed my mom. I missed my family. That's when we decided to move. That's when we decided to come here."

Pati, her other remaining sister, and the sister's two teenage daughters would follow the others and join their mother in Texas. María arranged everything from her garage apartment in Houston. She found a reliable guide and turned to her savings to pay a hefty fee.

"My mom wanted someone safe," Pati explains, "because of her experience, and the experiences they all had—my sister and my mother—when they crossed. It was really hard for them. So she didn't want us to go through the same thing. Especially because two minors were with us. My nieces were fourteen and twelve, plus my sister, their mother, and me. So we were four women, two of them young, and my mom didn't want the same thing to happen to us."[23]

In the beginning, all went according to plan. Their guides led them across the El Salvador–Guatemala border on a bus, and then all the way across Guatemala and through Mexico in a car. It wasn't until they reached the northern border across from McAllen, Texas, that the migrants' powerlessness caught up with them. In a hotel on the Mexican side, the women waited patiently for their guide to come through.

"Everything was arranged for us to cross over to here, but once we were at the border, he abandoned us. He told us, 'Someone is coming who will cross you over to the other side, and then I'll be there to take you to your mother.' But no. He left us there."

The sisters called upon María's resources once more, and after a week of waiting, a new guide arrived to lead them to Houston. In the passage, faraway wages transformed from letters and longing into concrete possibility, and the complex dynamic of the mothercoin redefined María's long-ago choices. No longer a last grab at hope from a place of desperation, María's migration had now become the strategic move of a powerful matriarch with enough social weight to deliver her children and grandchildren safely to her and place them each in homes as caring and reliable as the one she had known for almost two decades.

After a month of traveling, Pati and her sister and nieces arrived, and the family was together at last in their mother's home—a small garage apartment from which she had orchestrated six cross-border journeys over fifteen years of devotion and service to an American family that her children had never met. As the family squeezed back into each other's lives, the two older sisters and granddaughters moved into their own apartment and Pati and her brother stayed there with their mother in a home that had never been theirs but had for so long been hers.

In time, mother and children would redefine what it means to be family, and Pati would find her place in this new world. As María continued to fulfill her role in the American family she had found, Pati would discover how profoundly a person can love children who are not her own in a job that creates the feeling of family by the very force of its day-to-day interaction.

Hope, like food, shelter, and security, is a human need. For Pati and María and countless other women like them, the story of migrant hope is powerful enough to push them forward across borderlands marked by powerlessness and vulnerability, strong enough to endure the threat of violence and the more intimate attacks on moral worthiness engendered by the narrative of the criminal immigrant. Once across the broad border zone of checkpoints and evasion,[24] they will hold certain borders within. Lines will blur between here and there, right and wrong, love and labor as women, families, and communities feel together the mothercoin's reach.

Back home, those left behind will cling to the promise of return and to the sustenance of monthly remittances sent through Western Union transfers and MoneyGram wires. They will learn to sweep a little extra, cook a little more, play a little less. The most vulnerable among them—young children, those who are ill or elderly—will live their daily dependencies with lowered expectations. One fewer set of hands to hold, a little less patience with which to serve. Their communities will pick up the slack when they are able. When they're not, those most in need will suffer. Left behind at the end of a global chain of ever more strained resources, they may find their hope diminished. Overburdened grandparents will tire, distant children will turn away from studies and toward more immediate gratification, their taste for risk growing even as their sense of joy fades.

Meanwhile, in a small apartment half a world away, the women will scrimp and save and count dollars and days between phone calls and visits. Their daily work will present them with other foreheads to caress and other needs to meet, confusing the border between love and labor, as the world marches on to the beat of tariffs and trade and maquiladoras at the border, Guatemalan coffee and Dominican shortstops and the mashed Honduran banana on a baby's white plastic tray—made in China and wiped clean by a Salvadoran hand just in time for mom and dad to arrive home from a ten-hour workday with suits crumpled and shoulders slumped under the pace of their demanding lives. All of them doing what's necessary to survive and thrive.

PART II

THE FLIP SIDE

They forgot her name and gave her another. A name that barely
contains the story. A name that says she only weeps, only
knows how to weep. They gave her a name that
always makes her remember the beginning.
The name is a cage. A truth. A lie.

IRE'NE LARA SILVA[1]

Prelude

When Pati and Sara and the others arrive at their destination, they step into a larger story, the late-twentieth-century emergence of a global chain of care that leaves some regions healthy and nourished and attended to, and others wanting. This global "care drain" results from broad changes that have transformed how we organize and reproduce our societies.[2] In the wake of a demographic transition in which more and more women entered the workforce at managerial and professional ranks, families of the global north confronted new challenges in childrearing. At the same time, globalization fragmented processes of production and changed our relationship with national borders. In response to both of these shifts, carework has entered into the global web of trade. From nannies to elder companions to healthy wombs and babies for adoption, third world women have what more and more first world families have come to need.[3]

When parents bring in a nanny to take up the mothercoin and share the work of childrearing, they take a place in this larger drama. Much like multinational companies that shift the social cost of material production to the local economies that feed their maquiladoras with cheap labor, our first world families are able to shift the cost of their own increasing domestic and childrearing needs to immigrant women, whose own families absorb their absence and the untended labor they leave behind.

The personal cost for the immigrant nanny is palpable. At work in the receiving country, distance, separation, and the longing for touch are circumscribed by immigration policies that separate the worker from the family, erecting a solid barrier between labor and humanity. Calls for more humane family reunification policies are met with cries of "chain migration," accusing undeserving immigrants of entering the country on the merits of family members. As if workers were produced in a vacuum, absent of nourishment and maintenance and the sustenance of relationship. As if the work of family yielded no tangible value. Bolstered by such false logic, the system persists. The American workplace secures the labor, cheap and steadily available, but bears none of the costs of supporting and cultivating the human capital that provides it.

José builds our houses, but Honduras paves his roads and lights his home—when the grid is up and the hurricane winds are quiet. Rosalinda walks our kids to preschool and makes their cheese sandwiches while we go to work to shape markets and institutions, but Guatemala educates her own children—when the teachers aren't striking for a living wage. Yolanda helps our aging parents in and out of baths and toilets and slow, lonely afternoons, while her own parents are cared for by a remaining sister or cousin, likely hurried and stretched thin with left-behind children to watch and lights that are only sometimes on.

The worker brings the healthy labor to the receiving country, and the home country is left to take care of the workers' families. But social services don't rank high among the budgetary priorities of nations primed for export and debt repayment, and a civil society that is focused on throwing up some kind of bulwark against the encroaching power of transnational gangs has little time to walk arm in arm with an aging parent or sit beside a sick child. In the end, the care we import when the nanny arrives at our homes in the morning—fresh and willing and eager to watch the weekly envelopes multiply into security and opportunity— leaves a deficit behind that cannot be overcome.

Care is not an unlimited resource. The remittances an immigrant nanny sends home come at a cost. That bit of emptiness where once she raised children, or tended to the ill and the old, becomes a broad regional care deficit made up of a thousand local interactions.[4] A brave goodbye under a sleeping volcano, a debt incurred for guidance on a dangerous journey, a network activated across a kitchen counter—*Señora, my niece is looking for work, do you know anyone who needs a babysitter?* Or through an office door—*We need help with the new baby, do you know anyone we can trust?* An awkward interview on a Saturday afternoon couch. A shy smile, a tentative confidence, and a handful of lives unfolding on the flip side of the mothercoin.

CHAPTER 3

THE NATURE OF THE JOB

*There are so many women who come to this country
just to find one day of work, as simple as that.*

MAGDALENA

Sara

When Sara arrived in Houston, she slipped seamlessly into the shadow of her mother's working life. At fourteen years old, she had only just discovered the gravity of the distance that separated her parents' apartment from her village in El Salvador, and she was only just beginning to understand how her choice would shape her freedom. In the four-week journey that delivered her up to the mercy of the US immigration system, Sara had drastically changed her prospects. Though the narratives she encountered might cast her fortune in simple terms—the rise of the hopeful emigrant, the fall of the criminal immigrant—in fact, she had adopted a far more complex set of public identities that would determine the texture of her private life in important ways.

The leap from her *abuela*'s apron strings to her mamá's changed the nature of the choices available to Sara—now empowered by a service-hungry economy, now limited by shadow citizenship. As she made a life for herself in her new community, these choices collided with chances of fate to place her in more or less advantageous positions. She acquired a *machista* husband, gave birth to two US citizen children, and benefited from a temporary protected status for her and her compatriots, a designation that shielded her from the harshest vulnerability of the unauthorized.

The chance legitimacy offered by temporary protected status, or TPS, followed from a series of disasters at home, natural and otherwise. From 1998 to 2001, a number of hurricanes and earthquakes battered the region, along with other threats to regional reconstruction—floods and droughts, a coffee fungus, a plague of growing gang violence and unemployment. The US response to the loss of life and property wrought by these disasters would confirm what people like Sara and her mother readily understood: the economic value of a migrant abroad, legal or otherwise, is indispensable to her community at home. Within months of Hurricane Mitch in 1998, the Clinton administration suspended deportations to the region. In 2001, after two major earthquakes hit El Salvador, the Bush administration formalized the reprieve in the form of TPS granted to Salvadorans living in the US. The designation would be renewed continually until 2017, when the Trump administration's attempt to revoke the status launched it into a legal limbo, where it remains as of this writing.[1]

When the earthquakes tore into her homeland, Sara was already in the States, and like manna from heaven, legitimacy at work and on the streets fell into her lap. Her mother received the same reprieve, both women coming out of the shadows along with Sara's father, whose earlier 1994 arrival had granted him a more stable residency through a 1997 Central American relief measure passed in response to political instability in the region.[2] Sara's younger sister, Maribel, would not come for another three years, a choice that would relegate her and the young daughter she carried to the illegitimate margins of society as she took her place alongside her authorized family.

Liberated in her status and limited in her marriage, Sara would spend the next few years working at the side of a mother she'd lost to the mothercoin eight years earlier. Here, she slowly came to know the measure of an immigrant maid for hire in Houston, Texas—a value counted out in toilets scrubbed, floors mopped, and lunchtime sandwiches served.

She found her first job caring for the school-aged children of another immigrant in her community. This initial employer had been in the US for some time and managed to earn enough at a factory job to pay Sara ten dollars a day to take on her family's domestic work—cleaning, cooking, taking the children to and from school.

"Another immigrant?"

"Yes, with a lot more time here. They worked in a factory; their pay was low too. And, for me, ten dollars was a lot."

This was a typical move for the newly arrived, who often begin working in the home of a more established immigrant, cleaning and babysitting for a meager wage that seems a fortune to a girl still used to the relative poverty of home. Women like Sara often move up the ladder of domestic service as they gain experience and contacts and a growing cultural awareness of the local terrain.

Sara may have earned little in her first job, but she avoided the vulnerability inherent to the most common position for recent immigrants in the occupation, that of the live-in nanny-housekeeper. For a migrant with little knowledge of culture or language and limited mobility, a live-in arrangement can be a blessing or a curse. Working conditions vary widely, from jobs with concrete work hours, a separate entrance, and an open invitation to pantry and cupboard, to employers who heavily monitor access to the family's food and expect their maids always to be on call through sleepless nights and long, isolated days.[3]

For the uninitiated, it can be hard to imagine what might go on behind closed doors. The boundaries are so easily blurred, the power so clearly in the hands of the employers. In the best of cases, the job is one essential rung on the ladder to something better. In the worst, it can be a tale of trauma and desperation. Scholars and activists have documented wide-ranging abuse of domestics, both globally and within the US. Live-ins are particularly vulnerable because of their limited access to the community and their often unauthorized status. Employer transgressions range from verbal and psychological to physical and sexual.[4] In the US, the most extreme abuse is often encountered by the many migrant women who find themselves captives in the homes of diplomats and other authorized foreign residents, a form of modern-day slavery as prevalent as it is hidden.[5]

While the issues of outright abuse and labor trafficking are shocking, they can obscure the systemic problem that undergirds the industry. A foreign domestic who finds herself working for a "good family" may feel fortunate, but she remains as subject as any other to the imbalanced power embedded in the employer–employee relationship. In an industry that plays out behind the closed doors of private homes—where cash payment is the norm, employers routinely ignore labor laws, and many domestics avoid law enforcement as a rule—the potential for exploitation is ripe. Exercised or not, this power hangs over the relationship that develops between immigrant domestics and their patronas.

But time and experience can mitigate some of this vulnerability, as the newly arrived like Sara gather references and acquire a more nuanced understanding of the industry—the value of ten dollars a day, for example. In this "Wild West" of supply, demand, and limited power, a hierarchy has developed among women who perform domestic and nanny work in the US—from the least desirable positions as a live-in or a poorly paid muchacha[6] for a fellow migrant all the way up to the ideal: regular contract work cleaning private homes.[7] At the top of the hierarchy, the successful domestic has a robust network of employers and referrals, allowing her to maintain a steady series of homes that she cleans for a flat fee. She controls the pace of her work, collects her pay, often without interacting with her employers at all, and steps out the door holding a key ring jingling with access to regular casas and a car that allows her to get from one house to another and be home by three to pick up her kids from school.[8]

But it can take years to build up this kind of network, and a lot of energy and luck to keep it going. Every move counts. For Sara, the second move meant a job working seventeen-hour days for $150 a week. After six months, she changed course and took up a kind of apprenticeship cleaning private homes alongside her experienced and well-connected mother, Ana. Like the monthly remittances Ana had sent home and the coyote that brought Sara to the US, this move, too, was made possible by the groundwork Sara's mother had laid in the years they were apart.

"My mom would take me with her to clean houses. They would pay us sixty dollars to clean one house. We would work for eight hours and do everything, wash and iron the clothes and clean the home, for sixty dollars."

"Sixty?" I interrupt, "to clean, wash, and iron the clothes?"

I'm struck by the figure, far lower than the one-hundred-dollar norm in my neighborhood at the time—without the laundry. But Sara is not shocked. Her voice is even and matter-of-fact across the cool January air.

"Yes, we'd iron and clean for sixty dollars, the two of us."

She pauses as the story catches up to the figure, all those hopeful choices and hard lessons folded up into three twenty-dollar bills and a row of freshly pressed shirts.

"But then I got another job," Sara goes on. "Well, and I got married, too. I got married when I was fifteen after my quinceañera."

"Wow," I can't help myself. "Fifteen?"

I picture Sara at her fifteenth birthday—a dance floor and taffeta skirt, boys in cummerbunds, a Catholic mass, a *madrina*'s blessing, and cash tucked into a peach-colored silk purse. The *quince* is a celebration that means the end of something and the beginning of something else. For Sara, who had already left her schooldays and younger sisters behind, the transformation was irreversible.

"So yes, after my fifteenth birthday, I got married. I thought my husband was going to make a better life for me, because he always liked the best things, you know?"

"He was young too?"

"No, he was ten years older than me."

"Twenty-five."

"He was twenty-five years old."

A young girl's romance, then, shaped by stories that teach her where to place her hope—a longed-for mother, an American dream, a man to step in and make good on promises yet unfulfilled. But this tale reads like no love story I've ever known, and words like "bride" and "husband" feel wrong for the girl in Sara's story, barely past the threshold of adolescence.

There is such distance between the way we talk about womanhood and the reality of it. And in Central America, where teenage pregnancy and domestic abuse are as common as a migrant cousin, one can only imagine what it might feel like to come to know, in one painful encounter, the truth behind the promise of something better. In a culture where, so often, wives may be beaten into submission and girls might be taken like crops to be harvested, words like "rape" and "abuse" can be as foreign as the unknown *norte*, leaving a girl like Sara without the vocabulary that might call out such stolen innocence.[9]

As she entered into a new set of limits and possibilities at home, Sara's market value on the job was increasing. She was offered a position caring for a young boy and cleaning the suburban home where he and his mother lived. Sara refers to this third patrona as "*la morena*," the Black lady, and tells me she earned $175 a week with the woman, working five ten-hour days. She was expected to care for the child and clean the home. When Sara remembers her time with this woman, she smiles. *La morena* was a lovely person, she tells me, "*muy linda.*"

"She was very nice to me. She didn't speak Spanish, and I didn't speak English, but we communicated by signs. When she was leaving to eat or something, she'd go like this," she lifts her hands to her mouth to mime feeding herself from an imaginary fork, laughing at the memory.

"$175 a week for five days, ten hours?" I clarify.

"Yes," she answers. The pay works out to $3.50 an hour.

"She treated me well," Sara adds with a smile.

For Sara, to be treated well—at less than half the minimum wage—must have something to do with the humanity in these interactions, the mutual vulnerability. Neither woman speaks the language of the other, but both come together in smiles and gestures—poor immigrant teenage bride and single working mother of color, forging a relationship over a confusing terrain of limited options. These interactions are part of a complex coming together of individual and social identities, power dynamics, and personal histories. They are the stuff of relationship, and in an occupation that unfolds in the intimate spaces of home, relationship is everything.

Many domestic careworkers express an explicit desire for the kind of interaction Sara remembers with *la morena*. Distinct from the patronizing maternalism embedded in our history of mistress–maid relationships, this sought-after personalism is a two-way relationship built on confidence, communication, and interaction that recognizes the dignity and personhood of both women.[10] But many employers are uncomfortable negotiating such personal terrain with their cleaners and nannies. While their mothers and grandmothers often managed "the help" in a maternal style, with the attitude of a benefactress who protects and receives gratitude in return, the connotations of such interaction don't sit well with many women these days. And there is a certain historical weight to the mistress–maid dynamic that contradicts contemporary American values of equality and individualism.[11] To encounter the full humanity of your servant as she pushes a mop across your kitchen floor is to question your relationship to these ideals. Best to stick to business, then, clean envelopes and the heft of a coin in the hand.

Sara's job with *la morena* only lasted six months before the kind patrona packed up her child and her makeshift sign language and weekly $175 and moved to another suburb, leaving Sara to fall back on private house-cleaning work with her mother. Not long after, a different kind of proposition came along, one that allowed Sara to move from part-time co-cleaner and poorly paid muchacha to fully employed nanny-housekeeper for a well-off employer with a professional income and the ability to hire out the bulk of the family's domestic needs. As Sara stepped over the threshold into this improved station, she entered into another kind of relationship entirely.

By the time I met Sara at the park, she had worked for Leslie for eight years—sometimes full-time, sometimes part-time—and in that period, the two women had found the kind of volatile stability that carries echoes of a toxic love affair.[12]

"I've had a lot of problems with her, but she's also helped me a lot. It's like I've gotten used to her. She's yelled at me—sometimes she's made me feel really bad."

"For example?"

"Like, why don't I go back to my own country. Like, this isn't my country so why don't I go back to mine. She treats me like that sometimes, but I started to feel affection for her. It's like, you get used to being mistreated. But she always tries to help me when I need it."

"How did she help you?"

"Well, she gave me a job. And for me, that was . . . she gave me work when I needed it most."

Sara describes Leslie as American, but with perfect Mexican Spanish, though Sara couldn't say why. When she first began her job cleaning the home, picking up Leslie's son from school, and caring for the small family's menagerie of pets, she'd been shaken by the woman's tendency to scream in fits of anger. But the work Leslie gave Sara—a gift, in Sara's mind, independent of Leslie's own need or Sara's own value—paid seven dollars an hour, far more than she'd earned in any other job. And Leslie provided more than just a salary. As an attorney, she had given Sara legal assistance throughout the years, often wrapped up in judgment.

"She always tells me, if you need legal help, I can help you. But when I have something, like a traffic ticket, and I say, 'This country, it's horrible how they treat me,' she's like, 'If you don't like it, go back to your own country.' She'll say, 'What are you doing here anyway? I don't understand why you all came to a country that isn't yours.'"

She pauses for a moment. The wind in the park is low and gentle, the children's voices bounce from slide to swing to tree branches lost in a tangle of evergreen. I try to picture Sara's country, try to imagine "going back."

"One time," Sara goes on, "I got there like half an hour late, because back then I took a bus, and the bus was really late. She was furious. She yelled at me really bad, horrible, horrible screams, *horrible*," she rolls her *R*s with force, her voice high. "She yelled with words, her voice really loud, she made me feel so bad."

"Did you ever say anything back to her, when she screamed like that?"

"No, I'm afraid of her," Sara replies quickly, without hesitating.

Sara admits that she wanted to leave Leslie many times, but seven dollars an hour was hard to walk away from. "I would always say I was going to leave her, but I wanted to help my sister and my grandmother. So, I'd say to myself, 'If I quit working with her, I'm not going to find another job.'"

I nod along, lean in and listen, and try to understand the motives of one who would spit cruelty and another who would come back, day after day. But the complexity of relationships like these goes beyond simple oppositions like entitled and deprived, privileged and oppressed. Bound by distinct threads of public power and private histories, each of us meets our own strengths and weaknesses from our unique place on a tapestry of social categories that determines our access to power and freedom. Those categories teach us how to value each other and, in a very intimate way, how to value ourselves. For Sara, shaped by a personal history of loss and a habit of submission, something of this complexity keeps her bound to this angry patrona prone to fits of rage.

Sara continues to work with Leslie up until this day, though she managed to leave her briefly just after Sara gave birth to her first child. She only returned when Leslie's boyfriend, to whom Sara refers as her "angel," offered a kind smile and generous terms in the dark days that followed Sara's entrance into motherhood. It was a time when she would feel more intimately than ever the tightly spun threads that limited her freedom, and the impossible choices her own mother had once made.

Rosa

When Rosa woke up in a Los Angeles apartment in 1980, she was almost two thousand miles away from her children but one step closer to the future she wanted for them. If a weekly wad of cash laid out in her husband's construction-calloused palm was the way for Rosa's family to get ahead, then she would do whatever it took to be by his side and make sure he passed those bills along to her. Working, even if it meant being apart from her children, would have been natural for a working-class Mexican woman of the 1970s, and for a divided family like hers, leaving the kids behind was part of her mothering job.

So, after a year of parenting alone in Puebla, she had followed Arturo to Los Angeles, a sprawling metropolis already bursting with millions of Mexican transplants, more and more of whom were women. But for Rosa, the bustling city that rose up around these familiar faces took the shape of four thin walls and a lonely, sun-bright window in a small apartment with no children to care for or toasted seeds to peddle and no more laundry to wash than what little she and her husband wore in a day. For the first time since she could remember, Rosa was bored. So, when the wife of her husband's boss approached her with a casual offer, she was all ears.

"Rosa, what are you doing there at home?" the woman asked.

"Absolutely nothing!" she replied.

"Well, why don't you come over and help me in the kitchen? Why don't you come work for me?"

Rosa was itching to get out of the apartment and do her part, so for the next three weeks, she spent each weekday at this woman's house doing what she'd always done at her own home—everything needed to keep a large family clean and laundered and fed. In the morning, she made breakfast for seven people. Another meal at midday. Then, after spending the afternoon cleaning the house and washing and ironing the clothes, she made dinner for seven again.

"Guess how much she paid me per week?" Rosa asks me, an eager smile wide across her face.

I can't guess. I don't. How much would a full-time servant have been worth in LA in 1980? $150 a week? $200? How much did women's work cost back then?

"Fifty dollars!" she cries.

Rosa laughs and leans back in her chair, slaps a hand on my kitchen table. Her hazel eyes sparkle, set high above bronze cheekbones traced with years of living—joy and pain and hard-knuckled resolve, always laughter. She knows she's shocked me. She wanted to shock me. We're following a familiar script now. It's the one where I respond, "Fifty? No!" my eyes wide with disbelief, the one where she tosses her head back in response and cackles because she can see that I can see how scandalous it all is. How absurd to think that fifty dollars a week could compensate for all that work. When we both know what a woman's work is worth. When we both know, in our own way, what it costs to replace a mother.

Her husband didn't like it. He wanted her to quit. "Well what else am I going to do?" she challenged him, "I'm bored at home alone, sitting around eating and sleeping and getting fat."

Still he protested; it wasn't right for her to be earning so little. "Stay home and I'll pay you the fifty dollars," he said. His own job as a construction worker and bricklayer was bringing in a solid $350 each week. Bricklaying was a man's work after all—public, recognized, as visible as the apartment buildings and mansions it raised. Brick after brick shutting the private world of domesticity in tight.

Rosa's husband's work was so visible, in fact, that the tangible labor of builders and bricklayers like him was very much on the mind of policymakers and politicians seeking to overhaul an immigration system strained by the rising influx of migrants in the early 1980s. Increasingly, these Mexican migrants were women and families, many of whose husbands had gained legal entrée to the US as former Bracero workers and sought to take advantage of new family reunification policies that allowed them to send for wives and children. But as the ethnic landscape of communities and workplaces shifted, the significance of immigration acquired exaggerated proportions in the US imaginary.

The ensuing public conversation around immigration reform met a US society still reeling from the aftereffects of two tumultuous decades of radical identity politics and second-wave feminism. Public rhetoric located immigration conveniently within its ready-made frameworks. Mexican American cultural nationalism met with deep currents of American racism to fire up a debate about the assimilability of Mexicans and other Hispanic immigrants. And national passions around family values and the ugly narrative of the "welfare mother" converged with a growing pattern of woman- and family-based migration from Mexico to yield accusations of anchor babies and invading families of freeloaders.[13] In heated political debates around the 1986 Immigration Reform and Control Act, this rhetoric floated in and out of the narrative of the criminal immigrant that had begun to haunt the moral shadows of a changing American society.

But throughout these rhetorical battles, everybody agreed on the value of work in a man's world. Labor needs in construction and agriculture came up again and again as the thorn in the side of an "illegal"-free American economy, and a reality to contend with in any sustainable immigration reform effort. In fact, from agricultural exceptions to immigration enforcement to government-sponsored guest worker programs, the US government has consistently recognized that important sectors of our economy have developed around the cheap, benefits-free labor that immigrant men provide. Recognition of this work is written into the legal code, full of historical exemptions from penalty for farmers hiring undocumented workers. Consider the Texas Proviso, a provision in a 1952 Immigration and Nationality Act that sheltered Texas farmers from prosecution for hiring undocumented workers. The Bracero guest worker program, largely responsible for the family-based Mexican migration at the source of the debate, has its roots in the same need for cheap labor.

But when it comes to the feminine spaces of home and nursery, careworkers and cleaners rarely make it into the spotlight. In a notable exception, the "Nannygate" scandal of Bill Clinton's early administration shed a rare spotlight on the shadow world of immigrant domestic work. In 1993, attorney general nominee Zoe Baird, was forced to step down when it was discovered that she had employed undocumented immigrant women to look after her children and had failed to pay social security taxes on their behalf. In the heated debates of the early 1990s around both immigration and working motherhood, the Zoe Baird affair became a frenzied mess when a second nominee, Kimba Wood, was also discovered to have employed unauthorized domestic workers, along with two California politicians, Pete Wilson and Michael Huffington, both of whom had fashioned their campaigns on an anti-immigrant platform. Despite the visibility, the scandals did little to bring the labor of immigrant housekeepers and nannies to the debates, and the value of their women's work quickly receded back into the private spaces of dust-free mantels and vacuumed carpets—out of the public conversation and earning pennies on the dollar relative to men's manual labor.

The distance between Rosa's fifty dollars and her husband's $350 can be measured on the same network of social structures that debates the economic importance of the construction worker and ignores the productive value of the maid, because this architecture of policy and practice relies on a patriarchal organization of value that is as old as human society. In patriarchy, almost all human activity and natural phenomena acquire either a masculine gravity or a feminine air, the latter always somehow less. Reason is cloaked in the masculine and prized over emotion, which is made feminine in the pairing. So, too, the mind over the body, the public over the private, working father over stay-at-home mother, bricklayer over housekeeper. An entire sphere of human activity—"women's work"—is associated with the feminine, ceding its value and its visibility to the economics of Labor, with a capital *L*. And Rosa's husband earns seven times as much as she.

"Let me pay you the money," he'd said. After all, it was only fifty dollars.

But for Rosa, his work or her work didn't matter so much. Getting ahead was a family affair, and when an opportunity came up to earn more together, she was happy to leave a job where she worked so hard for so little. After a year spent in a lonely Los Angeles apartment and three weeks tending to a patrona with a brood to feed, the couple set their sights on Texas, where they'd found a good construction job for him and a live-in gig for Rosa. In this new position, they both could live together rent-free, earning and saving and sending their monthly remittances home to the five children who waited for them. And loving, of course. There in the same bed, where laborer and immigrant and Mexican and mother would soon converge with wife and lover, drawing the thread of sexuality into the tangle of Rosa's intersected identities and binding her ever tighter to a landscape of limited options and hard choices.

Elena

"But what will you do with these interviews?" Elena asks as she motions me to a chair at her cluttered dining room table. "What's your purpose?"

I take a seat and do my best to explain myself, taken aback by Elena's challenge and by her imposing presence—thickly lined eyes, broad shoulders, and swept-back auburn bangs. As I stumble through my pitch, I notice a book among the table's scattered papers and stretch my neck to make out the title: *Oppenheimer*, in severe black type, with "Fondo de Cultura Económica" stamped at the foot of the cover. The book rests casually beside us—Francisco Ayala's 1942 study of Franz Oppenheimer's theory of the sociology of the state and a favorite of mid-century Mexican intellectuals.[14]

I return to my explanation, and once Elena is satisfied with my answer, she leans in toward me, rests her elbows on the table and her chin on her interlaced hands, and nods at the recorder. I tap the red square and she begins her story in the middle, leaving it to me to sort out origins and first causes.

Elena never planned to emigrate. Only a year of classes and one thesis away from a business degree at the local university in Monterrey, Mexico, she had been drawn in by the promise of an immigrant domestic's earnings: $1,200 a month as a live-in nanny in New York, a pamphlet told her; $150 a day to clean houses in Houston, she heard from a visiting aunt. So she left her classes and her job as a sales assistant in a Mexican branch of a large multinational company and set her sights on the savings she would accumulate and the English she'd perfect after a year in the States. Upon her return, she'd have a healthy nest egg and an edge up in a competitive job market. As an added bonus, she would gain a little independence from her family home, where she had spent her youth tending to siblings and adhering to her single working mother's strict rules.

She made arrangements, finished up her last semester, and announced the move to her family just two days before leaving. From house to house, from grandmother to aunt to aunt, she explained to each of them, "I'm leaving. I'm going to Houston to work."

"In what job?" she tells me they asked.

"As a nanny," she replied, clear and direct.

Her family would surely have been surprised, as taken aback as I have been by the clipped tone of Elena's answers and the cool resolve in her voice. After all, Elena's choice implied more than just a new location. Her increased economic security would come at a cost—a downward shift in social class, troubled at the intersection of value, social hierarchy, and cultural differences.[15]

For a woman like Elena, migration was a bold choice among limited options, but it was not the survival strategy it had been for Sara's mother, or the only hope for something more that Rosa had understood it to be. Elena's middle-class urban upbringing had afforded her more choices in life and provided her with a cultural capital that opens doors, the kind of practices and knowledge that don't appear on a university degree. A taste for subdued colors, for instance, the careful pronunciation of a final *s* or an intervocalic consonant, or the impatient air from the other side of a counter that signals authority and communicates expectation. These differences influenced every facet of Elena's experience as an immigrant nanny in the US, starting with the crossing itself.

She secured a tourist visa with the help of a fraudulent letter from a former supervisor claiming that she was still employed in Mexico. Armed with compelling documents in a proper handbag and the right inflection in her voice, she was able to work the system.

"I had everything I needed to justify that I wasn't coming over to work. There wasn't any problem. They give you the visa for ten years. It's the permission that gives you problems, the one they stamp every six months. So, every six months I'd go and renew it, go again and renew it. I respected the rules and I never had any problems."

Everything in order. Respectful of the rules, and only technically illegal. Like hiring an undocumented construction worker or paying the maid in cash.

Once Elena arrived, she stayed with her aunt's friend, Chepa, counting on the older woman's church network to help her find a job.[16] When Chepa told her of a position caring for recently adopted newborn twin boys, Elena considered the job description and the pay and made her choice thinking only of earning and saving.

The babies were only three days old when she started. Seven hours a day, five days a week. They were, in many ways, Elena's. Because of the time the señora spent with her older daughter, Elena exercised exclusive control over the boys' weekday care. They were hers to shape as she saw fit, with order and rules and respect—and heaps of the kind of affection that, Elena insists, comes naturally to a *mamá hispana*. She took pride in the environment she created for the boys and in the values she imbued in them.

"I had it very well organized. I'd put them in the swing, let them fall asleep, then clean the kitchen. Then I'd watch them and give them their bottles and play with them, then put them down again and clean something else. As soon as a load was done, I'd put a twin in the swing and go take it out. I really don't know how I did it," she says with a laugh, "but that house was impeccable, always."

Like a regular Superwoman, Elena appears to have handled those domestic demands with the kind of ease that might inspire self-doubt in a less confident *patrona*; or relief, perhaps, depending on the sense of "mother" one chooses to adopt. But Elena assures me that there was never any problem with the señora. She was a lovely person, and of course she understood that the children loved Elena. That the children wanted Elena. That the children reached for Elena at the end of the day and cried out to her through tears in a Spanish their own mother couldn't understand.

"My name is Elena"—she'd remind the boys when their toddler's language turned her name into "Ma"—"and I'll be back tomorrow."

And as sure as the sun rising through a quiet apartment window all her own, Elena always returned the next day. And the next day, and the next. And year after year, until her mother and siblings finally gave up on the eldest daughter coming home to finish her degree and step back onto the path she'd started in Monterrey. By the time the boys had learned not to call her "Ma," Elena had made a life for herself in the US. In doing so, she traded some positions for others—citizen for illegal worker, closely surveilled daughter for independent young woman, and middle-class professional for something a bit more ambiguous. It became important to make distinctions.

"I say I'm a nanny and people think I'm sitting around watching soap operas," she tells me. "That's a typical nanny, right? She spends all day watching her *novelas* instead of playing with the children. Give the kids a candy or a toy, and back to the TV. I never do this."

It's a stereotype with which I'm unfamiliar, but Elena describes her understanding of "the typical nanny" with confidence. She knows these women, she insists. She talks with them in the park, just like I do. Despite the differences in social class, as a worker and migrant she shares an identity with the other women that I never will. All of us together there in the park—me, the white lady with the brown kids; they, the brown women with the white kids; and Elena, neither one nor the other. Her complexion more golden than the other women's, framed by thick auburn waves with red-tinted highlights that catch the light in her eyes. The twins' complexion, a touch darker than the other children in the park, small and sharp-featured little faces with racially ambiguous lines. Perhaps these other "typical" nannies told her things they didn't tell me, about the *novelas*, for instance.

Elena's observations are not casual. These women were an important part of her working life at the time. In an industry defined by individual experience and word of mouth, her fellow nannies held a good deal of power over Elena. For the most part, she felt good about her job and about the treatment she received, but then she'd hear the other women talking in the park about how well they were paid, how minimal their workload, and she'd head home wondering, "Wait, are my bosses taking advantage of me?" It colored the way she saw things the next day at work, wondering if she were getting the short end of some stick she'd failed to recognize.

"You go home and you see things differently, you know? Like 'my bosses are using me.' But then you go on and you think, 'No, these are good people. They treat me like family,' and you forget about it. Then later, you find out what the nannies said was all lies!"

All those ideal working conditions and fat wages, nothing more than lies told by gossiping nannies, Elena accuses. Those nannies in the park, the ones who spend their workdays watching soap operas and bringing each other down.

"Just think about it," she urges, "all the people who come here, how do most of them get here? Undocumented." Her tone is matter-of-fact, and I wonder if she considers herself "undocumented," with her visa stamped *tourist* and renewed again and again.

"They come out of need," she continues, "for a better future. But as soon as they see someone rising up, they'll pull them down. Pull another down, so they can rise up." She looks me in the eye and goes on with her explanation in an even voice, patiently didactic. "I mean, if I ask for a raise," she reasons, "the mom's going to say, 'But Elena, I pay you really well.' And then along comes Juanita, and she says, 'Pay me half of that and I'll do the same work and more. I'll work weekends.' Well, the mom's going to say, 'Juanita is cheaper, I'll stick with her.'"

Elena's opinions reflect the reality of the invisible economy that drives domestic work. Industry standards like wages and job descriptions are determined almost exclusively by informal conversations among fellow domestics and the information that employers choose to share with each other when making and receiving referrals. When it comes to going rates and employer expectations, the conversation at a patrona's dinner party is as important as the *comadres* chatting outside the preschool doors.[17]

So Elena may be right to say that there is nothing more to the immigrant nanny industry than a free-market wildcard going to the lowest bidder, but she also understands that the work of the mothercoin is subject to more than one logic and more than one system of values. While the nanny's paid labor trades in clean transaction—an hourly wage, a task fulfilled—the work of mothering is as much about the relationship it engenders as it is about the hands that push the stroller or the arms that sweep the floor. The logic of relationships is reciprocal, its rewards paid out in emotional bonds and the sense of self that is expressed through care. More than labor or hours, the nanny shares something of herself along with her vigilant eye and bouncing hip. A certain identity. A certain place in the order of a family and a home. Elena understands this, even when she perceives that others don't.

"People who have babies and hire nannies, they don't see it. They don't see that the love I give those kids isn't something you pay for."

For Elena, the job is about the love, unacknowledged though it may be. And in some ways, too, it's about the soap operas and the almost-business degree and the tourist visa and handbag, all those class markers that give her more power at the park and in her employers' home, but isolate her, too. And for Elena, the job is also about the things she knows and that she tries to teach the boys. How to respect your grandparents and obey your mother, how to see the other side of things.

Like the time in the car when one of the boys repeated his grandfather's complaint about immigrants stealing American jobs.

"He said, 'Oh, the economy is bad because there are a lot of immigrants here, so Americans can't get work.' No, no, no! I stopped the car and explained to him: 'No, señor! Do you see those guys cutting the lawn? Why do you think they're doing that? Because no one else wants to do it. And how many American nannies do you see? How many pretty, blue or green-eyed, blonde nannies do you see? None, because they don't want to do it.'"

Or the time she drove them to a certain stretch of road on West-park Drive where day-laborers and taco-sellers have their own lessons to teach about immigrants and the economy. Where, each morning, groups of men, mostly immigrants from Central America and Mexico, gather and wait for a half a day's work on the hot asphalt or in the shade of an overpass.

"Do you see those guys waiting for someone to pick them up and take them to a job?" Elena asked the boys as she drove slowly by. "Do you know what happens? People pick them up and they don't pay them. They don't give them food. After they do all that work."[18]

"But why don't they do anything about it?" the boys asked.

"Because they don't have any rights." Her voice is quick, strained in the retelling. "Because it's not their country. It's really cool to abuse those who don't have any power, huh?"

But as hard as Elena works to keep the boys from growing up with the wrong ideas, she isn't their only teacher. Evan, especially, struggles to sort out for himself the contradictions between his *nana's* lessons and those he receives from grandfather and television and news reports populated by dangerous stereotypes.

"Elena," he once reasoned aloud, "you're a good Mexican. But there are some Mexicans who aren't good. I know that you're one of the good ones, but there are bad Mexicans, too."

"Evan," she responded quickly, "don't generalize."

"It's these little things," she explains. "If I wasn't Hispanic, they would grow up with this idea that immigrants are bad for the country and they'd pass it on to their children. I have to explain to them the other side of the coin."

These kinds of lectures emerge from a certain meeting place of class, culture, and experience, an inflection of judgment that Elena doles out freely as she simultaneously chastises and defends a people that, for Elena, both are and are not *her* people.

"I love my culture," she says. "I love the food, I love everything. I just don't like to be caught up in Hispanic areas. Yesterday I went to mass. The little kids, three or four little kids and pregnant on top of it!" Her tone becomes evaluative, conclusive, "Hispanics are hard workers," she concedes as she leans into me across the table—close, in the manner of a confidante—"but they have too many kids."

For Elena, the logic reveals itself in observation, in nannies in the park who aren't strict enough for her style, mothers at church who don't curb their fertility the way she believes they should. They're all just so different than she is. There's so much more she feels she understands. She's not like those other muchachas, the ones who cross a river in the night and give their children too much candy, the ones who lie about working conditions and undercut Elena's pay negotiations. Too many kids. *Novelas* and gossip and Medicaid—that's not for people like Elena, with her tinted highlights and high cheekbones, with her port of entry smile and shelf full of books. But Elena does not question the values that inform her judgment of the other nannies, nor does she seem to direct her critique to the system that underlies their social immobility.

There is a place where the American Dream and American reality come face to face—the former, an available narrative of hope and liberty for those with desperate needs and bold aspirations; the latter, a history of stories told about those who deserve to serve and those who deserve to be served. For Elena, that place of convergence is at a park, squatting by the sandbox or a playground jungle gym surrounded by women and children who do not look or act like her or hers. Because the American Dream's promise of a rise through the ranks of society for those who are hardworking and honest and just a little bit extraordinary feels more available to Elena than to the other nannies.

These other women's American reality follows a different storyline, one that recognizes that this exceptional society of ours has always maintained a standing servant class. It is a group kept in its place through just the kind of nonstandardized wage negotiations that Elena refers to, which is legitimized again and again by just the kind of accusations of laziness and immature materialism that Elena implies.[19] When it comes to today's servant class, the problem is magnified by the shadow nature of domestic work and the reluctance of well-meaning employers to acknowledge the class implications in the industry.

Because the patronas' dinner party conversation is circumscribed by a cultural tradition saturated with a distinctly American rhetoric of social mobility and bootstrap ideology, ideals that generate a vague sense of unease in many employers of domestic workers. While America's class-blind focus on the hard-work-equals-personal-success equation has made us a nation in which upward and downward class mobility has historically been a real possibility, it has also created a way of talking about our social organization that ignores the hierarchy of social classes that does exist.[20] In this contradiction between how we talk about society and how we organize it, a dinner table falls silent and many a patrona shoulders the ambivalence of her position alone.

The realities of the mothercoin inhabit these silences and seep into the words we use, "I'm looking for someone to help me clean," we might say, "a girl to come in and watch the kids for me." Rather than hiring an employee, we seek a vague "someone," always there to "help." Because in a world of discourse and meaning that ignores the reality of the servant class and understands "women's work" as immaterial to larger economic forces, the outsourcing of such work is wrapped up in language of consumption, a guilty pleasure of the upper-class woman draped in white across the chaise longue.[21] As a result, families with real needs find themselves negotiating an industry with unspoken rules and vaguely defined practices, and cloaked in a hazy sense of entitlement that belies the urgency of their situation.

In reality, for the great bulk of American families, the situation is indeed urgent. Families in this country are working harder than ever to make ends meet, and childcare ranks as high as housing among oppressive costs of living.[22] Gender roles aside, most families couldn't afford the luxury of a single income earning model even if they chose it, and for families with young children, childcare has become one of the greatest financial and logistical challenges they face.[23] And they face it alone. Despite the "developed" moniker it enjoys, the US ranks far lower than its counterparts in its provision for childcare for its future workers, leaders, entrepreneurs, and consumers.[24] The reigning ideals of free market individualism have left families to foot the bill for that market's single greatest resource: its human capital.

These same individualist values have created a white collar culture of success that demands more working hours than ever before and a blue-collar practice of benefits-free part-time jobs that require round-the-clock shifts just to make ends meet.[25] Overlay this toxic mix with a stalled-out gender revolution in which the majority of domestic and childcare work is still done by the woman in most heterosexual American households and the frivolous lady of leisure begins to look a lot different. And a lot more desperate.

Yet even as we live these realities, so many of us still think of ourselves in terms of our ideals—equal, empowered women, class-blind, and egalitarian. The woman wiping the spilled milk off the counter when we come home at the end of a long day, the one who smiles and collects her things and hugs our children goodnight before slipping out the door to her own foreign reality, shoulders a legacy of servitude that may be something of a threat to those ideals. With one squeeze of a sullied mop, she has subsidized our feminism and reproduced the most glaring of global inequalities right there in our home, on a living room rug still warm with an afternoon of blocks and trains and light-up toys. It's no wonder these conversations make us uncomfortable.

And if conversations among employers are bound by a complex web of cultural values and social identities, the information exchanged between employees comes up against equally formidable obstacles. The fierce competition Elena references, the sheer exhaustion at the end of the day, these factors can complicate efforts to organize workers and professionalize the occupation. When a day's work is a day's rent for a woman accustomed to the invisible margins of her larger society, the promise of collective bargaining is a hard sell.[26] And from Elena's place on a bench at a neighborhood park, among nannies who are and are not like her, the job itself carries certain implications that impede solidarity.

Loaded with value assumptions about class and race, the nanny's identity as Elena knows it is rooted in an American reality that doesn't match her own modest dream—to earn, save, and move on. If only it hadn't been for the two small boys she's loved for thirteen years, who both do and do not belong to her.

It would take some time for Elena to sort out all the ways her bond with the school-aged twins differed from the relationship that the outside world recognized. The boys felt like hers in so many ways, but she knew that her love mattered only so long as her work was needed, and by the time she and I spoke at a dining room table cluttered with papers and books, she understood that her life with the boys was coming to a close.

"No, I think that it's not going to be the same anymore. They'll have more activities; they won't need me anymore. I still tell them, before I leave, that I love them. 'You know that I love you, right?' So they know that they're important to someone, you know?"

And after thirteen years, Elena is sure she's made her mark. "They have their values very grounded," she assures me, "*bien cementados.*"

Solid enough to know that Mexicans cut the grass because no one else will, that boys must keep their rooms clean, that mothers and grandmothers deserve respect, and that, though their *mamá hispana* may love them best of all, nannies are only part of the family for so long.

Magdalena

When Magdalena was nineteen years old, she arrived at her aunt's doorstep in Houston carrying little more than uncertain hope and the ambiguous memory of a South Texas beach and a border agent's apartment. By the time she was twenty-three, folding laundry in my neighbor's living room, she had married a fellow unauthorized immigrant from El Salvador, given birth to two young daughters, and cleaned the houses of a number of American families. Watching her work as I awkwardly pull an item or two from an overflowing laundry basket to fold as I listen, it's hard not to be struck by her beauty, the graceful lines from jaw to hip, the bright symmetry in her brown eyes and cascade of chestnut hair. The tale of the border agent and the movie theater lingers, and even as she launches into stories of demanding bosses and the injustices of her experience as an unauthorized immigrant in this country, the memory of her crossing persists. It will bleed into the conflicts she recounts—her defiance before an unreasonable employer, her submission in the face of a dominating man.

By the time we talk, Magdalena has learned a thing or two about living in the shadows of American society. More than anything else, she explains, it means work and fear. Work, which earns her enough to buy her daughters baby dolls and send them to a school with computers, to wire money home to a loved one in an emergency. And fear, the constant threat of deportation and immigration raids at a disco, a bus stop, her husband's work, so pervasive it moves her to warn the girls, "Take care of your things. Treat them well, because from one day to the next we might be back in El Salvador."

But in the end, the wages trump the fear. "In this country, when there's work, there's hope. There are so many women," she adds, pausing to shake out a pair of tights and dig for a matching sock, "who come to this country just to find one day of work."

Magdalena has worked for many days, for many kinds of women. Her experiences have all been different, but one truth holds across the families she has encountered: American children require a lot of attention. "The time and patience that I put into taking care of my two daughters, even four kids, that's how much time you need to care for one American child. And watching three American kids is like caring for twelve of your own. Everyone knows that American kids are really sensitive, and they need a lot of care and attention because they're your responsibility from the moment they're left in your care."[27]

I wince, finding myself on the other side of Magdalena's observations—how fragile my children seem, how fully they must therefore need me. Our perceptions of childhood and motherhood are deeply intertwined. The one creates the other. In the American middle-class world of turn of the twenty-first-century motherhood I've known, the sense of childhood as fragile and inviolable reflects a climate of political stability, social privilege, and a mandate to social class reproduction that focuses on nurturing and educating children well into young adulthood before sending them out into the world of white-collar competition.[28] These delicate, attention-hungry children are the social and cultural purview of the mother, who must therefore be a constant force moving before and about the child as a buffer to the world outside. So too, her hired replacement.

In Madgalena's experience, the American child's peculiar sensibility has something to do with the tendency of the American patrona to watch a caregiver's every move. "I've worked with so many people," she reflects, "and the experiences are very, very different. I've worked with señoras who spend the whole day with the kids and with me, and they don't make me uncomfortable at all. Because they don't say 'look, do this, or do that.' I just figure out how they'd like me to do things and I do it. But I've had others who won't leave even for half an hour, like they're desperate to be at the house."

It's a question of style, then. Of age and social class and personal histories. Each relationship unique, within a balance of power that always tips in the employer's favor. But Magdalena insists that she was no pushover.

"When I don't like something, I say so."

These confrontations, she tells me, would go something like this:

"You know what?" she'd say to an overbearing employer. "It makes me uncomfortable that you're here because you don't let me work the way I want to. And if you don't try to be a little more in the background, I'm going to have to stop working for you."

"I make you uncomfortable?" they'd say. "But why?"

"Because you're watching everything, always following behind what I do and watching how I clean and how I do things."

"Oh. Well," the patrona might respond, "if I've made you feel this way, I'm sorry. It wasn't my intention. I'll try to change a little."

And Magdalena, resistant and in the right, would emerge victorious. A woman like her may only have a few cards in her pocket to play in the game of power and choice, but when she's the sole author of her own story, she gets to lay them out with a fierce kind of dignity.

"Look," she recalls saying, "I know that you're the boss and I'm your worker, and I don't want to argue with you, but the truth is simply that I don't like how you're being and I don't feel comfortable. So I'm going to have to quit this job."

Not all of Magdalena's employers forced these uncomfortable confrontations, though. In some homes, free of constant vigilance and instruction, she felt free to make her own choices about how to do her work without judgment. That's how it was with the good patrona, the soft-spoken woman with the children whom Magdalena briefly loved.

When she started with this family, the children were quite young and Magdalena soon came to feel real affection for the baby and toddler, and for their mother as well. Like other "good patronas," this woman gave her employee the freedom she needed to do her job well. For Magdalena, this meant communicating expectations clearly. "Look," the woman would say when Magdalena arrived in the morning, "today in general I want you to help me with these three things. If you can't get to the rest, that's okay, but I need you to make sure you get these three things done."

This kind of direct communication about job expectations ranks high on a professional domestic worker's wish list. After dignity and respect, what workers say they want most is for the work to be treated as a legitimate job and for the worker to be given control over the work process.[29] The need responds to a prevailing sense of domestic labor as a private affair, an offshoot of femininity that is managed in knowing gestures and unspoken assumptions. "Of course, housecleaning includes laundry," an employer might assume. "Certainly, looking after the children means changing their sheets—every Monday, just like it's supposed to be done." When the work is treated as work and recognized as legitimate employment, written contracts can replace assumptions like these, performance reviews might resolve tensions, and an employee could have the chance to respond, "I'd be happy to change and launder the sheets—for twenty dollars more a week."

For Magdalena, the scope of her work with this family was clear—these three things, the daily work of a home with two young children, and two standing expectations. Magdalena laughs when she recalls the señora's reminder, "Make sure my husband's boxers are in their place, and the children's pajamas. Make sure that's done before you go." Her face and voice soften as she offers this memory, eyes steady on her deftly folding fingers.

Magdalena worked three eight-hour days a week for this family. When she started, the baby was only a few months old and the older boy was still small and affectionate.

"I had to put the little one to bed before I left each day," she smiles. "He wouldn't go to sleep on his own if he knew I was there. He'd rather stay with me than go with his mom. When his mom told him that I wasn't going to be working for them anymore, he said no. He didn't want anyone else but me."

The señora didn't want anyone else either, but their careful domestic balance could not sustain the contrary desires of each woman's husband. The señora explained to Madgalena that her husband insisted that their nanny have more flexibility.

"They trusted me," Magda insists, "the parents and the kids. They were very endeared to me. The woman even told me, 'If it wasn't that my husband wants someone full time, seven days a week . . . I don't want you to go, but well, I can't go against my husband.'"

Magdalena explains that it wasn't the seven-day commitment her own husband protested, it was the late hours. "They wanted someone who could be there on Saturday and Sunday so they could go out. And since my own husband won't let me work at night . . ." Her voice trails while she finds the words to help me understand. "My husband thinks only bad women work at night, *mujeres malas*." She pulls a bedsheet from a pile of linens and flips it sharply in the space between us, folds it against her chest and thighs, once in thirds, and then again. "My husband is very *machista*," she explains.

Magdalena assumes that I'll understand the word *machista* the way she does. Maybe she means to say that *machista* men are overprotective. Or that *machista* men are overbearing. Or that *machista* men are always jealous or suspicious. In any case, for her, *machista* is explanation enough as to why a man would think that night work is for bad women. I can't say if Magdalena intuits what I do about this sentiment, how it feeds into a perception of womanhood that allows for few options and no morally virtuous power.

In the *machista* meaning system that I'm familiar with, a good woman wears the saintly veil of the sexless mother, epitomized by the Virgin Mary; the bad woman is both oversexed and a traitor to men, the blameworthy Eve. Everywhere this Madonna–whore dichotomy surfaces, from Magdalena's rural Salvadoran hometown to the pages of Nobel laureate Octavio Paz, its purpose is to shame a woman's power—her work, her sexuality, her agency in a public world.[30] When the *mujer mala* is invoked in the *machista* context, it is associated with the *mujer pública*, the shameless prostitute. How dreadful it must be for Magdalena's husband to be a *machista* man in the emasculating world of the unauthorized immigrant. How necessary to control the pretty wife with the auburn hair. How important to dominate and protect, to be a man.

So for me, the word *machista* offers its own explanation for why Magdalena's husband made her quit her job. It has to do with a power dynamic that is unfair, some might say unjust, maybe even shamefully oppressive. But I am not the one who said goodbye for the last time to a little boy in fresh-pressed pajamas because of my man's machismo. I am not the one who needs to weave it into a personal story of defiance.

"So, what's your perception of this, your reaction to it?" I ask about her husband's prohibition.

"Simply that he's the one who works and provides for us. He can tell me if I can or can't go."

"But you work, too, right?"

"I work to help him, but if I can't, he does it all."

Like Rosa's fifty dollars against her husband's $350, a man's work counts more, even within the intimacy of Magdalena's marriage and her own perception. But where Rosa's labor was devalued in currency, Magdalena's is short-changed in power. The implications run deep.

Magdalena first met her husband in a laundromat. They flirted over the sounds of tumbling dryers and the boisterous exchanges of other migrants moving in and out of the machines' rumble in Spanish accents both familiar and strange. He was Salvadoran, too, a recent immigrant like her. She must have been barely twenty. As their relationship progressed, she learned of a girlfriend he had back home and protested that he spent all his free time at his sister's, on the phone with his "ex." It was a double life common among immigrant men, one lover here, one lover there. Magdalena complained, but he kept it up. She yelled, but he accused. To keep the peace they simply stopped visiting family—no more time spent at his sister's house, no more visits by Magdalena to the aunt who had taken her in. And it's true that, with all the work and so much fear, there was little time to make friends. And Magdalena would have liked to attend church services, but her husband says she only goes to catch a man, not to praise God.

"So, to avoid problems," she concludes, "I try not to go against my husband."

Pati

When Pati first found her place with the Stevensons, the complicated problems of work and family were stories other people told. In those early days after her mother, María, had found her the live-in position, she felt nothing but gratitude toward her new employers. And despite how it would all turn out, she still insists that the good fortune was hers. "I'll never forget the opportunity they gave me to work with them, with no English and no references, to accept me into their home and leave their two-month-old child with a stranger." It was more than she had hoped for.

The Stevensons really were something of an answered prayer for a recent arrival with slim chances in a network-driven business like domestic nanny work. But then, there was María. Though Pati had been devastated when her mother left home, the other side of María's mothercoin had garnered her a significant value proposition in the eyes of the hiring parents of Houston's nanny network. After eighteen years with the same family, María had earned respect and a reputation for honest dependable work. "Eighteen years," Pati reflects in the stillness of her afternoon living room. "It's a lifetime."

When she first arrived, Pati had tried to make a go of it as a seamstress, an occupation for which she'd trained in El Salvador. But overwhelmed by a demanding boss, unfamiliar machines, and limited advancement in an industry geared toward altering rather than creating, she quickly shifted strategy. After just two days with an overbearing supervisor and an insufficient skill set, Pati took stock and made a choice that would leverage the professional currency her mother had saved up over those long years of separation.

"Mamá," she announced, "I want to be a nanny." She'd always loved children; surely this was something she could do well.

Eager to transfer to her daughter the industry value she had earned, María turned to her employer's contacts to find potential positions. When an opportunity for work as a full-time live-in for a young family came up, it was María who made the contact. María who arranged the interview, who drove Pati to the couple's home and interpreted for daughter and employers during the entire conversation. With María's impeccable recommendation and fluent English to vouch for them both, Pati's prospective employers didn't concern themselves with the language gap. "The language isn't important," the señora had said through María. "What good is someone who speaks perfect English if they don't treat your child well? We'll figure it out."

"That," Pati explains, "is how they came to trust me."

Though Pati describes her job as a generous gift for which she'll always be grateful, I can't help but think of the eighteen years she spent earning this opportunity, a lifetime of relationship lost to monthly envelopes, sturdy shoes, and, somewhere down the road, the trust of a stranger. And though her gratitude is sincere, it minimizes the very real and immediate need she met for her new employers, trusting strangers who may have seen Pati as their own answered prayer. With two full-time careers and a second baby that would arrive in less than two years, the Stevensons needed Pati as much as she needed them. And they were willing to pay for it.

The conditions, as Pati relates them, were ideal. In the beginning, with just the infant, the job consisted of childcare and cleaning, eight hours a day, five days a week. The couple treated Pati's garage apartment as her private home, with a separate entrance and strict off hours. In those first few days, the señora would often come home unexpectedly to check on them. To Pati's knowledge there were never any cameras watching her, though she tells me she would not have minded if there were. She was invited to eat with the family when she was on the clock and to use the credit card she'd been given for work to purchase food and items for her apartment.

Pati's place in the family only became more secure as time went on, and the stability allowed her to turn her attention toward her adopted home. With the help of free Saturday classes and the books and dictionaries purchased by her employers, she studied her way to a mastery of English and earned her American GED. When she learned how to drive, the couple offered her a car, but she preferred to purchase her own. Through it all, she came to see her ideal working conditions as a reflection of her employers' good nature and her own value as an employee. The job made sense, she judged, and changes unfolded rationally. When a second baby was born a year and a half after she started, her employers changed the pay and the nature of the work. She would no longer be responsible for cleaning, and would now earn more. In Pati's view, this new arrangement was only reasonable. As parents, the Stevensons' job was to provide, in one way or another, for the attention their young children needed.

Over the seven years Pati worked for the family, the pay and hours and expectations continued to shift along with the family's needs— eight-hour days became nine, cleaning was reintroduced when the children started school. Pati was happy to adjust. She was young and single and the couple was kind and respectful. But Pati doesn't describe a passive kind of gratitude. She was ready to negotiate her terms if necessary.

"With friends or other nannies, when we'd get together in the park, they'd say '*Ay no*, look at what my boss did to me, she got home and yelled at me.' Or, 'she comes to me and she tells me I have to wash the shoes, like the mud that gets all over the little boy's tennies.' But I say, 'No, that's not part of the job.' Because I was always really clear, 'Okay, they hired me for this and this and this. I'll do it all.' But if they come to tell me to do something more, I'll say, 'Okay, you want me to do more? Pay me more.'"

She tells me about a negotiation with her señora, when Pati asked if she could be paid to replace the housekeeper, who would be out with a new baby. The señora resisted, but Pati pushed back. When I ask if she was worried about the risk to her job, she explains, "Yes, but I knew I was good, and I wasn't asking her to do anything unfair."

Sure of her own value and of the basic respect she felt she'd earned from the couple, Pati felt confident in her position. And despite how it all turned out, she assures me that she will always be grateful, not only for the job the Stevensons gave her, but for the model they provided of a couple who discussed decisions with each other, cared for each other, and disciplined their children with love and consistency.

"For me," she remembers fondly, "they were always an example to follow. It was a great schooling in every sense, in marriage, in parenting. They were always a model for me."

And then there were the children. And then there was the love. When I ask Pati to describe her relationship with the kids, her eyes grow wide and her body becomes lighter, "Wonderful! I adore those children. I always saw them like my own. I was with them all day long! From seven thirty in the morning to six at night. I was the one who took care of them when they were sick, feeding them twice a day. I watched them grow, saw how they developed. Beautiful, beautiful."

For seven years, Pati cared for the Stevensons' children, dressing them, playing with them, bathing them, and putting them down for naps and quiet times. She disciplined them with the same consistency their parents modeled, and doted on them when they were ill, even when she herself was sick. "All of us sick there in the house together, but I was with them." She tells me several times that she loved them like they were her own. But she never forgot the truth: they would not be hers forever.

The other nannies in the park warned her, "You shouldn't love those kids like you do. Don't love them like you do because from one day to the next you won't be with them anymore and it's going to be hard for you, very hard."

"But that's impossible," she would protest. "I love them!"

"But you should pull yourself away from them little by little," they'd warn, "because the day's going to come when the *patrones* don't need you anymore and they're not going to care what you feel. The families here are like that, once they don't need you anymore. . . ."

But Pati tells me she couldn't imagine doing her job any other way. "I don't care. How am I going to stop loving a child? To do my job well, I have to love them, I have to love what I do."

There on the playground, Pati got her first taste of the mothercoin's paradox: a nanny's work carries the expectation of authentic affection but responds to a logic of transaction that ignores the love. On the flip side, the nanny's left-behind daughter is asked to find the mother-love she misses in remittances received. For nanny and mother, the logic of the mothercoin can't account for the inextricable relationship between carework and parenting. The work engenders the feeling, and the feeling grows with the work—that day-to-day presence of hands that brush and tongues that cluck and hearts that beat close beside a toddler's small cheek. Pati's *comadres* in the park would have her ignore the emotion and swear off the affection, but for Pati, the labor and the love can't be pulled apart. "To do my job well," she insists, "I have to love them."[31]

There were other moments, too, when the logic of the mothercoin failed her. When the little boy was just a toddler, not even two, he began to call her "Mommy." Pati knew it had to stop, but she wasn't sure how. The boy's father asked her for help. It hurt his wife's feelings, he explained, and Pati understood. So, together, they taught the boy to call Pati by her name. The child seemed to understand and said "Pati" in front of his parents, but the moment they walked out the door in the morning, he'd turn to Pati and call out for his daytime "Mommy." It broke her heart to put an end to this. "Why are you doing this?" she would plead with the boy. "I'm Pati, Pati!"

Eventually, the child learned, as Pati and her mother had, that some relationships can't be named with the words available to us. In the same way, Pati's narrative forges its own language of love and logic. She remembers her left-behind childhood as a slow sadness, a building melancholy that pushed her north toward an experience of affection that might heal old wounds.

"I was happy. I even think that I came to love those kids so, so much because they helped me with a depression that I carried from my country, from leaving my whole life behind and starting over here. It was like I took refuge in the playing and the crying, in the good and bad times of a baby. It helped me to forget a lot of things, the frustrations and depressions that I carried with me from my country."

On this end of the chain of care, Pati experienced the kind of love her mother María must have known when María turned away from a six-year-old daughter and stepped into the life of another child the same age. This kind of displaced affection fills the empty arms of a nanny-mother with the small embrace of another child but does little for the Patis who are left behind. So many empty places that are never filled. Maybe this is what drives the resolve of left-behind children to join a far-away mother, despite the certain truth that she will have made a life of her own well before her daughter arrives. In so many ways, this worldwide chain of diminishing care breeds an ever-growing "global heart transplant" on a regional scale, with waves of broken-hearted transnational sons and daughters making their own journey north in search of the promise their parents followed years before. Waves and waves of them.[32]

For a time, Pati was able to fill the empty space with the love and affection engendered by her work with the Stevenson children. But even as she gave herself fully to this unnamed relationship, the warning voices continued to sound in her head and in the figures of wizened nannies tsk-tsking on park benches, or standing at bus stops with arms crossed and eyebrows raised. *They are not yours*, the voices said. *One of these days, you could find yourself separated from them, and there will be nothing you can do.* She could not have known that one of these days was soon approaching, heralded by tender breasts, a swelling belly, and a far more nuanced relationship to the work of motherhood.

This nanny work is different from other jobs. Here is one difference: feelings that emerge in an employee's heart through day-to-day acts of care—lifting and patting and wiping away a tear or a dab of morning yogurt. Here is another: work that involves the most precious and intimate aspects of an employer's life—small vulnerable creatures, dirty underwear and soiled bedsheets and arguments and caresses and bedroom doors slamming. There is the difference of the emotion that must be summoned—to do her job, Pati must feel the love, not just feign it.

There is the difference of the dignity that can be missed—for Sara, the value of warm smiles and gestures is greater than the cool dependence of seven dollars an hour.

Another difference lies in a kind of power that should be public but plays out in private spaces. The power to negotiate, to dismiss, to protest, or to accuse. To withhold pay, benefits, approval, to demand more or less, to accept or walk away. All these negotiations take place in kitchens and hallways and bedrooms, over washers and dryers and the scrubbed tile of a kitchen floor, a child's playroom lined with stacked books and sorted toys. They are spaces unaccustomed to the logic of factory and restaurant and construction site, or the sleek lines of a fourth-floor office. Within the home, the logic of power responds to personal relationships, not professional ones. It is a dynamic governed by emotional promise, punishment, and reward.

Joan Tronto has reflected deeply on this difference, concluding that—in addition to the emotion-laden power dynamic of the home, in which "noncompliance is often emotionally and psychologically charged," two more characteristics of domestic work set it apart from other kinds of wage labor. On the one hand, the maid and nanny is seen as a substitute for the wife, brought in to do "women's work" that is in many ways not considered "work" at all. On the other, the value of a nanny's work is measured by the quality of her relationship with the children. So that something as intangible as an impulse to protect, to comfort, or to elicit joy is forced into a system that would quantify it in terms of wages earned for hours labored.[33]

So different this work, saturated with emotion, informed by trust, and closed up in our private spaces. Yet at the same time, so fundamental to the economic drivers of our public world—remittances that shore up entire regions, services that enable full workforce participation for parents, daily care that cultivates a generation of workers, leaders, and consumers. In response to this contradiction, activists and scholars call for a professionalization of the occupation, reforms and messaging that remind employers and the broader public that these women—immigrant or native, authorized or not—are employees like any other, deserving of professional respect and legal protections.

These voices tell us that domestic workers want clear and fair directives, autonomy and authority in childrearing and work tasks, control over their own time when they clean, and the kind of acknowledgment of humanity that Sara's good patrona showed with her smiles and sign language. They emphasize the need for clear job descriptions laid out in written contracts, a safe working environment, and working conditions to which domestic workers are entitled by law and policy.[34]

Many employers are unaware that regulations covering regular breaks, overtime pay, and payment into Social Security and Medicare extend to domestic workers, regardless of immigration status. Notably, the Fair Labor Standards Act, which sets legal requirements for minimum wage and overtime pay, applies to household employees. State laws governing wages and hours apply as well, as does the federal Social Security Domestic Employment Reform Act of 1994, mandating that domestic workers above a certain earnings threshold be classified as employee rather than independent contractors, a classification for which employer contribution to payroll taxes is legally required.[35]

All this, and a word or two in the morning or across an evening farewell—*Is your mother feeling better? How did your roses do in the storm?* There are so many ways to mitigate the mothercoin's vulnerabilities. But its contradictions are deeper than generous working conditions, and more intractable than one woman's resolve to be a kind, responsible employer. Because the mothercoin will never be able to make up for a society that does not support its mothers and young children. And in a nation of working families left on their own to balance their domestic lives, nothing tests the limits of resources and good intentions like the complications of a baby on the way.

CHAPTER 4

PREGNANT COMPLICATIONS

They told me, "You're a good worker,
but we want someone without any problems."

SARA

Sara

When Sara's baby was five months old, he became ill. She had just gone back to work full time, leaving the infant with an uncle's wife.

"She didn't take very good care of him for me. I mean, I've never found a job where they didn't work me a lot—I've only ever worked long hours—and when I gave my son over to be cared for, the babysitter didn't take good care of him for me. He got sick. He lost iron and got anemia. Thank God I was able to cure him. He had Medicaid at the time, so I could."

By that time, Sara had been living in her mother's world of immigrant domestic work for four years. She had negotiated *la morena*'s kind smile and meager pay and her employer Leslie's angry fits and reliable hourly rate, all the while experiencing the mothercoin as something to know and choose, a thing to pick up, examine, and flip to this side or that. But after little Drew was born, the two sides became muddled, confusing the right and wrong of life as an immigrant mother and domestic worker. The lines between love, labor, and sacrifice blurred as she confronted a world that seemed set up against her.

"He had Medicaid, but I can't get it anymore. They took it away and told me I needed to give them papers that I didn't have. There's so much racism there in the office of human services.[1] The racism is mostly with the Black people. They help the Black people who are waiting first, and then the Hispanic people. So when I tried to renew Medicaid for the kids, they told me I had to provide evidence that I was a legal resident. I'm not a resident, I just have a work permit. So, they asked me for so many papers that I didn't have, I couldn't get them."

"But your children were born here, yes? I didn't think parents had to be residents for their citizen children to receive benefits."

"Me neither! It depends on the social worker you get."

I ask her about the social workers she's encountered. Are they all women? Are there Hispanic workers? "Has the good or bad treatment you receive depended on the race of the social worker, in your experience?"

"In human services, it's all women, but the majority are African American," she explains.

In her response, Sara switches from *morena* (Black) to *afroamericana* (African American), adapting perhaps to how I've primed her by asking explicitly about "race."[2] Though she struggles with English eleven years after arrival, she has mastered the language of social categories well.

"Did she speak Spanish?"

"No."

"And how is your English?"

"My English is okay, but when you have an interview with them, they get a translator. I do the interviews in Spanish. And they don't tell me, 'This is my decision.' They tell me to wait and then they send it in a letter, saying: 'Your case has been denied, and here are the reasons why. If you decide to appeal, you can call . . . ' But you can't win with them. It's impossible. They always have another trick to pull."

Sara has been speaking quickly, chasing after her own words in an effort to help me understand how it all works together. As I follow along and try to make sense of what she tells me, her story reaches me through the filter of what I know and how I understand—things like citizen children's right to Medicaid and the frequency of infant anemia, so unrelated to a babysitter's care. From where I sit, Sara's explanation of her son's illness at first feels naïve. But then, there is a real difference between breastmilk and the formula a caregiver would give, the former so rich in iron and the latter so often watered down by families on a budget or substituted with cow's milk and all its hard-to-absorb iron. And though Medicaid and CHIP are not tied to parents' status, the health care and legal systems are so complicated and difficult to navigate that misinformation and confusion can lead to self-limiting access and excesses of power at the gates of the human services office.[3]

But Sara has found her own way to understand what it has meant to provide and care for her child, and she speaks from experience I've never known. Sara's words paint the picture of an entire system set up to make it impossible to mother her children the way she feels she should. Through confused filters of translation, misunderstanding, and imperfect explanation, more and more is asked of her. At work, impossible hours. In the health services office, papers she doesn't have, status she can't obtain, and time lost to plastic-bucket waiting-room chairs and fluorescent lights where she sits and waits and watches others move in and out, others who don't look like her but who do look like those in charge. This is what Sara sees. This is how she explains the injustice she feels, as tangible as the shrill admonition of a demanding boss or the pale of her baby's sickly pallor. She seeks, as we all do, someone to blame. And the story she tells me is peopled with the villains she perceives. Where I see broken and unjust systems, Sara sees faces—a racist social worker, a lazy babysitter, a despotic employer, all with a role to play in the tale she weaves.

When her son was a few years old, Sara found a stable job with the Taylor family. Five days a week, eight hours a day, she stepped into the family's home and took up all the tasks required to ensure domestic harmony. "I did the wash, picked the little girl up from school, walked the dog, picked up the dry cleaning, prepared the meals, bought the food. I did everything for her," she tells me, adding later, "I was a slave for them."

Everything for *her*, she says, a slave for *them*.

During this time, little Drew continued to be a source of concern for Sara. He often became sick, always with some problem or another, and in her job with the Taylors she couldn't take any time off. Her *patrones* had their own professional commitments and if Sara called in sick—for herself, for her son—who would watch the Taylor children?

Though Sara did not leave her son with a final embrace and an 1,800-mile-long promise as her mother had once left her, she has stepped into a local version of the same global care chain that compromised her own childhood. In this drama of the shifting cost of care from the first world to the third, Sara plays an outsized role. As a child enduring her mother's absence, as a migrant bound by her commitment to grandparents and sister back home, and as a mother giving her son over to subpar care so that she can give the best of herself to the American children she nannies. From societies to governments to families to individuals, women like Sara bear the burden of unsustainable economies and social systems in a broad global workaround that leaves their own children wanting. And Sara learns to understand her troubles as hers alone, a private experience of mothering that remains off the clock and out of the line of public sight.

When Sara began working with the Taylors, she was able to hide such concerns from her employers. Her son's needs and complaints belonged to her personal life, relegated to her inner thoughts and fears and pulled out into the light only after she got home—at 6:45 p.m. every weekday, when, certainly, she would turn to her own domestic tasks, to the cooking and the cleaning and the parenting. There at home, the work of parenting and homemaking would be indistinguishable from mothering, unquestioned woman's work that was hers alone. Because that man she married—the one ten years her senior with a taste for finer things—turned out to be less than an ideal husband. "My husband . . ." she'll tell me in a hasty aside, "is not the best husband around, you could say."

For a while, these conflicts could remain tucked away in her home and in her heart, allowing Sara to be, in her words, "the perfect babysitter, perfect servant, the one who did everything." But when she became pregnant again, things changed. For a working woman, nothing complicates the fragile line between private and public life like the pregnant, birthing, and breastfeeding body. And, though Sara insists that the quality of her work during her second pregnancy was not affected, the fact of her pregnancy—the visible swell of her belly and the impending needs of the child within—conspired against the value of Sara's mothercoin in ways that left her speechless.

"I told them as soon as I found out. I mean, I had told them I was married. When you're married, this can happen at any time, right? So, I got pregnant in July. That same month that I found out, I told them I was pregnant. Then, they started to treat me badly, the *patrones.*"

When Sara made her announcement, the Taylors' second baby was only a couple of weeks old and the señora was still home on maternity leave, ever-present and ever more demanding. "She was the kind of señora that, if I was supposed to work eight hours, it was eight hours I had to work. They didn't give me a break; they didn't give me anything. When she was there at the house, she was strict about everything.

"And the babies that she has," Sara goes on, "they're the kind that cry and cry and cry all the time for three months. And she wanted me to carry the child all the time, and he cried and cried and cried."

"Did she ask you to clean too?"

"Yes!" She sits up straighter, her eyes round and voice loud.

"She was there with me. Sometimes she would help. She would take the baby and tell me to watch the little girl. But when I told them I was pregnant, they changed with me. They made me clean the windows outside and it was very hot. They wouldn't let me take a lunch break. They made me do everything. Made me clean, take the little girl to different activities, whatever it was. They wanted me to quit. If I quit, they wouldn't have to pay me my severance. They wouldn't have to pay me anything, because I would be quitting. They wanted me to quit, but I couldn't quit; I'd just gotten a house, so I couldn't stop working."

In the brief pause that follows, I try to step into Sara's story, carrying my ignorance alongside what I do know. I see the error in Sara's assumptions about her position with the Taylors. That her pregnancy wouldn't compromise her job security, that employers who violate labor laws related to mandatory breaks, safe working conditions, and pregnancy discrimination would adhere to an employee's expectation for severance upon being let go. But mostly, when I close my eyes and try to enter into the story Sara tells, I imagine the sensation of cleaning windows in Houston in July. Even in January, I can feel the summer heat that descends on this swampy, semitropical city, the thick mantle of a hundred-plus degrees and heavy humidity that saturates concrete and asphalt and hot aluminum ladders.

Under that oppressive summer sun, two cultures come together to conspire against Sara's employment. One, an employment culture in this invisible industry that is often ignorant of its responsibilities to its workers and sheltered from sanctions. The other, a Latin American tradition of domestic employment grounded in the paternalism of old, yet carrying its own modest expectations, like severance.[4] Like many domestics, Sara finds herself on the losing side.

As her pregnancy progressed, the pressure and the working conditions began to weigh on Sara. When her son got sick again, it became overwhelming. "I got depressed," she says, "because of the pressure from work, my pregnancy. It was really hard for me."

Up against the mothercoin's paradox—a system that can't reconcile the economic necessity of mothering work with the personal and cultural demands of motherhood—Sara would soon discover that the system has its own way of managing this kind of breakdown.

On a Friday afternoon in August, almost a year after she began working with the Taylors, the couple called her into the study. The señor spoke first.

"I'd like to talk to you," he began.

"Okay," she replied, and followed them both into the room, where her boss turned to her and said plainly, "You can't work for us anymore."

"Why?" Sara asked in surprise. After all, she had endured the demands, the sweat and the colic and the relentless pace.

"Look, you're an excellent worker," he went on. "You work hard. We're not going to find another worker like you, but we want someone without any problems."

Sara pauses for the story's effect, her eyes on me.

"The pregnancy was the problem?" I ask.

"The pregnancy was the problem." She holds a beat before she resumes, "I wanted to die, because what did I do wrong?"

"What did you say to them?"

"I didn't say anything to them. They just said, 'Look, here's your check. We've paid you for two weeks. If you want references, give us a call. Or we can recommend you to friends. But we don't need you anymore. We already have someone else who's going to work for us.'"

It was the last bit that dealt the final blow, the replacement the Taylors had hired. "They hired that person and I was right there. But I didn't know what they were talking about. I was there when they hired the new person, and I didn't know what they were saying because it was in English."

If only she'd mastered English in her young life of iguana-hunting and border-crossing and red-cheeked window-washing, Sara might have better understood liability of the pregnant muchacha in America. Tremendous vulnerability. Because while her childcare and housekeeping work has been quantified and made to fit into a wage-based economy, the biological labor of pregnancy and childbirth has always been cast as incompatible with the public domain of work.

Contemporary US writing on motherhood is saturated with reports of workplace discrimination against pregnant women in both working-class and professional occupations.[5] And though all pregnant workers are protected under the law, some are more empowered to protest than others. When the balance of power is tilted away from an employee like Sara, unchecked in a shadow occupation marked by the pervasive fear of the unauthorized, a pregnant domestic who has been fired or subject to worsened working conditions is left to accept her fate alone.

But no matter how unfair the system, infants will be born, children will grow, and caregivers will respond to their needs—often outside of the logic that would discount them.

Sara reflects tenderly on the Taylors' youngest child, "I miss the little girl a lot. She was a wonderful little girl. She called me 'mommy' all the time. I tried to be nice to her all the time, to be a good nanny, because it made me feel bad that her parents were always working, working, working. They didn't take care of the kids at all. I had to be there for everything. So I always tried to put on a smile for her."

So many children, so many needs. The conflicts imbue Sara's story with a profound ambivalence—tenderness for the child whose parents neglect her, shame for the unmet needs of a son to whom she gives all. "He's always been sickly," she says, then lowers her voice as she confesses, "in part because of my neglect, because of my work and all the attention I didn't give him."

A human face for the villain. As she did with the unyielding social workers and cruel employers, Sara looks for someone to blame. And where I perceive a system set up against her and her young son, she turns inward to herself and only sees a mother who hasn't given enough.

Sara's reputation as a hard worker picked her up from the blow the Taylors dealt her, as did her complicated relationship with her former employer, Leslie, the Spanish-speaking lawyer with a penchant for rage and remorseful generosity. Though Sara had left Leslie's employ shortly after Drew was born, she still cleaned one day a week for the woman's boyfriend. Aware of his housekeeper's plight, the man, whom Sara calls her "*señor ángel*," offered her an upgrade from one day a week to two at a flat rate of $100 a day.

When her baby was born, he showed his generosity again. "He gave my daughter two hundred dollars, a gift for being born. So he's my angel. He's amazing." And for the mother, a gift more valuable still: "When my daughter was born, he said I could bring her with me. She was seventeen days old when I went back to work. With my financial situation, I couldn't be at home any longer. I brought a friend to help me."

When Sara strapped her two-week-old to her chest and returned to work with a friend in tow, she followed a pattern familiar to many a working mother in a country without paid maternity leave. She took it upon herself, privately, to patch together her own leave—less than three weeks' rest and a shared workload with diminished pay, all made possible by a benefactor with a healthy income and a generous disposition.

The cost of caring for a newborn is tangible and real. In Sara's story, that cost falls disproportionately on her shoulders, but she is not the only one who feels its weight. Her private chain of diminishing care traced a line of unmet need that ran straight from the Taylor's little girl, through Sara's pregnant body, all the way to the growing boy who watched as his mamá became ever more tired, ever more drained, and ever more unavailable to give him the attention he would one day demand. Little Drew would soon take a resentful stance, informed by the years he spent in the care of his aunt—Sara's once left-behind sister, who would never learn to forgive.

Rosa

In 1982, as a mother of five children under the age of twelve, Rosa was no stranger to the complications of the pregnant body. So when she and her husband arrived in Houston from LA and made their home in the small bedroom that had been set aside for them in her new employers' house, she was careful to save a space on the shelf for the birth control pills she'd been taking for years. She'd come to the US to work, after all, to raise up the family she and Arturo had already made and lift them into a life where they could make something of themselves. But nature had a different idea, helped along by a doctor who was sure he understood Rosa's body better than she.

"Congratulations, señora!"

In the local clinic, the doctor's hearty greeting grated on Rosa's nerves. Just a few weeks before, she had been in his examination room complaining of general discomfort and disinterest in sex. He'd told her the birth control pills were making her sick, that she should stop taking them. "No!" Rosa had protested. "If I stop, I'll get pregnant." But he assured her, "Oh no, you've been taking them for years."

On this second visit, not even two months after she'd taken his advice and gone off the pill, Rosa met the same doctor's congratulations with skepticism.

"Congratulations, why?" she asked.

"Because you're pregnant. Why, is something wrong?"

"Doctor," she responded—too resigned to the implications to appreciate the irony in his question—"I have five children already."

"No!" he'd said, as surprised as any who had not taken the time to ask, as surprised as any who had not considered that an unwanted pregnancy might not be cause for congratulations. "Well, anyway," he went on, "you're definitely pregnant now."

"My husband was thrilled," Rosa tells me. Her voice is as low and tired as it would have been that day in the clinic—when her husband would have smiled and the doctor might have chuckled and Rosa will have placed a red-knuckled hand across her belly and said to herself then, as she says to me now, "But I came here to work. I came to get ahead."

A few months later, as Hurricane Alicia blew fast and furious across Houston on 115 mph winds and a twelve-foot storm surge, Rosa and Arturo welcomed their sixth child into the world, a US citizen whose relationship to national privilege would set him apart from siblings and cast his own identity in an ambivalent shadow.

It was a complicated time for Rosa. She'd already been navigating the emotional landscape of living in a big city in the US while her children carried on life at her parents' rural home in Mexico. It had been three years since she had headed to LA and left them in their grandparents' care, and things were going well for her and Arturo. Rosa earned $135 a week, along with the room, and Arturo continued to ply his trade in the meantime. They'd been working and living comfortably for two years in Houston, providing for their children through hefty remittances and regular phone calls; the free long-distance calling that Rosa's employers provided was an important benefit of their living situation in a time before cell phones.

But at times it was hard to know what to make of the inevitable comforts of their American life, when they knew what they did of the lives their children were living in a rancho too small to call a village, with aging grandparents and unpredictable school days.

"The youngest was two and a half years old," Rosa reminds me. "It's hard," she reflects, "to leave children there and you're here and you're living well with them over there. . . ." She trails off, then catches herself quickly. "They were fine," she says, her voice becoming stronger as she assures me, assures herself, that the children were doing well. "Because we sent them money. Ever since we started working, we've always sent them money so they wouldn't suffer. They ate well." *Comían bien.* Which is to say, they ate more than rice and beans and the fruit of a shrinking orchard. Which is to say, they were already getting ahead.

But the distance remained as real as the separation was unnatural—mom and dad here working, kids there waiting—and now, an infant. Rosa's job at that time consisted mostly of cleaning; the family's children were adolescents, the older two away at college and the youngest already fifteen. This kind of cleaning work is demanding, but more predictable than a toddler's needs or a young child's schedule, and Rosa found a way to work around the maternal complications in which she found herself.

Her employers allowed her to stay on with the family and keep the baby in her and Arturo's room, as long as she could keep up with the work. So she devised a system all on her own for tending to baby and to work.

"I breastfed him, because mother's milk is the best. So I would feed him and then go to work until I couldn't take the pressure in my breasts anymore and I felt like I was about to burst."

"But where did you leave him while you worked?"

"In the room, I left him in my room."

"And this didn't worry your employers?"

"My *patrones*? No, no. They said as long as I could do it, there wasn't a problem, I could keep working."

As long as she could make it work. Such a familiar condition to working mothers. From my own academic world of late-night laptops and early-morning feedings, I feel the familiar squeeze, how we tuck away the private tasks of reproduction into the twilight hours, shut it up behind closed doors. So expected, it's easy to forget to question it.

For Rosa, a compromise like this was as anticipated as a doctor's careless advice. From the clinic's white coats and stirrups, to the belly she'd carried alongside broom and mop and the swollen breasts that kept her working body in tune with the needs of a hidden infant, Rosa had negotiated the most intimate expressions of her private sexual identity in constant dialogue with the public realities of healthcare and productive labor. In Rosa's case, these tensions worked themselves out in the isolated spaces of a family home where she worked for pay, and a closed bedroom door behind which an eight-month-old, desperate to be close to the laboring body that had left him a few hours before, learned to climb out of his crib.

"The little one would get out of the crib," she tells me. "He'd hurt himself. Every time I'd feed him, when I said, 'I'm going now,' he'd let loose crying, the kind of crying that breaks your heart. I'd leave him crying, Elizabeth—" She calls me by name, "*Elizabeth*," me, because it's important for me to listen to this part. It's important for me to be there with Rosa in some way, in the thirty-year-distant room she shared with a needy child whose cries still bring her to tears. "I'd leave him crying there and when I'd come back half an hour later to check, he'd be asleep. It hurts, Elizabeth. Because—" She stops, swallows, and shakes her head slowly, overcome by the emotion of a past she still carries in her body, breasts that still remember the tug and the pull and the need, "—our children's suffering, that's the hardest."

"One day," she pulls herself together and back into the telling, "I found him asleep there on the floor. He would get out of the crib and fall onto the mattress on the floor."

By the time Arturo got home from work that night, she tells me, she had made up her mind. "Our son's not suffering for diapers," she said to her husband, "he's not suffering for food. But he's suffering when it comes to the best in life. No," she declared to Arturo in their little room in another family's house, "I'm going home."

Not long after, Rosa showed up at her own mother's door in Puebla and announced her return: "I'm back now," she said. "I'm taking my kids back. I can't be over there working anymore. My little one is suffering there, and I am too."

After almost four years working side by side, the couple had saved enough money to buy a small house in Mexico. It was an old house, nothing grand, but with what they had earned in the north there was enough to furnish it all and still have some savings in the bank. "It was what I'd wanted," she explains, "a place for us to live."

So, Rosa and her six kids set up a house of their own in Chietla, close to the rancho and to the memories of a different way of life, and Arturo headed back to Houston to work. He would earn his American wages, send money to his family, and come home on holidays to visit for as long as the ever-more-imposing border would allow him.

"Nine years," Rosa says slowly, her tears dried and her memory clear, "Nine years in Mexico. Alone again, with my six kids."

These were Rosa's choices. To follow Arturo along footpaths and bracero pathways trod out by generations before them, fathers and grandfathers drawn to seasonal labor across a fluid border. Back and forth, these men had dug deep trenches of social networks paved with a cultural legacy of migrant labor. When Rosa accompanied Arturo to LA, then to Houston, she was one of many wives who took up this tradition in following their husbands to the other side—*el otro lado*, where one goes to work, but not to live. That was one choice.

Here, was another. A choice made in a cultural tradition on the flip side of the migrant worker legacy: the divided family—transnational by definition but different in feel and experience for Mexican families than for those separated by continents and oceans. For transnational children and mothers like Sara and Ana, Pati and María, the US–Mexico border is a place of distanced imagination. But for Rosa and others steeped in the familiar rhythm of circuitous migration—there for the harvest, here for the holidays, there for the bricklaying, here for the baby-making— the border is a real, tangible space: imposing, defining, dividing, but in the late 1980s, still a thing open to casual transgression.

"In those nine years, I came over here three times. He sent me the money to come. So that I could pay the coyote and pay someone to come watch the kids."[6]

These were the occasional encounters with savvy coyotes and corrupt cops, empty gas canisters and another woman's baby placed on her lap as cover for a risky crossing, the occupational hazards of a left-behind wife. Just as the mother in her had pulled her back home to her children in Puebla, the wife and lover in her drove her to risk the crossing, all of it a casualty of her landscape of choice.

Throughout my conversation with Rosa, my youngest has been popping in and out of the kitchen—she's cold, she wants to watch *Mickey* but *Handy Manny's* on, she brings me a gift, a flower from the patio, some bit of fabric or a small toy she's picked up off the floor. She climbs up onto my lap, she is soft and warm and full of needs. "Go watch your show, baby," I say. Something in her need draws my attention back to the baby at Rosa's chest, to the fetus in her womb and the man in her bed, the room in the home and the weekly pay for the woman's work she did. The fallen eight-month-old asleep on the floor. The dust on my floorboards, the three-year-old on my lap. There is no extracting sex and birth and belly and heartache from wage and market and the cultural logic of transaction and labor. Nothing is private. Not in Rosa's story. And perhaps not in mine.

This, then, is Rosa's landscape of choice. To live the fullness of her relationship with her husband, she must make herself vulnerable to the arbitrary power of the border and its illicit economies. To work with diligence and pride, she must ignore the tender ache of breasts, full for a child who cries for her on the other side of the closed door—ignore, too, the fear that she may be living better than the five children who wait for her on the other side. And to live out fully her understanding of what a good mother is—one who keeps the family together and raises them up to get ahead—she must sacrifice a part of herself. For four years in LA and Houston, it was the presence of her children, the braids and the meals and the laughter. For nine years in Mexico, it was the closeness of her husband, the touch and the embrace and the moment so many couples look to at the end of the day, when one or the other stops for a moment, leans into their partner's embrace, and relinquishes, just for a bit, the responsibility for the choices they have made. Worker, lover, mother, woman.

Alicia

Alicia is a thirty-two-year-old Mexican woman whose story unfolds sixteen years earlier, on the threshold of her emerging sexuality. From the moment she arrived in this country, to the day she talked to me on a neighborhood playground where her young charge crawled and climbed, her developing sense of self has struggled against the steely power of *machista* brothers and vigilant employers—a power almost strong enough to silence her voice. Almost. As we follow Alicia's fair-haired charge from jungle-gym to playhouse to sandbox to swing, my little one running in tight circumference around my movements, Alicia tells a story about a river and a desert, her siblings' tight control, and a serpent that struck without her knowing.

Urged to leave Mexico for Texas by a boyfriend who would be waiting on the other side, fourteen-year-old Alicia and her twenty-two-year-old sister made the eight-hundred-mile trek to Houston from their home in Hidalgo, Mexico. Alicia's pueblo was a small town that rolled down the western slope of the Sierra Madre Oriental,[7] where she left behind an imprisoned father and a mother who had spent years in severe depression after losing a child. Alicia's older brother accompanied the sisters. "My brother came to take care of us," she explains, "because of all the things that can happen to a woman on the journey."

A cousin served as their coyote, leading them across a knee-high river at night, where the first dark mystery struck.

"What happened was, I was bit by a snake, or something, on the foot, and it started to swell up a lot. My foot was hurting me a lot, and they were like, 'No, we're just going to walk a little.' But then we walked for sixteen hours. Toward the end, I could barely walk, and my brother and sister carried me. They were like, 'No, it's nothing. It was just a worm.' But it wasn't nothing, it was a snake that bit me, a snake."

After traversing the line and the checkpoints, she and her siblings arrived at an aunt's house filled with an extended family of immigrants, some recent arrivals, others less so. Here, Alicia discovered that, even in the US, her family was poor.

"I was kind of surprised to see how they were poor too, and I said to myself, 'Well what did I come here for if we're going to be just as poor as in my pueblo?'"

For a young girl whose idea of America had been shaped by 1990s TV shows like *Family Matters* and *The Fresh Prince of Bel-Air*, this encounter with poverty dealt a blow to the hope and promise she had learned to associate with migration. But the explanation for her family's poverty remained a mystery to Alicia, along with so much else that she never knew to ask.

Alicia's brothers were house-painters, and she and her sister started their laboring life in America trailing behind the brothers and helping to clean windows and other odd jobs. "That's how I got this scar," she tells me, tracing a thin finger along her upper arm, a pearly pink line of skin, broken and grown back together taut and tough. Soon enough, the siblings found Alicia a job of her own, working in a Mexican-style cafeteria where no one ever asked about age or status. Pushed out by the female owner's insecurities, she left the restaurant after two months to take up her first position as a nanny. The child she would care for was four years old. Alicia was still fourteen.

"The little girl loved me," Alicia's voice is soft and warm. "I still carry a picture of her." She pulls out her wallet and opens it to a photo, creased and worn in its thin plastic sheath. A small girl grins through thick bangs and apple-blossom cheeks. Alicia smiles at the picture, her round face bright and auburn hair falling forward as she leans in to study the image.

As a weekday live-in, Alicia earned $110 a week working for this American family, Monday through Friday, from 7:00 a.m. to 8:00 p.m., cleaning the house and watching the little girl. A sixty-five-hour work-week at less than $1.70 an hour. On weekends off from her nannying job, she returned to the crowded home she shared with her siblings—a sister, two brothers, and a sister-in-law with a child of her own.

"I was a girl taking care of another little girl. Fourteen years old, naïve, and coming from such a small town."

"And they never asked about your age?"

"They didn't ask about my age or my papers, nothing."[8]

On the cool November afternoon in 2008 when Alicia first talks to me, her story quickly takes the shape of the child and the photo and the low tone and whispered cadence of her voice—as tentative as her furtive gaze that scans the sand and equipment and buzzing lights on her cell phone. Later, I would revisit the details of her story and understand more fully. Especially this: the adults who kept Alicia in their home, paying her less than a maquiladora assembly line worker would make on the other side of the border, were parents of two teenagers of their own. They knew what a fourteen-year-old girl was, and what she wasn't. They had to know. And they looked the other way. Later, as I set Alicia's story to words on a page, this would be the first detail to make me cry.

The little girl with the apple-blossom cheeks became Alicia's happy companion, filling the empty spaces beside her as they made their way through the days. "I taught her Spanish," she recounts proudly. "She knew a lot of Spanish when I was done."

As she folds the billfold to put it away, I notice a second photo, the face of a teenage boy with a strong jaw and dark eyes.

"I would have liked to go to school," Alicia picks up her story, "but I didn't have the support from my older siblings."

"Did you ever ask them?"

"No, I was more focused on working, on sending money home to my parents."

From her very first job in the Mexican cafeteria, Alicia had been sending money home. She still does to this day, eighteen years later. With no formal schooling beyond the ninth grade, Alicia's education would come from the spaces that marked her world. The corridors of apartment complexes filled with migrants as poor as she. The rooms assigned to her in the homes of American families eager for the cheap labor of an adolescent hand. The tree-lined residential streets where she would push a stroller alongside other nannies. And the small corner in her siblings' crowded home where she would hide away her secret.

Like most teenagers, Alicia immersed herself in music and television to the point of perfecting her English.

"I mostly learned it listening to music in English and watching shows, the ones with Black people. There were like five shows I watched and I liked them a lot, a lot. I didn't understand, but I liked watching, the comedy. And then, music. I've liked country music ever since I was in Hidalgo and my brother would bring me CDs."

"Who's your favorite artist?"

"Alan Jackson. And George Strait. Of course, George Strait comes first."

"Of course." We laugh, her perfect pronunciation of the Anglo name feels light and easy in this painful telling. George Strait, of course.

When Alicia talks about Alan Jackson and *The Fresh Prince of Bel-Air*, it's hard to reconcile her mature age with the youthful light in her eyes. It's as if there is still something in her that burns bright with new ways of life to imagine, something still just on the verge of becoming. In her hushed giggles and tentative words, I recognize a quality of youth that seeks to give voice to her experience, to name the snake that bites.

"I was sixteen when I got pregnant. My family turned their back on me and I was left alone. Ever since my little sister died, I'd thought to myself, 'When I grow up, I don't ever want to get pregnant.' And then, it was the first thing that happened to me."

"Because you didn't know how it worked?"

"Yes. The first time I was with a boy, I got pregnant."

"And no one had talked to you about all that?"

"No one. It's a very closed off town, people don't talk about these things. They don't really teach that stuff in school. No one even told me that I would get my period. When it happened to me, I was like eleven or twelve, and I started crying when I saw it. I was afraid."

From the start, Alicia had navigated the mystery of sex and reproduction on her own. No lessons from mother, no aunts or sisters or teachers to fill the gap. Like poverty in America and the love of a stranger's child, sex was a lesson Alicia learned in the doing, outside of language and very much alone.

By that time, she had left the job with the cherry-cheeked child and moved on to another nanny position, where she cared for a little boy and cleaned for $160 a week.

"It was fifty dollars more," she explains, "but the house was a mansion. When I worked in that house, I would beat my belly. I would pummel myself and tell God over and over again that I didn't want to be pregnant. Because I know my brothers. I know how *machista* they are and I knew that something was going to happen."

A phone buzzes in Alicia's pocket. She pauses to check, leaving me to fill in the silence that trails behind her stubborn belly and menacing brothers. She places the phone back in her pocket and returns to me and the park and her sixteen-year-old desperation.

The rest of her story happens in three movements.

Movement one.

The pregnancy progressed despite the self-inflicted beatings, and when Alicia confessed her plight to a cousin who was also pregnant, the girl suggested they both visit her sister in Dallas who would be able to arrange for an abortion. "So I left the house where I was working, because it was the weekend, and went to meet my cousin at the cafeteria where I used to work, because she worked there. I had my suitcase with all my stuff, and we were going to go to Dallas. But before all that, God or something—I don't know, I can't explain it to you because I don't even know—made me, like . . . leave. I left. I can't explain this part to you because I don't know. It's not like I don't remember it," she insists. "It's that I don't know what happened. It just happened."

Movement two.

Alicia became friends with another nanny who worked across the street, "Because the nannies, we go out walking with the kids a lot," she explains. She confessed her situation to her new friend, who went straight to her own patrona for advice. This employer, an Argentine woman with two children of her own and one on the way, would later tell Alicia that, if it weren't for her own pregnancy, she would have adopted Alicia's baby herself. Instead, the woman guided the young nanny toward an alternative to abortion.

"She took me to the doctor. She paid. She paid for the checkup and she didn't even know me. They did an ultrasound. That's when I found out it was a boy. Then she took me to a church."

This check-up would be the only doctor Alicia saw for the duration of her pregnancy. At the church, she listened to a Spanish-speaking woman explain the organization's adoption process. The center would cover all her costs and place the baby in a good home on her behalf. She paused to consider the papers placed before her, the doctor bills she would not have to pay and the labor she would undergo right there in the center, and she leaned forward to sign the forms, carefully, deliberately.

"Then, when we were leaving, I started to cry and I said, 'No, better not to. *Mejor no.*' Just like I'm telling you right now. '*Mejor no.*' I said it to myself, 'Better not to.' I stood there like that, you know? Like, 'No, better not to.' And that's how it ended."

The third movement takes some time to develop.

Eight months into Alicia's pregnancy, her sister and sister-in-law called her in to talk.

"We want to talk to you," they said, "We want to know if you're pregnant."

She looked across at them, her sister and her brother's wife, and asked them why they wanted to know.

"Because we want to help you," they responded in earnest. Alicia may have believed them, or wanted to, or she may simply have been out of options. Either way, she confirmed their suspicions and hoped for the best.

But even if they had wanted to support Alicia, the women's hands were tied. Theirs was a world of men, governed by a tradition of *machista* power in excess. It was the brothers who held the power in Alicia's family. Brother who shadowed the sisters across the border. Brothers who contracted her out to work, whose word could grant her the chance to study or not. Brothers who would not forgive the sexual sins of a teenage girl. Though these men may have talked in terms of honor and shame, the rules they lived by had little to do with values and everything to do with shoring up a social structure from which they benefited. In a patriarchal order where men are served and women are controlled, the power of women's sexuality and procreation is a threat that must be contained, a danger to be expelled.

"They didn't care about me anymore," she says of her brothers. "They said, 'We don't want you in our house anymore. You're going to have to leave now.'"

And when the labor pains overtook her just a few weeks later, the brothers once again held all the cards, because the men were the only ones who knew how to drive.

"They wouldn't take me to the hospital. They just kept cursing me, saying, 'Goddamnit, *chingada madre*, who's the father? Who's the son of a bitch? 'Cause we're gonna kill him!' And I wanted to die because the labor pains had already started."

Her sister-in-law begged the brothers, "Come on, take her to the hospital. Can't you see she's going to have the baby?"

As the brothers argued and the sisters pleaded, the sensations of a confused labor came over Alicia in powerful waves, tight and unrelenting and magnified by fear. "I wanted to die because of the pains."

Finally, the younger of the two brothers relented. The sisters packed Alicia into the car, helped lift her out when they got to the hospital, checked her in, and left. Within minutes of arriving, her water broke. In an hour, she was a mother. Sixteen years old and alone.

When the Spanish-speaking labor and delivery nurses asked her gently, "What name will you give him?" Alicia didn't know.

"I didn't know what to name him! I didn't have clothes, or anything. Nothing, nothing."

Sometime in the months leading up to that day, Alicia had gone out on her own and purchased a baby blanket, a bottle, and some rubber nipples. It was all she knew to do to prepare for something as unimaginable as motherhood. "I kept them hidden," she tells me, "so the others wouldn't find out." Now, that hidden corner was the only home she and her baby had, and she didn't know if she could go back.

"When you have a baby, they tell you when you can go home. But I was afraid, because I thought, 'Where am I going to go? They aren't going to want me now.' They never even came to see how the baby was or to meet him. Not until I called them to say could they come get me please because the hospital wanted me to leave."

The siblings did come for her, with a baby carrier and hard-set faces that would remain cold and distant for the weeks it took Alicia to find a job and another place to live. All the while, her oldest brother told her he didn't want her there, and her sister watched impassively as Alicia cried alongside the tiny creature at her chest.

"I didn't know how to take care of him. I'd cry along with him because I didn't know what to do. My sister had kids, but she was, I won't use the word *mala*, she wasn't a bad person, just cold, very cold. The baby would cry, and she didn't teach me anything. It was me all alone."

Two weeks after the birth, Alicia got a job at Jack in the Box, a $3.25-an-hour gig she secured with the help of a fake social security number purchased at the flea market.[9] But the job barely covered the amount she paid a neighbor to watch the baby, and it was hardly enough to get the baby the clothes she so badly wanted to buy. As her older sister had done, the world watched on impassively as Alicia struggled on her own to make a life for herself and her child.

After an interview for a restaurant dishwashing job, she met a young woman at the bus stop who would be the first to open a door. Whether it was something in the stranger's eyes or the simple gesture of friendship in her question—"Did you just interview? I work at the restaurant, too"—something about the warm stranger inspired a sense of security in Alicia, and she let loose a torrent of words and tears and the story of those tumultuous months. The next day, Alicia's new friend and coworker invited her to consider moving into the house where she herself lived with her three-year-old daughter. The home was owned by an older couple.

"The man was American, and the woman. They had little rooms that they would rent to people. She started taking care of the baby for me. But I paid her a lot, almost half of my check, plus I had to buy diapers."

Despite what the woman charged, Alicia knew the couple loved the boy. And in those early years, such love was a complicated proposition.

"I didn't love him—" her phone sounds in her pocket and she reaches to quiet the buzz. "For three years, I didn't consider myself his mother. I took care of him, of course. I never left him alone or gave him to anyone or anything. I didn't abuse him or hit him. But I didn't love him. If he fell down, it didn't bother me. For three years. Not now, of course."

"Of course," I think, recalling the dark poetry of feelings a mother isn't supposed to have.[10]

Now a handsome sixteen-year-old whose photo has found a place in Alicia's wallet, the boy eventually won his mother's heart and the two have forged a life together in the years since. But back then, Alicia tells me, it felt different. Back then, the American couple loved the baby without ambivalence, the tiny thing Alicia left behind each day in order to earn a paycheck that would cover his care, his diapers, his constant need for clothes and food and a roof over his head. A paycheck that must also find its way back home to a dad in jail, a mother in depression. And Alicia so all alone.

Back then, when the couple offered to adopt the boy and make him their own, it took some time for Alicia to give them an answer. Like many women, maternity was something that had simply happened to her, far removed from any conscious decision. And in the exaggerated patriarchy of her brother's machismo, reproduction and choice were as incompatible as power and a sixteen-year-old girl. From the moment she cried at the blood in her panties, to the lonely hospital phone call she made to siblings who rejected the infant in her arms, Alicia's experience of her own sexual power was as confusing as the dark forces beneath the surface of the Río Bravo—a presence she felt but could not name.

But even where language and understanding fail us, there is power in desire. And something moved Alicia to choose to be a mother to her baby. The same kind of impulse, however uncertain, that caused her to meet me at the park that day, watch me hit *record*, and tell me about the choice she made.

The third movement.

"I was close to saying yes," she says of the couple's offer. "Because, like I said, I didn't feel that love for my son, I just knew he was mine because I'd had him. But—" The phone sounds again, insistent. "Wait, just a moment."

She brings the phone quickly to her ear, her shoulders hunched and chin tucked low. "It's my boss," she whispers, "*Es mi jefe, el señor.*" She crouches into the phone and swings her body away from me, lowering her voice and moving quickly toward the boy to sort him out from child and cloud and mulch and playscape.

I take a step in her direction. "Well, if you have to go . . ." I call after her, but there is a new panic in her eye when she insists, "*el señor*, from my job." And I understand that we won't be finishing her story today. Nor the next, when she does not return my call.

Mejor no, she must have decided. Better not to.

Pati

After several years with the Stevensons, living in a garage apartment that felt like home and loving the two young children who felt like hers, Pati met the man who would become her husband. The couple knew it was serious from the start, and Pati felt that her employers recognized and respected the relationship.

"Little details. She let my husband, when he was my boyfriend, he practically lived with me in the apartment. He would come on the weekends and stay with me. They never said anything, they never reproached me, they were wonderful with me. Maybe it was taking advantage of their trust, but I said to myself, 'I'm a single woman who's old enough to meet someone and make her own family.' They understood. I always respected their house, their privacy. My space was my space. The children would even say, 'That house is your house, Pati.' And I'd say, 'Yes, that's my house.'"

When Pati found out she was pregnant, she told the Stevensons right away. "If you want to find somebody else," she added, "you have all the right. Because I'm pregnant, and I don't know what I'm going to do."

But the Stevensons were happy to adjust, and Pati had other concerns to tend to. She and her not-quite-yet-husband found themselves in a complicated situation. As the pregnancy moved on, he lost his father to a sudden, aggressive cancer and now found himself the sole caregiver for an elderly mother who, as Pati put it, "also needs a bit of care." Where before, there had only been the Stevenson children to tend to, now the need for care had begun to multiply—a new infant, an elderly mother-in-law. With new needs, new compromises.

Pati turned to her patrona for advice. "I don't want to move into his parents' house," she confessed.

"This is your house," Ms. Stevenson told her. "If you want to live here, you can live here with your child. You don't have to leave."

For Pati, the Stevensons' willingness to adapt to the new circumstances of her pregnancy were signs of their good-hearted nature and of the respect and affection she herself had earned in her years with the family. It's also true that her employers had invested a good deal in hiring and training Pati, that she performed her work well and had proven herself trustworthy and capable, that to find someone new might be more of a disruption than the pregnancy itself. But narratives have a way of reinforcing themselves, and in Pati's tale, each new accommodation, each adaptation to changing lives, became a sign not of negotiation and partnership, but of her employers' charitable kindness and her own good fortune.

The adjustments the Stevensons made over the next weeks and months only fed Pati's gratitude. An additional cleaner brought in for household work, plans for a temporary replacement for Pati's six-week leave—"I told her, 'I'll come back after four weeks,' but she told me, 'No, that's too short. You relax and rest' "—and a running conversation with the children about life after baby: "Baby Melanie is going to be here, there's going to be a baby here," the American children's mother would tell them. "You have to be good children, because Melanie is going to see your example."

Pati's words are soft and warm when she tells me about five-year-old Ellie Stevenson's excitement about the baby. "She would hug me and hug my belly. She took care of me. She brought me my vitamins and told me, 'Take your vitamins because they're for Melanie.' She'd tell me, 'Don't drink coffee, your baby can't have coffee.' "

She pauses and sighs, full in the memory of a little girl's unconditional love and all the child didn't understand about when it is safe to give over your heart, and when it is not.

One memory of this time is particularly bittersweet. Early in Pati's pregnancy, an infection resulted in a doctor-ordered five days of bedrest. Unaccustomed to missing work for illness, Pati assured the Stevensons that she would still watch the kids, even if she couldn't pick up around the house and clean. She understood as well as they did how much she was needed. But the señor didn't like the idea one bit. "No, no," he responded. "Go on and get back in bed—now!" Pati mimics his voice when she tells the story, smiling as she drops her own pitch low. "Your child is more important, Pati, the pregnancy. We'll take care of the kids. If you need something, call me on the phone, we'll bring it to you, whatever you need. For now, rest." And then he said the words that would stay with Pati for a long time, long enough to find new meaning across her quiet living room sofa. "Your job will be here another twenty-eight, thirty years," he had said. "Whatever you need."

The pregnancy progressed, along with her relationship with her employers, and Pati made choices with full confidence in what she understood to be the Stevensons' special affection and respect for her. At seven months, after making it clear that living with her husband's newly widowed mother was not an option, the couple found their own small apartment. It's the same one she and I sit in now, one child sleeping and a second resting heavy in Pati's womb, a home of their own due in part to the wisdom her husband received from his mother: "Pati needs to make her own nest," she had explained to him. "She wants to create her own little burrow."

Pati's mother-in-law understood what most women are taught to see, that a family needs a cultivated physical space, a "home" that is both metaphor and mantle, refuge and safety and trodden carpet and soft sheets. Pati chooses the word "nest" in conveying her mother-in-law's advice, recalling the "nesting instinct" to prepare a safe and comfortable refuge before giving birth. Though it all seems to fit together—mother, child, home, woman—there is little evidence of a direct link between nesting behavior and biological motherhood or femininity.[11] The association is created in the practice, the closeness of woman to infant, infant to nest. These images confuse biology and leave us all with little time to question the naturalness of a woman's connection to homemaking. For women like Pati, and perhaps her husband's aging mother, making home and family is simply a feminine task, naturally.

The assumption reaches across culture and region and social class, so that Pati's patrona, too, carries an unequal domestic burden in the family. "It was her that I spoke with," Pati tells me, "almost always with her, more than with him."

I ask her about this shared experience, prompting comparisons. "You two are in more or less the same situation when it comes to starting a family and making compromises around working and being with the kids," I suggest, "but she had the option of hiring you. . . ."

In response, Pati tells me a story:

"One day, when I was pregnant with my daughter, I said to her, 'I'm not going to leave my daughter to go to work. I can't leave her.' Two days later, she talked to me about it. She'd taken the comment personally. She thought that I was telling her she was a bad person for leaving her children with someone else, with me."

As Pati tells me this story, I can't help but feel the sting of my own working-mother insecurities. But for Pati, to work and mother is no cause for guilt or shame. It's only in the nature of the work that conflicts arise.

"No, señora," she recounts her response. "It's just the opposite!" In the retelling, Pati takes on the countenance of a parent smiling at a child's misunderstanding, the tone of someone older and wiser who takes the time, patiently, to explain.

"Do you know what the difference is between me not leaving my daughter and you leaving your children? It's because you go to an office, and I would be going to care for other children. What would my daughter say? 'Why does Mommy take care of other kids and doesn't take care of me?' How could I spend all day with other kids not knowing how my own child is? I wouldn't feel good for one moment playing with other children, feeding other children, and not knowing how my daughter is. The work is different. If I had to work like you do, I would look for a good person to take care of my kids and I'd leave them. I can't leave my daughter to go and take care of other kids, but you don't go to work with other children. Your kids know that.

"The work is different," she insisted to the señora. "It's different," she repeats now to me. "I don't judge her, it's just the opposite. I don't judge her."

As the left-behind daughter of an immigrant nanny and a nanny herself, Pati knows that the work of caring can blur the line between love and labor and wound the trust between a nanny and her own child. Pati has learned firsthand how the emotional alchemy of loving for pay and working for love can confuse a woman's deepest sense of herself. "No, no," she insists to Ms. Stevenson, "You don't understand. The work is *different.*"

Peering into this intersection between work, family, and emotion, sociologist Arlie Hochschild has developed a vocabulary for these tensions and teased out the space between what we are supposed to feel and what we do feel. "Emotion work" describes that personal effort to feel as we are expected to—the child who must try not to resent an away-mother who works for her child's benefit, the mother who must try to love a little less the child that is not hers. "Emotional labor," refers to the workplace endeavor to perform emotions required of the job—the nanny who smiles patiently at a disrespectful child, the domestic who listens without complaint to a mistress who seeks a confidante. In the case of a nanny who leaves her children to care for others, the emotional labor required of the job generates a more intimate emotion work as nanny and mother struggle to feel the right thing for the right child at the right moment. In all the confusing spaces in between, authenticity can be compromised, wounding our "source of self."[12]

Pati has made a life for herself within this nuanced landscape of feeling rules and suppressed emotions. And when she learns, in a handful of bittersweet moments, that the affection she feels for the Stevenson children is the same love her mother has known for twenty-five years, her body can no longer contain the effort not to feel as she shouldn't. Through tears and trembling shoulders, she explains that this love is what makes the nanny's work different for the child left behind. Then, she quickly tucks away her tears and sniffles, pulls herself together, and declares, "I don't judge my mother, I don't judge her. It's just that life isn't what one would want it to be."

Though she forgives her boss and her mother, Pati is not willing to leave her own child in order to care for others. She'll do everything she can to be there for them all. It will be her job and her responsibility. The señora's guilt. María's choice. All of it, a feminine affair.

What kind of society have we created such that a mother like Pati must pay the cost for her pregnancy alone? What good is there in a social system that pushes the Taylors to rid themselves of the pregnant nanny in the wake of their own hard-won maternity leave? And in what world does it make sense for Rosa to leave an infant alone all day behind closed doors to clean house and pick up after a fifteen-year-old? This is the reality we have created by insisting that family is a private, feminine responsibility.

The drama that plays out in an American home when the Central American nanny gets pregnant reflects a larger theatre of smoke and mirrors that insists that the personal is somehow not political, that the world of work and finance and policy is always just on the other side of the domestic threshold. This false division separates children from the society that produces them and which they will grow to reproduce, and parents—mothers especially—are left to negotiate the tremendous cost of caring for their children on their own. When it comes to the mother-coin, the "problem" of pregnancy and childcare in this country is passed along from those with means to women with fewer resources and fewer options, bound by the limits of social class, race, and citizenship. At the losing end of this care drain, Sara and Rosa and Pati are left to bear the cost of society's failure to attend collectively to its own survival.

Rather than address this failure, American feminism has ignored the experience of poor and working-class women of color and given itself over to a shallow rhetoric of equality that pretends women can somehow separate their maternity from the public sphere of work and power. And with good reason. There is much to lose in acknowledging the complications of working motherhood. So much for women to lose if we can't find the words to name the problems without punishing the women. So much for all of us to lose if we can't look beyond the faces of individuals forced to choose from a limited field of options and see instead the systemic agents at the root of the conflicts. Policies and practices that reproduce inequality and reflect a cultural logic that devalues children, women, and the work of home and family.

There is another way to view the labor of childrearing and home-making. When we understand the economic value of mothering work through the lens of social reproduction, its value is as clear as day. Social reproduction is the labor and resource-intensive process of reproducing our societies' human capital, all the work of birthing and nurturing children, keeping their homes clean and safe, feeding them, educating them, protecting them and keeping them healthy.[13] Despite decades of compelling arguments by economists and policymakers, the productive value of social reproduction has not been incorporated into macroeconomic models in the US or elsewhere.[14] This omission makes it all but impossible to argue in economic terms for federal policies that support pregnant women and mothers—and all parents of young children who struggle privately to shoulder the bill for our future workers, consumers, and leaders.

It takes a certain resolve to ignore the economic value of childrearing. A kind of willful blindness is required to believe that a society's children are the responsibility of their parents alone. And it takes a power structure invested in maintaining the unpaid labor of women to insist that a woman's child is her private responsibility. Despite the hard-fought battles to bring women into the public realm and expose the myths of biological difference, it is still "mostly with the señora" that the nanny deals, and it is still somehow logical to say, "I know I'm pregnant, you don't have to keep me. But if you do, I'll try to work just as hard."

So the señoras find a way. The working mother with means has certain choices available. She can tap a network, seek out trust, take a chance, and stop at the ATM on a Friday afternoon. But in time, she, too, will discover that the choice to trade in the mothercoin is a complicated proposition.

CHAPTER 5

LAS PATRONAS

We're hiring essentially a housewife.
We're hiring you as a housewife.

LAURA

Laura

"I was like, 'Look, I need someone full service who will do everything. We'll pay you well, but here's the thing: we need you to do everything.'"

Laura lifts a scoop of salad onto her plate. Her volume rises as she describes the offer she made eleven years ago to their longtime nanny, Diana. "'Like, we're hiring essentially a housewife. We're hiring you as a housewife. You're going to be the next housewife of this Daniels household. The kids are the most important thing, and when the kids nap you wash clothes and do the dishes and clean the house, and food is the less important thing.' We hired her to cook, too."

"But she wasn't a good cook," Eric interrupts.

Laura shakes her head in agreement. "I mean, she cooks for the kids. But she likes to clean. The house is always spotless."

Laura is a Colombian woman whose family immigrated to the US when she was a teenager. The political violence they fled was recognized, their authorization granted, and the family transitioned into an American professional class that set her on a particular trajectory. Now a successful attorney in her early forties, she lives with her American husband, Eric, their two children, one cat, and a home that stretches sleek and pristine from floor to twelve-foot ceiling.

She looks me in the eye as she explains the evolution of the work

Diana has done for them over the years, pausing to fork a cucumber from the Greek salad I picked up on my way over, a prepared dinner offered in exchange for an after-work evening of conversation about their life with their nanny.

"I mean, that's what we needed," Laura goes on, munching on the salad as she loosens her lock on my eyes and returns to her plate. "Someone to clean, take care of the kids—"

"The kids always came first," Eric interrupts as he tops off a glass of wine placed before me. "We always said, first the kids, then the other stuff."

"Absolutely," Laura nods her head vigorously. "Kids first."

"What about the administrative stuff?" I ask. "Repairs and maintenance, all that."

"No, not in the beginning," Laura responds quickly in her matter-of-fact tone. "Although we joke that she's reached a managerial stage now."

Diana has been with the Danielses for over ten years. When she arrived, their daughter was two years old and the boy would be born two months later. Now at thirteen and eleven, the children have grown up with Diana in a way that is both tender and quite practical. Laura and Eric devote significant time to their careers, and the couple fully acknowledge the essential role Diana plays in their family.

"I thought of her as an insurance policy for our lives," Eric says.

In the decade that Diana has worked for the Daniels family, the relationship has evolved as they've all learned each other's ways. Over the course of our evening meal, I learned about Diana through her employers' eyes: she's not a cook but she's a hell of a cleaner, she's always on a diet, sometimes she lies, she spoils the kids, she only knows how to work one TV in their house. Her relationship with each of the children is different—with the girl, there is more distance; the boy, who was given into her arms twelve hours a day from birth, she protects fiercely.

Laura describes the terms of the work. "She's been with us full time, always. Every two weeks, she gets a paycheck, whether we're on vacation or not, whether she's back home visiting in El Salvador or not. She has other jobs on the side—part-time jobs and contract cleaners and rental properties—but she's always been full time for us."

In exchange, Diana must be always available. The house must be clean. The children must be cared for and delivered and picked up promptly

from all scheduled activities, fed, managed to a reasonable degree. The re-
pairmen must be met, the packages delivered into waiting hands. The cat
fed. In short, a housewife.

For Laura, who grew up in a professional home in Colombia—her
mother was a physician, her father an engineer—the kind of job that Diana does has nothing to do with the domestic servants of her childhood.
"The kind of nanny we need has evolved tremendously from what my
parents needed."

There are explanations for the disconnect between the Colombian muchacha of the 1970s and 1980s and the US nanny of the early
twenty-first century. In a region with a standing servant class, all but the
humblest Colombian families historically employed at least one full-time
servant in their home. These servants—often indigenous and from rural
communities outside of the urban centers where middle-class families
lived and worked—were responsible for the cleaning and the serving
and the childcare in a way that a contemporary US nanny-housekeeper
might be, expected to take up the most basic tasks of housecleaning and
child-minding and deferring always to the lady of the house.[1]

But Laura and Eric's needs are different. Rather than a shadow presence ready to serve as a pair of hands to wash or arms to hold, the Danielses
have hired someone to make decisions, to arrange playdates and plan the
menu, to manage deliveries and supervise the children's activities. More
than the extension of the role of the *ama de casa* that Laura knew as a
child, the US version of the muchacha has become a household manager
and proxy for intensive mothering. This twenty-first-century iteration
of the job pays relatively well, $32,000 a year in Diana's case.[2] All of it
under the table. All of it outside of the calculations of economists, social
policymakers, and ideologues of immigration. Because, although Laura,
Eric, and Diana may understand what a housewife is worth, somewhere
along the nineteenth- and twentieth-century way, American society as a
whole has forgotten.

The story of how the American housewife became economically invisible is an important part of the immigrant nanny story, because without the smoke and mirrors that hide the social role of household labor,
the industry would look a lot different. When the industrial revolution
gave way to an emerging capitalist economy in the mid-nineteenth century, the relationship between a family's livelihood and its home shifted.

No longer an extension of the family farm or a site of production of household goods—clothing, furniture, soap, etc.—the work of home narrowed its focus to housekeeping and childrearing, tasks that, in turn, became more demanding.

In a changing economy that required new kinds of skills and preparation to compete for industry jobs, the project of rearing children took on a new intensity. At the same time, a social distance grew between "women's work" within the home and the money-based, public sphere of "men's work." Domestic economy divided along gendered lines, home management shifted from making goods to buying them, and a new language emerged in mainstream culture in which mothers became the keepers of the spiritual and emotional life of the family—innocent, clean, morally righteous, and separate from the worldly realm of work and money. In the cult of domesticity that developed in the early nineteenth century, housewives became rhetorical angels of the hearth, and domestic servants receded into the shadows.[3]

The consequences for a woman's relationship to property and wages within marriage were profound, manifesting not only in legal restrictions, but in deep cultural perceptions as well. The reality of the nascent wage-earning economy created a new financial dependence among wives, who now needed their husband's wages to manage their homes. This shift in power inspired strong feminist resistance and a fight for economic equality in marriage that, in the end, proved more challenging than the battle for suffrage. While women in the US earned the right to vote in 1920, their husbands remained the sole owner of wages and assets acquired in marriage until 1970.[4]

For early-twentieth-century feminists, equality in marriage seemed a more distant goal than equality in the public domain. So they turned to the vote, to wage-earning and other political and legal battles, and tossed the domestic sphere to the rhetorical wolves that would insist that the dynamics of power within the home are unrelated to the public world beyond its threshold. By the turn of the twentieth century, two attitudes toward motherhood and household work had developed among middle-class white feminists in the US. The first camp held that the recognition of the social and economic value of the mother and housewife was worth fighting for. The second, that the drudgery of childcare and housebound work was an undesirable burden from which women must escape via waged work.

While a budding twentieth-century feminism was turning its back on mothers, an emerging language of capitalist economics was doing its part to ensure the political invisibility of the unpaid labor those women performed. First, wives were stripped of their productive value in the census: they were given the wage-neutral occupation of "keeping house" in 1870, and, by 1900, counted as an economic drain and labeled "dependents." In full recognition of the actual value of household work, the forty percent of African American women employed in domestic service at the time were included in the measure of productive labor, earning the title of "housekeeper."[5] In this way, the same job that entered into economic models when exchanged for wages, became publicly insignificant when construed as a labor of love.

In the twentieth century, the value of household labor took another hit when it was erased from national models of economic growth. Though unpaid labor, the majority of which is performed by women, is responsible for nearly half of a nation's economic activity, it is excluded from the gross domestic product. By midcentury, the GDP had become the sole indicator of the economic health of a nation. As a result, the source of data that would determine broad economic policy around social structures like education, welfare, childcare, and parental leave now officially excludes the productive labor of childrearing and housework.[6] Women's work erased.

The will to ignore this story is powerful. It is strong enough to deny the reality of the housewife's value in public conversation, even as her resource-intensive labor is acknowledged in hiring and promotion practices that penalize mothers and in welfare and immigration policies that ensure a steady supply of maids and nannies.[7] For feminists, the story is steeped in the errors of essentialism, that slippery slope of logic that would point to women's potential maternity as a signal of her fundamental difference from men. To open the door to this tired debate is to jeopardize the conceptual equality we've earned. But as babies continue to be born, children need tending, and homes require managing, equality in the abstract can't account for the need. And women—no matter how enlightened—continue to be the ones who choose.

"So I have a tough question for you," Laura says, turning to Eric.

"Me?"

"Yeah." She leans toward him over discarded dinner dishes and take-out boxes, her cheek resting on one hand. "Did you ever resent me for not taking on a bigger part of the family household?"

Eric considers his wife's question for a moment, leaning back in his chair. "No. I mean, when we were first married and without kids, and we had that conversation—"

"See, my mom always worked," Laura inserts. "Eric's mom always stayed home."

"Yeah," Eric continues. "So we had a conversation then, and Laura said, 'I think I want to work.' And I was like, 'I'd rather you stay at home when the kids are born and manage them.' But then we had that conversation, and after then, not really."

"But," Laura digs a little deeper, "I mean, because it also has meant a lot of sacrifices for you. A lot of your friends, they come home and dinner's made; they don't have any obligations. And I'm like, 'Here's your jobs for the day.'" They both laugh, we all laugh, sitting around a kitchen table talking about demanding wives and sacrifices and choices made.

"Not really," Eric smiles softly.

The question leads to a discussion of work–life balance, and Eric tells me about a conversation he recently had with an up-and-coming employee in his firm. "I was hoping he'd be my successor. He was having a difficult time making it to these meetings in the morning, so I just sat him down and I said, 'Look, I need to know where your head is. Are you going to be one to want to be here and actually do what it takes to get to the next level, or are you just happy where you're at?' And he's like, 'I'm just happy where I'm at.' They both work, and he's got some stuff going on at home, his mom's sick and other things. Which is fair, completely fair. That's, you know, work–life balance."

Laura chimes in, "I have actively made the decision to not promote people or put them on my succession line, because they just can't do it."

"Because they choose not to? Or—" I ask.

"Family." Eric answers for her, "Family, family over—"

"No," she quickly cuts him off. "It's not family. I choose family, too. But I choose to have the support so I can have a family and have the flexibility to say, 'Diana, I'm going to be late tonight because my boss just asked me to do x, y, z. So I need to stay late.'" She pauses. "Look, this is a personal choice. It's entirely a personal choice."

"Choosing not to be on that track?" I ask.

"Mhmm," Eric leans back and nods.

"Yeah," Laura continues. "Look, I wanted to be general counsel; it was a career goal of mine, and I knew what it took. I'd seen it. My boss, before I became general counsel, she essentially had married a guy who didn't work, and I had seen the hours it took. I didn't have a stay-at-home husband, so I basically had to hire somebody who was willing to take on that responsibility for me, for a price."

I consider the sentiment. The price gives me pause. If professional success, the pinnacle of American self-realization, is framed as a choice that inherently conflicts with family, then family and the work it entails will always be at odds with professional success. In this dynamic, only those with the means to fill in the gaps of our flawed practice of equality will really be able to choose.

For thirty thousand dollars a year, Laura and Eric are able to pursue professional success and still develop deep meaningful relationships with their children. With Diana at the helm, mom and dad are free to leave work for a class party or a doctor's appointment, to take one-on-one parent–child trips, to set aside time and space for the important conversations. The kind between mothers and daughters, for instance, about the choices of a working mom.

"She used to ask me, 'How come you're hardly ever home?' At first I used to say things like, 'Well you know so we can buy this house, and provide for these things.' But the reality is, I never wanted that for me. So, having the confidence now to be able to tell your kid, 'Look, honey, I love practicing law. I love it. And I'm a better mom because I work.'"

Laura's approach to teaching her daughter about women's relationship to professional fulfillment is heartfelt and powerful and only possible because of Diana, who will always be the substitute for the housewife and stay-at-home mother that Laura chose not to be.

For Eric, choice doesn't enter into the equation.

"I definitely don't have those thoughtful of responses," he reflects, his eyes on his wife and a table dressed in half-drunk wine and unwashed plates. "But it's worked out well."

But of course it has; they've had Diana.

Jenny

"She's not 'the nanny I used to have'; she's Nora. And everybody knows who she is when I say Nora. They all know that she was the nanny who took care of my kids, and she comes to birthday parties, and my friends know who she is. We've had her come to parties when the kids aren't even here. So we just all became friends. It felt like family, and I trusted her with my children. I knew that they would be safe with her and taken care of."

Jenny sits on a stool in the renovated bungalow she shares with her wife and three children in a comfortable family neighborhood in central Houston and tells me about her family's relationship to their long-time nanny. Her ten-year-old son practices gymnastics in the next room while her eight-year-old twin daughters play in the back. It's a summer day, and Jenny's teaching job allows her to be home with the kids while her wife, Rene, works a year-round, nine-to-five job. It's always been that way, and summer is Jenny's happiest time.

"I would have probably stayed home, at least for four or five years. I could do this housewife thing. I think this would be fun. Summer time is great. People are like, 'What camps do you do?' I'm like, 'Mommy camp.'"

If circumstances had been different, the couple might have found a way to live on one income while the kids were small, but public policies around family leave, childcare, marriage laws, and health insurance made staying home impossible for Jenny.

"I had to go back to work. I stayed home as long as I could. I stayed home seven weeks. But as a teacher we don't get paid when we're home. After you run out of your days you're just, you're done. And I couldn't afford not to work because I wouldn't have had health insurance, and my daughters wouldn't have had insurance either."

The girls were biologically Jenny's and, because Texas didn't recognize the couple's marriage until 2015 and adoption takes time, there was no way for Jenny or the children to access Rene's employment-based health insurance. If she'd left her job, Jenny would have risked losing healthcare at a vulnerable time for her newborn twins.

"They were born in September. I stayed home for those seven weeks, and I went back in November, right before Thanksgiving, and then I didn't get a paycheck until almost January. My paychecks were negative, because I had to pay back my health insurance. I ran out of the ten days, because I had spent all ten days, because I had just had him two years before that, so I had nothing in the bank."[8]

Bound to work despite the negative paychecks and the pull of her babies, Jenny returned to the classroom, dropping all three kids off at their nanny's home each day before the morning bell. For both Jenny and Nora, the arrangement was a godsend.

The women had found each other two years earlier, in what was for Jenny a moment of desperation. The crisis was triggered by a phone call at work from the daycare center where she had left her ten-month-old son.

"They wouldn't hold him," Jenny's voice is strained as she recounts the experience, still angry with the memory. "They wouldn't hold my baby to give him a bottle. He was really small—failure to thrive—and he couldn't hold the bottle and they wouldn't hold him."

Jenny had spent that summer interviewing nannies and visiting daycare centers, only reluctantly settling on the one that felt the least wrong. "It was clean. The staff was friendly. It looked like he would have room to roll around." At $800 a month, the cost had only just been manageable for her and Rene. But the phone call was the last straw.

"I was walking out the door and I was crying, and one of my coworkers said, 'What's wrong?' I told her what had happened between me and the daycare center. She was like, 'I know a lady.'" Jenny pauses, letting the sentence hang in the air, then picks up her coworker's voice again. "'But I don't want you to be a snob because she lives in a really poor home. But her house is clean, and she takes really good care of her kids. Her name is Nora Martínez.'" Jenny stops to catch her breath. "I was like, 'I know who that is.'"

Nora's child had been a student in Jenny's class, and Jenny liked the woman and was ready to trust her. "As a teacher, you can tell. There are some parents who don't do anything, and you could tell she was a parent who does everything. You could just tell. I felt like she was going to take care of my kid."

She thanked her friend, and by the end of the day, she had picked her son up from daycare for the last time and visited Nora at her home, where the Mexican woman regularly took in children in an informal home daycare. The place wasn't yet set up for a crawling baby, but something about Nora and her house inspired trust, that intangible gut feeling that forms so much of the nanny industry infrastructure.[9] So Jenny said yes, and she and her mom and Rene headed to the discount store for floor mats and a high chair and anything else that Nora's modest home was missing. For the next two years, Jenny paid a hundred dollars a week for her baby to spend his school-year weekdays with Nora and the other kids she cared for.

The arrangement worked well, but when the twins came along at the same time as another client had twins herself, Jenny knew Nora wouldn't be able to tend to all the children. So she asked Nora to make a choice: keep Jenny's family on as her exclusive clients during the school-year or lose them all together. The choice, in Jenny's view, was clear. She was one of the few parents who paid Nora regularly.

"Nora has a hard time saying no. Her children came to me and told me that the other woman didn't pay her. But Nora can't say no. She just loves babies and she loves children. So when the woman would show up with a kid, she was like, 'I can't say no to the kid. Where else is the kid gonna go?' That's what she's thinking. So she would always take the kid, and then when the woman showed up and didn't pay her, she just kind of got screwed. And it happened to her a lot.

"But we paid," Jenny declares. "We always paid. We never showed up on a Friday and said, 'I don't have your money.' And other people did. Other people would show up and go, 'I don't have the money, can I pay you next week?' And next week turned into next week, and so when it came down to it, I was paying."

Nora's other clients were likely facing the same obstacles that she and Jenny were, all of them managing a reality that requires they work outside of the home for wages and healthcare, but doesn't give them any recourse to affordable quality childcare. As many middle-class and working-class parents have discovered, the childcare options available to the average American family these days are grossly inadequate, and the cost can be insurmountable.

Next to housing, the cost of childcare is the single greatest expense that American parents face. A 2016 report from the Organization for Economic Cooperation and Development (OECD) reveals that families in the US spend an average of 25.6 percent of their income on childcare. For single parents, that percentage increases to 52.7. In Texas, childcare costs surpass the cost of tuition at a four-year public university and childcare for two children averages 27 percent of a family's take-home salary. For perspective, the US Department of Health and Human Services considers childcare affordable if it costs 7 percent or less of a family's income.[10] Globally, the US falls far short of its peers in supporting its very young. Of the thirty-four countries in the OECD, the US ranks near the bottom in early childhood education and is still the only advanced economy that does not guarantee maternity leave for working mothers.[11]

For Jenny, securing Nora as their exclusive nanny saved her from tripling the cost of a daycare center, but it also meant a significant responsibility.

"In the summer, I'd take them over to her once or twice a week. When you have daycare you have to pay all summer for the daycare, and she wasn't getting any money, with me being her primary income. So on holidays, when I would be gone for two weeks at Thanksgiving or Christmas, I would pay her anyway. I would call it her Christmas bonus and give her the money that she would have made. I did that because she sacrificed other children for my kids. So I tried to take care of her.

"And then," she pauses, "my parents bought her house."

Jenny explains that, as the families became more enmeshed, the relationship between them acquired a more personal, intimate feel. So when Nora's family came home one day to find an eviction notice on their front door, it felt natural for Jenny to find a way to help them.

"They got evicted. They paid rent to live in the house. The owner let his house foreclose while they were living there and kept taking their rent, and they had no idea until one day someone came and put a sign on the door evicting them, telling them, 'Look, you've got thirty days to get out.' They're not here legally, and they felt like they couldn't do anything because, they're gonna call the cops and report this man, and then they're illegal. So my dad contacted the bank and bought their home, and they just paid my dad the rent to live there."

When Jenny's father steps in to fill in the gap between the realities of immigrant life and social protections that rely on status, the line between personal lives and political realities becomes confused. The private reach of public policy emerges once and again in Jenny's and Nora's stories. Both women negotiate relationships and emotions within social structures set up against their mothering desires. Jenny pays half her underpaid teacher's salary to leave children she longs to be with in the care of another. Nora takes in children whose parents don't pay and manages her work and home in the shadows of her unauthorized status. The common thread between them, Jenny's need and Nora's livelihood, is the way their lives have been shaped by the myth that childcare is a private affair, separate from state support and community responsibility and belonging always to the realm of the feminine.

Here again, feminism's cry that the personal is political has come up short for mothers. Though women are constantly bombarded with the rhetoric of choice—as a right, as a source of power—the empowerment it promises is largely about choosing away from motherhood, not toward it. With its overwhelming focus on abortion and birth control, the feminist discourse of reproductive rights has coalesced around the choice not to have biological children, a move that has become conflated with freedom from gender roles. As a result, the political dimension of the personal experience of motherhood is tossed aside, leaving no feminist language to assert a mother's right to be supported in her maternity or parents' rights to be supported in their childrearing.[12]

But motherhood is political. And our collective political history favors a certain kind of mother. She is usually white, middle- or upper-class, and married to a man. At its most extreme, this ideology has resulted in the forced sterilization of immigrants, racial minority women, the mentally ill, and the incarcerated.[13] At its most expansive, the mid-century welfare system created an institutional safeguard: the designation of "employable mothers" to ensure that the right kind of mother could stay home with her children, while the others—poor women of color—remained available to "help."[14] From welfare policy to marriage laws to a healthcare system conditioned on full-time employment, mothers who don't conform to the white, middle-class, heterosexual ideal often find themselves out of luck.

Where political structures meet the rhetoric of choice, moral judgment rears its ugly head. In the same way that pundits and ideologues tell us that the poor who struggle must somehow deserve less, conversations around childcare, welfare, and workplace discrimination come back over and again to a shame-laden construction of choice. Wrong to choose to mother if she's poor, wrong if she's unmarried, if she's unauthorized, if she's gay. And those on the wrong side of choice are left to manage on their own. So Jenny must return to work for negative paychecks, and look for trust in the little things—a clean house, an involved parent, someone she can talk to. Someone who may come to feel something like a friend.

After Jenny and Rene's kids had been staying with Nora for a while, the relationship between the three women began to take on a quality much like friendship.

"She started asking us to stay, like, 'Why don't we just sit down and have a drink?' So we started doing that. Then, she would invite us to parties, like a birthday party for the kids or her grandkids, like on a Saturday night. We started coming over and spending time, as friends, you know, and hanging out."

"Did you ever feel any awkwardness, any social class difference?"

"Not really. I mean, they had less money than me, and I was her employer, but I didn't feel like there was that big of a difference in our class. And she has an engineering degree. She can't do anything with it here in America, but in Mexico, she was very highly educated." Jenny explains that Nora came here for love—fell for a less educated man, had a couple of kids, conceded reluctantly to his immigrant dreams.

But social class isn't enough to explain Jenny's uncomplicated sense of the friendship between her and Nora. Many immigrant nannies come from middle-class backgrounds. The ability to migrate requires certain resources that have historically meant that immigrants are rarely the poorest of the poor. In Jenny's case, there's more than similar education and background that closes the gap between the women.

"I mean, as a parent and a teacher, we started off in that relationship, where it was almost like I'm working for her. As an educator, you feel like you work for the parent. So it started off that way, the roles kind of went back and forth. And then, she was watching my kids when I had her twin in my classroom."

Something in this power dynamic creates a more balanced relationship than what other patronas describe, but the difference feels deeper to me than parent–teacher meetings and college degrees. I recall a comment Laura made when I asked her and Eric how negotiating with their nanny compared to discussions with employees at work. "She's more like family," Laura had responded. "It's more like negotiating with an older kid. Like, 'Fine you can have that nicer phone, but what are you going to do for me? Then you need to start taking out the trash two days a week.' It's like you start negotiating for more chores or something. It feels a lot like that."

The distance between this kind of power struggle and the relationship Jenny describes with Nora is hard to explain. The home is part of it—dropping her children off makes Jenny more of a client than a boss and it sidesteps the awkward intimacy of dirty laundry and heated arguments in the next room. But there's something else going on here, too, something to do with the sense of social power a teacher holds relative to a successful attorney or corporate executive. There is something limiting in Jenny's negative paychecks and ten sick days a year that may be familiar to Nora, the shared experience of a world set up for a different kind of mother, a different kind of woman.

Nicole

For others, the relationship between nanny and employer is more complicated.

"I wasn't particularly crazy about the fact that I was offloading basic mothering to some other woman," Nicole confesses over a lunch-hour meal on a bright spring day, "but I had to work."

With her liberal leanings and tremendous ambivalence about her dual roles as mother and breadwinner, Nicole has struggled with the implications of her position as employer to a full-time domestic worker. Over the two-hour span of our conversation at a glass-windowed café on a university campus, she sorts through the privilege and the need, the guilt and the gratitude that marked the eighteen years during which she employed full-time nannies.

In the early years, when she was still married to her first husband, the couple only had one child, an infant. At that time, the realities of Nicole's marriage made a nanny the only option. "I was working full time because I was the primary breadwinner in my family," she explains, "and I had to work. I was the one providing health insurance, so I didn't have a choice. My ex-husband, my then-husband, he wasn't going to quit. We were actually paying the nanny more than he was earning, but to maintain an element of peace in the family, it made more sense to have a nanny. He wasn't about to stay home, so I made an economically foolish but socially responsible choice."

Hyper-aware of the imbalanced power and the perception of unchecked privilege, Nicole sought out a nanny with few mothering constraints of her own. "I wanted a nanny who had raised her own kids. One, because I wanted someone who understood the stress of parenthood. And two, I didn't want a nanny who was having to leave her child with somebody else to take care of mine. That just feels weird. I don't want to feel like I'm causing a mother to leave her own child."

She soon found Marta, a Mexican woman with three nearly grown sons, who spoke little English, loved babies, and would care for Nicole's infant son, and the brother and sister that followed, for the next ten years. Marta loved the kids, and their parents trusted her completely. She spent every weekday with the children, caring and cooking and carting them to school and spending the night when necessary.

Nicole was hesitant to embrace her identity as a patrona to a Mexican nanny. More than her own working-mother ambivalence, it was the nature of the relationship that made her uncomfortable, the intimacy and the dependence. She recalls her ex-husband telling Marta that she was one of the family. "I'd say, 'Don't say that. I'm her boss.' I mean, you're not really family if I can fire you," she reasons. "It's a really complicated dynamic."

But the feeling of family persisted, and over the years the two families became more and more entangled. Nicole helped Marta navigate the financial landscape of credit and debt, getting Marta's ex-husband off her mortgage and advising her on credit card interest rates. She recommended one of Marta's sons to an industry job, threw a graduation party for a daughter-in-law. She helped the family when another son was caught stealing. "It was challenging," she says, "because at some point you end up taking care of the family as much as they take care of you."

Amid all the closeness, the ambivalence and the concern, the relationship only became more confused when Nicole's needs changed. As the kids got older and Marta's limited English didn't match new tasks and contexts, the gap between the demands of the job and her ability grew. Marta relied on the second son's strong Spanish to interact with others, which compromised her authority, and she was less comfortable managing after-school schedules as the kids moved into junior high. Like Laura and Eric, Nicole increasingly needed someone who could "do everything."

And then there was the episode with the shirts.

"There was one incident we had with Marta," Nicole begins. "She was trying to do a little bit more and my ex-husband had her take his shirts to the dry cleaner, about fifteen shirts. So I came home from traveling and I got to the dry cleaner, and I said, 'Where are all these shirts?' He said, 'We don't have any of that.'"

Back at home, she told her husband, "Something's wrong," and picked up the phone to talk to Marta through her daughter-in-law's translation. "Are you sure you dropped everything off?" she asked.

"Yes," Marta insisted. "Yes, I did."

Nicole thought for a moment, considered the dry cleaner's location, right next to a Goodwill donation center, and asked, "What did the place look like?"

"I realized what had happened," she explains. "She took all of his clothes to Goodwill. Nice, custom shirts. It was terrible. She felt horrible. That's when I realized I can't ask her to do these things. I can't morph this job into something else because it's not a good fit. And I need more help."

So, she gave Marta plenty of notice, calculated a six-week severance pay according to her own industry standards, and helped her find a new job caring for babies. "And then," Nicole adds, "I paid off her house."

As she rationalizes this $12,000 move, Nicole offers two explanations. "She was probably close to seventy by that time, and so part of what I wanted to do in paying off her house was to take care of some of her fixed costs so that she would have more flexibility. Really, in my heart, I thought, 'She's old enough that she shouldn't have to work anymore.'"

But mostly, she admits, it was the guilt. "I felt really guilty about letting her go, and I figured if I gave her a good severance and helped her find another job and paid off her house I could stop feeling quite so guilty."

The guilt and ambivalence that mark Nicole's identity as a nanny's boss isn't unique. It's a natural outcome of the mothercoin's transaction. Because an immigrant nanny crossing the threshold of an employer's home every morning brings with her a world of injustice that is hard to ignore. To engage with her—to write the check and ask after the family and look her in the eyes—is to confront one's own place in a society that can often be cruel. A world of regional inequality that forces the conditions of migration but punishes those who cross the borders. A world of domestic conflict that casts the work of mothering and homemaking as an undesirable burden but shames the working mother for her absence.

No matter how big an employer's heart, no matter how genuine her concern for her employee, the domestic worker in her home is there because she has fewer choices than her employer does. And Nicole knows that no matter how caring and fair she may be as an employer, Marta will always be grasping at the short end of a stick that Nicole herself feels powerless to change.

After letting Marta go, Nicole put an ad on an online childcare brokering service. "The posting was for a 'house manager,' somebody who could manage the house, who could manage meeting an appliance repair person, taking the car to get serviced, doing the grocery shopping, going to the dry cleaners, and initially it was cleaning."

In Adimu, an educated immigrant from central Africa who answered the ad, Nicole found the support she would rely on for the next six years—through a demanding, successful career, the changing needs of three school-age children, and the stress and upheaval of divorce.

For both women, it was clear that Adimu had taken the place of the traditional housewife of the home. "This is going to sound awful," Nicole confesses, "but it was everything that a traditional wife would do if I wasn't working full time. We would joke about it. I was like, 'I hired a wife.' And she's like, 'It's funny you say that because I say that too. People think it's really weird.'" Nicole laughs at the memory. "I was like, 'But that's what you are. You do all the stuff that I can't do.'"

Adimu took over the day-to-day operations of Nicole's home. She shuttled the kids to and from school, ran errands, managed home repairs and related bills, and in the beginning, cleaned. After some negotiation, the evolving job description dropped the cleaning and Nicole hired a housekeeper three times a week. As the children grew and personal lives unfolded, the two women became close. But Nicole is quick to point out that they weren't exactly friends.

"The power dynamic was funny, but we were the same age and sometimes we would just talk as women. With me being aware that I had to be careful, because as vulnerable as we would be with each other, she still works for me. But we would talk about marriage and children and everything. I mean, a high degree of intimacy, though not an equal partnership by any stretch of the imagination. She had lots of marital problems, and then her son was not very healthy. She was working for me when there was a bombing at a mosque, so we talked about being a Black

Muslim woman in Texas. We talked about race. We talked a lot about values, tolerance, what's happening in the country.

"So it was probably not like we were friends, because she worked for me. The power dynamic was funny. But again, she was in my home, she saw my marriage fall apart. She was able to witness everything and basically saw it coming a mile away and had some definite opinions about my marriage."

When Nicole did end her marriage, Adimu made all the difference. "Having her support enabled me to have more control over my life. My career didn't take a huge hit. I wasn't so distracted by the divorce. If you've got a nanny that enables you to work, you know, a portion of your success is probably attributed to the fact that you've got somebody at home taking care of the kids. My divorce was all right because I had a woman who was able to serve as my support. People say during a divorce, for two years your career is probably just cooked. I took a little dip, but not much, and a lot of it's because I had someone to help me get through it."

More than help managing the divorce, Nicole admits that Adimu's role in the family home empowered her to choose to leave a failing marriage in the first place. "There's no questioning the fact that I was set up to leave that marriage. I had the infrastructure."

But even someone with the means to hire nannies and house-managers, someone who runs companies and manages employees and departments and budgets, is powerless to combat images and rhetoric that insist on the story of a good mother who is attentive and nurturing and sacrificing, uncompensated and always present. Powerless, too, against the cultural narrative of the bad mother, the busy professional who dismisses her domestic duty, passing it off to a hired replacement.

"When we got divorced, I was afraid if we went to court they'd try to paint me as a neglectful mother because I worked so much. I wanted to say, 'Okay, look, I'm not what you think. On paper, it may look like, "Oh, here she is, she offloaded her kids to the nanny and she outsourced her parenting, and he was so supportive."' I know how this story gets told, and that's not our story. I was gearing up for the fight. 'Here's the evidence; that's not who I was, so don't paint me as this cold person.'"

While Nicole defends her truth against the false narrative so often construed by divorce lawyers, she doesn't question the assumption at its heart—that the woman is supposed to give more and do more, that the woman, by virtue of her motherhood, is morally bound to the home in a way the man is not. I'm not surprised by the silence. In fact, I've learned to anticipate it in my conversations with employers. Though women like Nicole and Laura are deeply aware of the feminist implications of their choices as working mothers, they never challenge the assumption that the hired help is there to substitute the wife, that managing the maid is her job.

I hear it in the little things. The pronoun Nicole uses when she reprimands her husband for telling Marta she's one of the family: "Don't say that," she told him. "*I'm* her boss." A story Laura tells about Diana's poor judgment in dropping off a child at a summer day camp without walking her in: "It turns out—lo and behold—*I* made a mistake and it was not her week." And the woman is the bridge when families become enmeshed: it's Laura who fixes Diana's divorce, Nicole who buys Marta's house. Even Jenny adopts the singular: "I was aware I was her only income," she says of her arrangement with Nora. Never "we," always "I," always in the feminine.

If the women are the ones managing the maid, it's because, despite its language of choice and liberation, feminism has failed to denaturalize the woman–home connection in broader culture. Because the loudest feminist voices have refused to take up the theoretical task of maternity, the whole project of gender equality has developed on a false foundation.[15] Ironically, in an attempt to erase the expectation that women *should* be the ones who tend to the children, feminist discourse has ignored the fact that so many still do. Studies of household labor in heterosexual couples find over and again that the woman does the bulk of the unpaid work, regardless of the nature of her paid labor. An analysis of 2018 survey data on time use in the US found that, on the whole, women spend 37 percent more time on unpaid household and carework than men. This gender gap increases for women who work part time in the paid labor force and shoots up to almost 50 percent for Hispanic women.[16] The sense of a feminine responsibility for the home—from decorating to dinner planning to social calendar management—remains intact. For women who can afford to compensate these injustices with a domestic hire or two, there has been little incentive to buck the system. On the contrary, the system has become more emboldened.

Somewhere in the late twentieth century, the ideal of good mothering intensified and the scope of "women's work" skyrocketed. Many mothers found themselves responding to a certain something in the air that demanded a mother be more available and attentive than her own mother ever felt she needed to be. That she dedicate herself to shaping and molding her children through constant micromanagement, selfless emotional giving, deftly orchestrated enrichment and social activities, and a steady supply of nutritious snacks. It is an intensive style of parenting, characterized by guilt, stress, and an ideal that seems only to be attainable by mothers with the means to finance art classes and sports equipment and either not be employed or hire out a permanent domestic presence with a driver's license and enough command of English to negotiate a Mommy and Me class.[17]

When Laura tells me, "The nanny that we need today has evolved tremendously from the nanny that my parents needed," she's referencing a framework of intensive mothering that the modern nanny both enables and reinforces. But this approach to parenting sets an impossible standard for the bulk of mothers in America who must manage childcare and work and family budget without "help." And as long as mothers of means who are leaders in their fields and influencers in their communities use their nannies to sustain the image of a supermom capable of doing it all, then the ideal will persist.

Even as domestics are hired and workarounds develop, the standard, like the shame, intensifies. These days, American mothers must live up to an image as unsustainable as a Barbie doll. Selflessly attentive to her children's emotional, physical, and intellectual needs, a good mother cures colds with supplements, manages pony league pitchers and budding stage actors, and ensures college prospects through years of extracurricular grooming and elbow-to-elbow late night homework. Again and again, she falls short. Especially when she must also respond to the demands of working-class realities: insecure housing, an income that pales in comparison to her children's needs, subpar public education, and access to healthcare that is tied to her job or her partner or to a gold card she fears may be compromised by paying taxes on the job she performs every day for a woman who can afford to try to have it all. When the stakes are this high, everything a mother gives often feels like not enough. Even for the patronas.

A moment remains frozen in my mind. Nicole and I walk away from the restaurant where we have met to talk. We speak of our own children, our families and personal lives. Our kids are the same age; they share schools, sports teams. Just before we part ways, she begins a story that becomes a confession. Her young stepdaughter recently went to a party filled with popular kids. Something told Nicole that she should take the girl to the party herself, scope out the lay of the land and the vibe among the queen bees and wannabees. But caught up in the busyness of a demanding career and three other children, a new husband and a new life, she allowed her son to drop his sister off instead.

"I should have been there," she says as she pulls out her phone and scrolls through her pictures. She flashes a photo in front of me: her ten-year-old daughter smiles awkwardly and stands far to the side of a group of girls who somehow have chosen the right clothes, the right pose, the right way to be. Nicole's eyes tear up, "I really should have been there."

In the end, we mothers can never seem to give enough. Whether it be the social minefields of a private school party or an empty seat in a crowded auditorium, the expectation that mothers can and should manage every moment of our children's lives is a harmful burden. And the ideal of the constant, selfless mother—somehow naturally feminine—does real damage. From middle-class American intensive mothering to the entrenched domestic gender roles of rural Mexican and Central American cultures, the burden of our children's needs continues to rest disproportionately on a mother's shoulders. It sends women across borders to supplement the food and education and healthcare their children aren't receiving at home, and it inserts them into a home and a relationship often burdened by the guilt and ambivalence of one who must make up for all her personal "choices" in a confusing landscape of emotion and regret and stunted feminism.

So Nicole will cry for the photo she could not prevent, and Sara will feel shame for the child's illness she failed to ward off. Rosa will throw her migrant dreams to hell for the baby she's found asleep on the floor, and Jenny will leave work with red eyes and a heart aching for the skinny little thing who can't hold his own bottle. All of them suspecting, deep inside, that they are the ones who are really at fault—for the absence, the unmet needs, the performances missed and applications botched, all of it somehow a reflection of the wrong choices of a good mother.

In time, Adimu's job with the family came to a close. The kids were older, Nicole explains, her new husband had taken over a lot of the home management, and grocery delivery services could compensate the shopping. The separation was painful, especially for Nicole's thirteen-year-old daughter. "She was in tears," Nicole tells me. "She really missed her. Adimu was a big part of their lives."

Looking back, she thinks about the choices she might have made and reflects on the ones she did. "If I could have afforded it, I probably would have . . . maybe not stayed home full time, but I would have definitely considered it. But I didn't have a choice. I didn't want to work the way I did," she reflects, "but I had to. And I couldn't have worked the way I did without them.

"Chris Rock has a joke," she adds with a reflective smile. "He says white women shouldn't complain about their nannies, or something. And on the one hand, he's right, total first world problems, *Oh, my nanny didn't get the organic soap*, or whatever. But then, it's a very peculiar dynamic. You try to be a 'woke' employer, but the whole thing is just kind of weird. I mean, at one point I was a little embarrassed by it." So she buys Marta's house. She hires a housekeeper at Adimu's request, and when Adimu's son needs afterschool care, Nicole increases her pay. She does what she can to manage the power differential in a way that honors her own moral values. But the discomfort persists, because something is still not right in this relationship.

For women like Nicole, the idea of hiring a "housewife" feels like an inadequate solution to a very real need. The proposition "sounds awful." She feels a little embarrassed. Because the word "housewife" means things these days—dependence, weakness, triviality. The job description is as concrete as dinner on the table and collecting kids from piano lessons, but its rhetorical value in the American imaginary is null, economically insignificant, and just a little bit shameful. But turning to the mothercoin to escape these associations and resolve the need has real consequences. For patronas, for nannies, for all of us.

When we replace the housewife with a low-wage, publicly invisible muchacha, we maintain the same system of gender-based power that women have been resisting for ages. Because the feminist revolution did not dismantle patriarchy, it only allowed some women to participate in patriarchal power.[18] At home, mothers still find themselves on the losing side of a hierarchy of power with intimate reach. Winners and losers are reproduced in the shadow market for domestic service, and the nanny-housekeeper suffers doubly for our diminished sense of what a housewife is worth.

More broadly, trade in the mothercoin reinforces the unsustainable parenting standards that so many of us come up against. Broad cultural ideals around intensive mothering, expectations for corporate success, and the illusion of personal choice are fed by the steady supply of low-cost labor coming in from places like Rosa's rancho and Sara's cantón. All the while, a certain deception unfolds behind the closed doors of upper- and middle-class American homes. Daughters are told they can have it all, mothers tell themselves they've found a way to have it all, and couples cease arguing about who will clean the bathroom or miss work to pick up a sick child from school. Equality achieved—as long as we can ignore the maid scrubbing the bathroom floor, who likely faces the same conflicts she's been hired to resolve.

Of all the forces that feed the need for the immigrant nanny and determine the conditions in which she lives and works, the greatest is the occupation's intractable association with the idea of "woman." In avoiding the association, feminism has ignored the mothercoin's conflict of values and failed at resisting its injustice. If we recover the value in the work of childrearing and homemaking, we risk regressing into the trap of essentialism. But if we don't, our children will continue to learn what the world is set up to teach them—lessons in value about who matters and who doesn't, about which mothers are good and which are bad, and about the children who deserve to be loved and protected, and those who must learn to expect far less.

PART III

VALUE PROPOSITION

I am visible—see this Indian face—yet I am invisible.
I both blind them with my beak nose and am their
blind spot. But I exist, we exist.

GLORIA ANZALDÚA[1]

Prelude

A system set up on shaky moral ground will fight like hell to justify itself. It will bend perception, mete out reward and punishment, cast strategic doubt, and offer selective praise. It will paint images, tell stories, and try to teach the world to see its own skewed values in the faces it encounters. For those who trade in the mothercoin, these lessons coalesce around an ideal of the good mother that burrows deep into a woman's sense of self. But the ideal is not attainable for all. The standard of moral motherhood in America has always grown up in tandem with its flipside—a standing servant class of women whose own parenting is charged with a different kind of cultural meaning.

Throughout this country's history, immigrants and women of color have been routed again and again into positions of domestic service—Eastern Europeans in the northeast, African Americans in the south, Mexican Americans in the southwest, Japanese and Chinese in the far west. As daughters of European women moved out of the domestic service sector in the early twentieth century, those of the darker-skinned maids were tracked by teachers, social policies, and federal programs back into the homes of more privileged women. Late in the century, this dynamic began to shift as women's migration from Mexico, Central America, and the Caribbean picked up, and African American granddaughters actively resisted the tracking and the expectations, saturated with mammy stereotypes and kerchiefed Aunt Jemimas.[2]

In response to these changes, the system moved its gears to ensure the supply for its unspoken demand, spinning the tales that would make the exploitation feel not so very wrong. From mid-century welfare policy to late-century immigration reform, politicians and pundits told the country which groups deserved support and which didn't, and their rhetorical value lessons taught us why. The Black welfare queen rose up as a lazy and immoral foil to the more palatable widow or victim of a deadbeat dad. The immigrant mother of anchor babies emerged as a deceptive trickster out to take advantage of chain migration and American social welfare.[3] This shame-generating face of the system teaches a lesson with deep implications: these women's mothering is less valuable, their children less precious. The framing makes it easy to extract their labor from the context of mother and child, making it a quantifiable resource to be given over to other mothers and other children, who somehow deserve this "help."

There are other voices to listen to. The cultural meanings of motherhood in African American communities look quite different from the homebound angel of the Anglo-Saxon tradition, incorporating the importance of breadwinning, "othermothers," and community-based childcare into cultural ideals of good mothering. Hispanic mothers bring nuanced understandings of working motherhood and the integrated place of mothers in communities.[4]

These alternative ideals hold transformative potential, but they confront a daunting reality in the gears of the machine. When a mother is cut off from social welfare by poverty, status, and patriarchal violence, needs that run deeper than soccer cleats and SAT tutors tug at her parenting self. Because what kind of a good mother can she be when she can't protect her child from fear or disease, from an ambivalent caregiver, gangs on the streets, or the hard lessons of a world that compensates its shortcomings by choosing who deserves to be protected and who will be blamed? As policy and ideology continue to punish and reward in public arenas, and cultural forms of resistance emerge and succumb, women like those in this book will weigh the value proposition of the mothercoin against their own mothering ideals. They will make their way through a cultural battlefield of blame and praise as they secure their children's most basic needs—nourishment, safety, health, hope.

While in the crossfires, the children watch and learn.

CHAPTER 6

LOS NIÑOS

We are all children of God.

TERESA

Sara

Sara's son Drew spends a good deal of time with his aunt Maribel, watching. After school, holidays, summertime, whenever his mom works, he and his little sister are with their *tía*, following her closely as she tends to the children whose parents pay her to care for them. They are with her now in the park, responding to her calls and requests, little Drew with one eye always on his mom. Who sits next to me and works to tell her story, which is, in some ways, Maribel's.

"My sister thinks that it would have been better if my mom had stayed home, that enduring the hunger, but everyone together, would have been better than giving us the comfort we had later on. Because my sister thinks that the love and affection was better, being with our mom. That the hunger didn't matter, that we would be poor, but we would have survived.

"My sister, since she didn't grow up with a mom, she got married when she was twelve. So, she had her baby girl when she was thirteen."

I try to find the lines of a twelve-year-old girl in the woman resting on a picnic table one sandbox away, curved and heavy with the needs of the four children surrounding her. I try to see her as a vulnerable, motherless child in a place that does not protect its girls—where underage pregnancy numbers in the tens of thousands a year, and rape is a common cause.[1]

"My sister decided to migrate with her husband and two-year-old daughter. It cost us $12,000 to bring her over at that time, all three of them. But the coyote wasn't able to cross the baby, so they decided to leave my sister with Immigration and let the agents decide if they would cross her over or leave her there. So they passed her over to Immigration, and they were like, 'Well, you have a baby, you're a minor, and your parents are here . . . ' So they gave her permission to cross over."

"Permission" is a slippery word for migrants, caught up in the confused legal landscapes of residencies and work permits, green cards and suspension of deportation. The temporary protected status that protected Sara and her mother offered a mix of deportation protection and work permits that sheltered them from the greatest vulnerabilities of illegal migration status but kept their claim to civil participation fragile. Amnesty is different. Though the word carries the connotation of categorical pardon, in practice, immigration-related amnesty invokes a patchwork of legal designations that together offer a degree of legitimacy to the migrant who happens to be in the right place at the right time.

While older migrants, like Rosa's husband Arturo and Sara and Maribel's father, benefited from IRCA and NACARA amnesties, with an eventual path to citizenship, others were more temporary.[2] Together, this hodgepodge of policies and programs makes up a tapestry of limits and opportunities for families like Sara's, one in which debates about "chain migration" and merit-based policies overshadow the damage done to the children who are caught in the confusing landscape of partial legitimacy.

The permission granted to fifteen-year-old Maribel and her two-year-old daughter, Celia, ushered them into a family separated by complicated intersections of status: renewable TPS for Sara and her mother, NACARA protection for her father, citizenship by birth for Sara's two children, and for their aunt Maribel and cousin Celia, a veil of illegality that would deny them security and access. Criminal in its association, racist in its application, and brutal enough on a school playground to send a tearful young girl pleading to her teenage mother to take her back to a home she never really knew.

"The girl," Sara continues, "my niece, she wants to go back to El Salvador. She wants to go back because at school the kids call her a wetback."

"But there are a lot of Hispanic kids who go to her school," I respond, yet uninitiated into the pervasive confusion that tumbles through the halls and classrooms of an inner-city public school—*Mexican, Hispanic, Black, mixed, chino, mojado.*[3]

"Sure, sure," Sara responds. "But you understand, there's a lot of racism in schools. And she wants to have a lot of things that the other kids have. A lot of times she'll say, 'I want to see my grandparents.'"

She pauses and her gaze rests on the child who plays in the chilled breeze with sibling and cousins. "My niece, she has a problem. She has a thyroid problem, but because she doesn't have papers, she can't get medical insurance. The sickness she has, it's that she eats and eats and eats and she doesn't get full. As you can see, she doesn't look like a seven-year-old girl. And she can't get treatment because she doesn't have insurance."

I look at the little girl pushing a sister on the swing set. She would be about seven years old, but she doesn't look it, her flesh stretched and full in tight-fitting clothes. Dark curls frame her face the way a little kid's do, wispy and tousled by wind. She breathes heavily, always pushing the swings, never being pushed.

"What kind of treatment would she need, medication?"

"Yes, because it's a sickness that she has in the glands, here," Sara raises her chin and keeps her eyes on me, directing my attention to the center of her neck. "My sister's trying to get the gold card for her, that's the one that helps immigrants."

"But where has she had medical care up until now?"

"She hasn't."

"Not even preventative?"

"No."

I imagine the ER, maybe at Texas Children's Hospital where my own kids' run-ins with table corners and slippery pavement have landed us a night or two—3:00 a.m. and a hundred-dollar copay with my employers' insurance, nothing to fear but the small bones and thin skin of their fragile bodies. Waiting rooms filled with coughing children in tired parents' arms, so many of whom have no recourse to doctors or nurses outside these understaffed and overburdened emergency rooms. It must have been in a place like that where young Maribel learned that her daughter has a problem. That the problem is in the thyroid, "here, in the neck," the hurried doctor might have signaled, where glands that are supposed to tell her to stop eating don't work.

Though Celia makes her life north of this global divide, her geography, race, and status are inscribed on her young body. Here on the losing side of the global care drain, the nanny's children—and the gardener's and the maid's and the elder-care worker's—continue to receive less. Less time, less attention, less care. Some would call this care a right.

A number of thinkers have developed a nuanced understanding of the moral imperatives that inform the practice and value of caring. Taken together, these imperatives form an "ethics of care" that illuminates the moral disconnect at the heart of the mothercoin dynamic, so dramatically revealed in young Celia's story. The foundation of care ethics is both simple and profoundly transformational: we are relational beings, and our moral practices are shaped by the care we give and receive within our relationships, even those we don't choose, even those in which our power is limited.[4]

When our core selves are constituted through the care we give and receive, then an unfortunate situation like Celia's and Maribel's becomes a cutting examination of our collective morality. If Celia deserves the same care her cousins receive and all of them deserve the same care that Sara's young charges receive—with their illnesses treated and fears soothed and questions sorted—then the situation that unfolds at a neighborhood park where global migration meets domestic labor for hire represents a collective moral failure. Such unequal care becomes a violation of fundamental rights, for the children and for their mothers.

Mothers like Sara, who frets for the hours she leaves her own children alone while she chases after an American boy who kicks and slaps and screams that he does not want her.

"A couple of months ago, he started to give me problems. He treats me badly. He tells me that he hates me and I should leave, that he doesn't want me in his house and I shouldn't come back."

The little boy is six. She's been working with him for two years now, and when she tells me that he was there the day I first met her in the park, I search for his image but only find the memory of a sandy-haired blur running past. The family are good people, she assures me. She's cleaned the patrona's mother's apartment as well. Good people, lovely. It's just that they've spoiled the boy, and the situation has gotten out of hand.

"He kicks me. Three weeks ago, he slapped me twice, hard. The other day he threw a ball at me, it hit me here, and I said, 'No more, no more!' But then when I wasn't looking, he threw another one and it hit me here—" She twists her body to show me the spots on her back beneath a thin T-shirt and cardigan, curves and flesh and a target that yields only when the victim is turned and running away.

"One day, I had to lock myself in a room because he was following me around with a sword. He wanted to hit me. So wherever he got me, he would start kicking me."

"So how did you react?"

"Nothing. I can't do anything."

"What did the parents say?"

" 'I'm sorry.' Most Americans, they fix everything by saying 'I'm sorry.' "

But they really are a good family, she insists, even the little boy, before all this started. Gentle, she assures, polite. "Just last Saturday, he tells me very politely, '*Please*,' " she mimics the child's voice, parroting his English, " '*don't come back my house*.' I feel bad, because I leave my own kids to come take care of these kids"—she's gone from singular to plural, from one boy to all of them, one job to an entire career—"I treat them better than my own, because I have to be sweet to them, to be available for whatever they need."

Whatever they need. But what a child needs can be complicated. The Taylors' daughter, for instance, needed something her parents didn't give. "The little girl, the one from the job where they fired me? I miss her a lot. She was wonderful. She called me 'Mommy' all the time. And I tried to put on a good face for her all the time, to be a good nanny. One, because she wasn't my daughter, but also because something about it upset me, because her parents worked all the time. Work, work, work. They didn't pay attention to the kids at all, and I had to be there for everything."

With the new job, the little boy, she's tried the same approach. "I try to do the best I can. If he wants me to do something, I always say, 'Yes, yes.' All the time, even if I'm tired, because the parents are paying me to be with these children and give them affection and care and treat them well, like their parents would."

"So you never punish them?"

"No, no. First, because they're not my kids. And then, because this country has very difficult laws. You can't yell at a child, because that could get you into trouble. My upbringing was different. In El Salvador it's very different than here. In El Salvador, if a kid is rude, you can punish him—give him a spanking or send him to the corner or tell him he can't do something. But here you're only supposed to talk to them nicely, explain things. They haven't given me permission to put him in timeout—"

"Have you asked?"

"No. Normally in my jobs, the moms will say 'Entertain the kids and if they don't behave put them in timeout.' But not her. She only says, 'Say I'm sorry.' And I'm like, Okay, so the kid knows that as long as he says a couple of words to me, that's it. In his mind, he'd think 'If I say it nicely, then she'll take what I give her.'

"They're really nice people," she repeats, "but I can't control this situation."

Faced with his kicks and slaps and insults, Sara remains silent, appeasing without license to protest. Instead, she's forced to speak nicely, to explain things, *Your words hurt my feelings.* In the silence and acquiescence that follows, the little boy becomes bolder, angrier, freer to take his frustrations out on the dark-skinned woman before him, the one who picks up his toys and prepares his after-school snack. All he has to do is say, *I'm sorry.*

For Sara, these experiences weave themselves around each other inextricably, so that motherhood and occupation and immigrant and American all play out along the same continuum of power. I hear it in the way she associates one thread of her story with another. The story about a boy who learns that the consequence of bad behavior consists of an insincere two words leads into an aside about Leslie, her former employer.

"The one with the dogs?" Sara's voice is animated, her pace quickened. "She would yell at me really bad, really ugly. But then she'd find me and bring me a little present to say, 'I'm sorry, I understand now,' a little regretful. But it would only last a little while. She'd get angry and yell again."

And the story of the boy who acts without consequences that led to the story of the patrona who acts without consequences leads to a statement about the life of an immigrant: "They're experiences that a person has, how can I explain. Being an immigrant is very hard. It's a cross to bear in this country. The first question is always, 'What country are you from?' and the second, 'Do you have papers?' Here, it's papers for everything, health insurance, a job contract; where you're from matters for everything."

In recounting her experience with a boy who slaps and his mother who takes insincere apologies as atonement, Sara tells a story of powerlessness derived from status—"*el origen de uno*," where you're from. And the young boy, who does not know where Sara is from but learns nonetheless that she does not demand the same respect as other grownups, will work out his own explanation—round face, dark eyes, a target that gives.[5]

Rosa

It had been nine years since Rosa returned to her children in Mexico and set up house as a left-behind wife in a divided family. By that time the two eldest had already left for the US. They had finished the basics of their education—a secondary degree that in Mexico roughly equates to a ninth-grade education—and set their sights on their father and America and all the promises that evaded them in the modestly furnished home that their parents' remittances had afforded them in Chietla. The oldest had been the first to announce her plan to emigrate north, followed quickly by the second. Their father Arturo wouldn't hear of it.

"He didn't want to bring them," Rosa says. She mimics her husband's scandalized reaction, "*¿Cómo? ¡Son mujeres!* They're women!"

But Rosa knew he was wrong to protest. And though it may have hurt her to let them go, she understood that mothering meant doing what she had to do to get her family ahead and keep them all together. Like so many times before, one would have to take precedence over the other. No stranger to putting her foot down against Arturo's wishes, Rosa took his *no* in stride and sent her daughters anyway, to be with Rosa's own siblings in California.

"It always hurts when the children leave," she reflects. "But I say, if they want to survive and get ahead, go right ahead. Because if you can't give your kids what they want, then let them go find it themselves."

A few years later, the family once again gathered at their home in Mexico, this time to celebrate their second daughter's wedding. The groom was a fellow immigrant from Puebla, and bride, groom, and relatives had all made their way home to mark the marriage. It was a southbound ritual they would repeat time and again for future weddings, funerals, holidays, any time life meant living and not working.

At the wedding, Rosa's son Miguel approached her in the midst of the drink and celebration. "Mom," he said, "I'm going with my sisters. I'm going with my sisters," he repeated, "or I'm going with my dad."

Miguel had finished his basic schooling by then, and Rosa might have expected this. But as she looked at the boy in front of her, raised alongside the two sisters who were only home to visit and the younger three who would be hers who knew how much longer, a resolution began to form inside of her. By the next time Arturo visited, she had made up her mind. Rosa recounts the conversation in full character.

"Either you stay," she declared to Arturo, "or I go. Which will it be?"

"No, you're crazy! What are you going to do there?" he protested.

"Look, I only have three kids left here," Rosa reasoned. "Why should I spend the best years of my life here, when I could be with you?"

Stunned, Arturo wouldn't give in. "You're crazy."

"Well, if you don't want us to come, then let's get divorced. I'm not willing to be without a husband anymore. Should I look for another?"

Arturo scrambled, "How much time will you give me to get an apartment set up?"

"One month, and I'm not giving you any more. And don't worry about sending me money to pay for it, I'll figure it out here."

And that was that. After selling every electronic device in her house— "televisions, stereos, tape recorders, video cameras, everything electronic"—Rosa scrounged what she needed to secure her and the children's passage. It would be Rosa, thirteen-year-old Lila, and eleven-year-old Martín.

After passing their nine-year-old citizen brother off to their permanent-resident father in Laredo, the two siblings and their mother gave themselves up to their coyote's instructions. They walked five long hours into the night, and at 3:00 a.m., they arrived at a hiding place in the brush, covered by trees and littered with water bottles from migrants who had gone before. When a pick-up truck approached, the coyote ordered them into the open bed, where the children were to hide in a closed box. For half an hour, Rosa tucked behind the box where her children crouched. Later, the kids would say it felt like they were suffocating. Then, the truck stopped, the coyote bought them all soda pop, and by 5:00 a.m., the family was together in Houston.

"We took off our shoes, and it felt like our feet were on fire," Rosa tells me. "The pads of our toes were raw and bleeding. You took off your socks, and there was blood all over. We'd crossed through a bit of desert, or something like that, covered in nopales, and my son fell in the cactus thorns. I had to pick out the thorns with tweezers. But there were so many! He'd fallen in a hole covered with cactus thorns, and us with our feet split open, split open."

But not everyone suffered from the cactus and the desert and the truck's dark cargo box.

"Ha ha! You guys suffering and us in a hotel!" bantered young Eddie. Born into American citizenship in the little room in Houston in a house Rosa once cleaned, the nine-year-old now smiled smugly at his stunned sister and brother. "We went to the movies. You guys were suffering, walking all that time, and we were at the movies eating popcorn!"

To a child caught up in the back-and-forth banter of sibling relationships, the contrast was funny, all that sneaking his brother and sister had to do and him so free. A lucky win for the baby of the family. Eventually, no one would have to sneak around. The younger Lila and Martín would find their way to citizenship along a line of luck that led from their father's IRCA–enabled reprieve to his naturalized citizenship to his own petition for his wife and children. Their older sisters benefited from the status of their American husbands. By 2019, the whole family, save for Rosa's daughter-in-law, would sport a US passport among their travel documents. But back in the early 1990s, each member of the family had a different relationship to American legitimacy—and therefore, a different relationship to hope and to fear.

In those first few days and weeks, the family was gripped with excitement and anxiety. Banter and conversation tossed about in a kitchen stocked with the pots and pans that Arturo had collected from left-behind belongings at the apartments where he worked. "There's a food store," he had told Rosa when they first got to the apartment. "Go and give them the money and make some food, so we have something to eat." The kitchen soon sizzled with onion and chile and cooking oil, the children dizzy with the afterglow of their first days in America—bloody toes and movie theaters and giant grocery stores on wide city streets.

"Ay Mamá," the boys exclaimed. "It's so nice!"

But Lila cried and cried. "She didn't like it," Rosa explains of her thirteen-year-old daughter. "She would see police and run to hide. She was afraid when she heard the sirens. She'd heard that here there was a lot of *migra*, and if the *migra* caught you they'd kick you out. So every time she'd hear the police, she thought they were coming to take her away."

As days passed and the boys became more enchanted, Lila felt ever more estranged. She begged her mother to return, telling her, "I go to school, Mami, and they talk different. I don't understand them. They tell me stuff and I don't understand. I don't know what they're saying. Let's go to Mexico, let's go back, Mami."

While Rosa soothed and shushed and explained that there would be no going back, the boys were less understanding. "What's wrong with you?" they'd say to their tearful sister. "Are you crazy? It's awesome here! Dad takes us to get hamburgers and takes us to the park and all over!"

But Lila would not be consoled, until she met a neighbor friend who helped her with English. Until she learned to navigate the world of a teenage immigrant in Houston. Until she found all the security she wanted in a seventeen-year-old boy with a charming smile and the promise of forever.

"She got married really young," Rosa explains across the years and across my kitchen table. "I told her to study. But if they don't want to, there's no use. The older girls got married too, in California. Only two of my kids finished twelfth grade. The one that was born here was the most stubborn. He wouldn't finish school! The one who had the chance to go to college, the one who was born here!"

For the baby crying on the floor in 1983, college was an option that he chose—freely—to reject. For his sister and brother, like so many child migrants brought over as minors, the option to access affordable university studies or legitimate careers would be wrapped up in the radioactive politics of the Dreamer movement. From the DREAM act to DACA, over almost twenty years and three administrations, the "Dreamers" have become a kind of political bargaining chip with a rhetorical heft that outweighs the numbers.[6] Meanwhile, the young adults whose future depends on such legislation hold their breath and steel themselves against the slings and arrows.

The struggle of the Dreamers may not yet have affected Rosa's mixed-status brood when they arrived in Houston in 1992, but the fear of the *migra* that gripped their daughter is familiar to anyone who is, or loves, an unauthorized immigrant. Countless studies have documented the damage that chronic fear related to immigration policy inflicts on children in immigrant families. Children need stability to thrive, they need safety and routine and the calm hand of trusted adults to guide them. For a child like Lila, who has learned that police and sirens mean uniforms coming to get her and firm hands sending her or her parents "back," stability and security is evasive.[7]

In the history of US immigration policy, fear has been a targeted tool that expands and recedes according to changing political winds. For the hardliners, workplace immigration raids have long been instrumental in ratcheting up the anxiety. In the 1980s, raids were as common as apple pie, dying down somewhat as the century came to a close and spiking again in the later, post–9/11 Bush years. The most visible were the 2006 Swift meat processing plant raids that rounded up 13,000 workers, and a 2008 field raid that wiped out 20 percent of the population of the town of Pottsville, Iowa.[8] These tactics are about the spectacle; their purpose to generate fear. As an immigration enforcement tool, they've done little to affect the numbers. In fact, under Obama, known by some as the "deporter in chief," raids dropped dramatically even while overall apprehensions and removals surged. Since the administration targeted only recent crossers and criminals, the Obama years left established immigrants with less to fear, lulled into a sense of stability.[9]

When Trump's presidency ushered in a new era of increased immigration enforcement in 2017, the feel of the thing shifted dramatically. In the first months of the administration, hot off the heels of rescinding DACA and the TPS designation for six countries, the Department of Homeland Security (DHS) increased apprehensions and returns, reopened myriad cases that had been administratively closed, and announced an end to Obama-era prosecutorial discretion.[10] As resistance flared up—from sanctuary city policies to know-your-rights rallies and volunteer monitoring of Immigration and Customs Enforcement[11]—the department shifted strategy and began hitting migrant groups at their heart. Arrests moved from jails and workplaces to the community itself. People were subject to detention at their front doors, dropping their children off at school, coming out of churches, at the park. No categories were spared, not the non-criminal immigrant who had been regularly checking in with authorities for years, not the pregnant woman with no criminal record, the refugee seeking humanitarian status, or the bystander caught beside a targeted migrant at the time of arrest. All of them became subject to a knock at the door or a boot turned in their direction.[12]

In response, a certain chill in the air froze business and activity in immigrant communities. School seats went empty on days after an anti-immigrant tweet from Trump. Anxiety multiplied. The spectacle was the thing. Children may not grasp subtle differences in status and origin, but they sense the fear. When one in three children in Texas has an immigrant parent—and five million US children have at least one undocumented parent—status becomes irrelevant on a playground charged with the terror of deportation. Kids talk, hear, and put together the pieces as best they can. Very young children often don't even know their parents' status. And assurances based on legal terms or papers or even national origin can't compete with the specter of the loss of a mom or dad.[13]

So when Rosa tried to calm her daughter's fears as the children gathered around the frying pans and soda pops in their Houston apartment in 1992, she was up against a beast that would not be quieted. And in 2010, when Sara's niece Celia cried for home amid schoolyard shouts of "wetback" and an unchecked disease with no access to medical care, she joined Lila and a chorus of children who cried over a world in which they or their parents could be taken away. A world where only some have a right to college and jobs and driver's licenses, to medical insurance and the freedom to walk unafraid from school to park to home. They cried over a world where, for them, to be poor and foreign meant to deserve less and, always, to be afraid.

Teresa

It takes a complex machinery of ideology, rhetoric, and policy to justify a social order that protects only some of its young. But it only takes a few words to remember that they are all equally innocent.

"I believe that all of us are children of God, and all of us are equal."

Teresa sits across from me at my kitchen table on a late August afternoon. The dryer runs as we talk; the air smells of lemon-scented cleaner. My older children are at elementary school, and my two-and-a-half-year-old daughter, Amelie, sits on a couch in the other room, watching cartoons and swinging her bare feet. Teresa has filled in for day-school today, which doesn't start for another week. She has spent the day playing with my little one, washing the dishes, folding the laundry. Now she takes a seat and tells me about her life, about her decision to migrate and the child she left behind.

Teresa begins her story at the meeting place of emerging womanhood and public shame.

"*Pueblo chico, infierno grande.* We say 'small town, big hell,' because everyone in a small town knows everyone else, and everyone knows your business."

Teresa's small town was a little *pueblo* near the northern coast of Honduras. Her *infierno* began when she was fifteen years old.

"A neighbor lady told my mom that I was pregnant. They punished me without even asking me if it was true. I wasn't pregnant, I'd never had anything to do with a boy, and they were going to take me to a gynecologist for a test."

Teresa is small and bright and her voice becomes animated as she talks, dark curls bouncing about her round face. Despite her thirty years, she still has the air of a girl.

"I went through the shame and embarrassment of them punishing me and slandering me. So I left and went to live with my boyfriend. I had been studying, I was in *tercero de ciclo,* like ninth grade, and I was going to finish that year but I decided to leave and go with him, to get married. Not *married* married, like with papers or anything, but together, me and him."

Two years later, she had become a mother to an infant son and a partner to a man whose taste for drinking and racing cars would land him in multiple accidents, paralyzed, and left in the reluctant care of his young almost-bride. At seventeen, she made her choice. "I said to myself, 'This love, or the illusion I had of it, is over. The dream is over.'"

She went home to mom and dad and found a job in a men's clothing store earning 350 lempiras a month, about twenty dollars. It didn't take long to see what kind of future stretched out before her. "No, I said to myself. This is no kind of life. I'm never going to get ahead like this."

So she borrowed the cash for a coyote and traveled north with a cousin and aunt—over 1,800 miles in buses and car trunks, the scoop of a dump truck, a raft on the winding Suchiate river. She took shelter with a community of native Maya people in southern Mexico—"*indios,*

indios," she tells me, her eyes wide—then headed north by car to spend five days in a smuggler's safe house before wading across the Rio Grande. All the while, she became accustomed to a certain absence in her arms and at her chest.

"What happened with your baby?"

Her voice falls a bit as she responds. "I left my child."

"With your mother?"

"I left him with my mother." Her eyes on mine, a space of silence.

"How old was he?"

"He was two years old . . . and a few months. Two years, three months."

She holds her smile in the quiet. Through an open doorway, my daughter sings along to Mickey Mouse.

"Like Amelie," I say.

"Like Amelie," she replies.

The dryer turns. The sun stretches longer across the kitchen table.

Once she arrived in Houston, it took some time for Teresa to establish herself. She worked as much as she could—in a factory, in restaurants and private homes—astounded at what she could earn and quickly gathering enough to pay back her debt. In the back of her mind, her little boy, Rubén, waited.

"How long did it take you to gather the money to get your son?"

"I brought him over two years later."

"Oh." I am overcome by the understanding, the dull ache of two empty years. "He was four years old?"

"*Sí,*" she responds. Yes. The word is small, muted by her posture. Her chin tucks into her neck, tightening the vocal cords and sinking into her body.

She offers her explanation. Two long years of missing her child had been enough for Teresa to find the courage to take the risk, so she began asking around. "I started working in a restaurant, and there, well, you meet all kinds of people."

In the restaurant, she met a man who said he could bring Rubén across, and the two made the arrangements amid the din of the restaurant kitchen, clanking forks and mashed frijoles and a mother's measured breath. The coyote explained the plan: He would secure a Mexican visa for the boy and fly with him from Tegucigalpa to Monterrey. Then, the two would travel by bus to the border.

"From there," Teresa explains, "it was a question of turning the child in. Cross the river and wait for Immigration to pick him up. Immigration gives them permission, and you go get them."

Meanwhile, Teresa would wait on the other side.

"So, Rubén came with this person the whole way?"

"Yes."

"And you trusted him completely?"

"Mm-hm."

"Completely?"

A phone rings on the chair next to us. Neither of us acknowledges it. One ring, two rings, three. Cartoon voices drift in from the next room. Teresa keeps her eyes on me, the question still between us.

"Enough to bring my son over. The need to bring him over—you can't be a hundred percent sure about people, but you have to risk it, because the need to see him, to have him there with you, it forces you to risk it."

Amelie in the next room and an imagined scenario: gone two years from my arms, from the place where she rests on my right hip. Yes, desperation.

"They were en route for four days," Teresa goes on. "When they left, he called me: 'I have the boy, I'm leaving. I'm heading out with him now.' And he didn't call me again."

Over the next four days, Teresa had no communication with the man. "Four days, total. I was desperate. I felt like I was dying. I didn't eat, I was crying the whole time."

On the fourth day, at 6:00 a.m., she got the call and rushed to the immigration holding facility to receive the boy.

"How was the reunion?" I ask.

"Oh," she melts. Her entire body is joy and memory and release. "It was the best thing in my whole life."

In 1998, when Teresa retrieved her son from a South Texas border patrol agent, she trusted in a set of policies that were specific to a certain political moment. Twenty years later, as I transcribe and narrate and slip into the feel of the thing, I find myself asking, *What would have happened today?*

The first time this question came to me was in 2017, when I learned that an executive order of the Trump administration had mandated that ICE begin targeting unauthorized immigrant parents and relatives who retrieve their unaccompanied children at the border. If the parent appeared, they would be apprehended. Deportation a guarantee, criminal prosecution and prison time a real threat.[14] The question of Teresa's fate came to me again in the summer of 2018 at a rain-drenched protest in Houston's East End. We had gathered in front of a detention center slated to house the growing number of children fallen victim to DHS's new "zero tolerance" policy.

Under the new protocol, any migrant attempting to enter the US between ports of entry would now be prosecuted criminally and detained in a federal detention facility while awaiting proceedings. Bound by a 1997 Supreme Court decision governing the treatment of children in immigrant detention, CBP chose to separate children from detained parents.[15] The children were taken from their mothers' and fathers' arms and placed in holding areas before being sent to shelters. Toddlers and schoolchildren, nursing infants. So many children, in fact, that the authorities erected makeshift chain-link holding pens and placed the children inside, wrapped in a silver blanket. Waiting.[16]

On the street, in the rain, I closed my eyes and saw Teresa and Rubén, Rosa and Lila, Maribel and Celia. Mothers who love their children as much as I love my own. I know they do, because I've watched them and listened to their stories—beside the sandbox at a neighborhood park, across my kitchen table.

"A parent always protects their child," Teresa tells me as our conversation comes to a close. "You always want the best for your kids. So it doesn't matter what place you're in or anything. It doesn't matter what level you're at either, because when you're a mother, the most important thing is the kids. All of us are equal, and all of us are children of God."

The dryer buzzes again. My Amelie becomes restless. Teresa and I say our goodbyes. Before leaving, she pauses with her hand on the handle of the kitchen screen door.

"My sister Daniela just got here," she tells me, almost as an afterthought. "She left her children behind." Her voice is low and soft as she tells me how her younger sister had been abandoned by a migrant husband and left alone with two young children and infant twins. After two years trying unsuccessfully to support her family in Honduras, she made the choice to leave them with their grandparents and join Teresa in the US.

"She's so sad," Teresa reflects. "At night she sleeps with a pillow under each arm."

She holds my gaze for a moment before saying goodbye.

When she steps out of the house and into the long summer sun, her sister's two pillows remain. One for each twin. They seep into the familiar sounds and spaces of my late afternoon kitchen—the dishwasher running, cartoons singing, and dryer tumbling, my daughter small and safe in the next room. I place a hand on my hip, palm flat, to stay a sudden truth. The empathy is almost unbearable.

On February 22, 2018, the US Customs and Immigration Services quietly changed its mission statement from the duty to "secure America's promise as a nation of immigrants," to the charge to "administer the nation's lawful immigration system . . . while protecting Americans, securing the homeland, and honoring our values."[17] Within months of this erasure of our nation of immigrants, over fourteen thousand migrant children would be held in indefinite detention, over four hundred parents deported with no knowledge of their children's whereabouts.[18]

That we are all children of God is not a hard lesson to learn, but somehow the proposition of equal human value has been lost in the mothercoin's transaction. That she must leave her child. That her child must meet chain link and cold shelters and separation and fear. What, then, could it mean to honor our values?

Pati

As a girl, Pati learned early that children need more from life than tender affection. "You can't survive on love alone," she declares. But as a woman, she has come to understand that the love she missed and the love her mother gave to others are two sides of the same coin, and that she has paid an irrecoverable price in the transaction.

The clarity came to her on a Monday morning drive. Her mother, María, at the wheel, Pati in the passenger seat, and the youngest of María's charges in the back—a teenager who had grown up with his *nana* an arm's reach away.

"That day, she was taking me to work and taking this boy to school, and she said to him, when she said goodbye, she said, 'I love you, sweetheart, *mi amor, te amo*,' and gave him a hug and a kiss and said goodbye to him."

The story is meant to make a point about all the ways this work is different, but somewhere between the logic and the reason, the feel of the thing overwhelms her. Her voice catches, her shoulders tremble.

"I know that my mom loves us more than anything. The hard part was, when I came here she didn't tell us. She shows us that she loves us, but she doesn't tell us. She doesn't come up and hug me and tell me 'I love you.' Because, twenty-five years not doing it, she's not going to start doing it now. And when I came here and I saw my mom with these kids, the youngest was eighteen, telling them 'I love you, sweetheart, take care,' in front of me—" she loses the words, becomes tight tears and staccato breath, "—in front of me. I was like, 'Why? Why with him and not with me?'"

A moment passes without stories or explanations, only Pati's sobbing body and a hushed lullaby on the baby monitor, a tissue box untouched on the coffee table.

"The same thing happens to me," she goes on. "I never had my mom to tell her, 'Mamá, I love you.' I try to say it to her and I can't. *I can't.* It doesn't come out. I want to hug her, and it's really hard. It's because of the kind of life we've led, far apart from each other. That day when she told the boy 'I love you,' I analyzed it all, in that moment. I thought, 'It's logical, it makes sense. I want to tell her but I can't. So it's the same with her.'"

She pulls a tissue from the box and blows her nose. Her shoulders shift and straighten, her spine lifts, her chin. She glances my way and dabs at her eyes and face, as if she is suddenly aware of the wounds she's exposed, as if she regrets having invited me into the moment when she understood that what had been lost was irretrievable.

"It's logical," she concludes. "It makes sense."

But there is little logic to the powerful feelings of a left-behind child, nor to the lessons they learn.

In 2002, journalist Sonia Nazario followed a young boy named Enrique from his home in Honduras as he attempted to travel north to be with the mother who had left him when he was five years old. In the eight attempts he made, Enrique was shaken down by corrupt cops, sent back seven times, and brutally beaten by gangsters who tossed him from a train and left him for dead. Laid out in a makeshift cot along the trail, beaten black and blue, he tells the woman tending to him, "I am going to find my mom." When he finally arrives, he and his mother struggle to know each other again. In the last words of the series, Enrique urges his girlfriend in Honduras, mother to his infant child, to come meet him in North Carolina. "If I have the opportunity, I'll go," she assures him. "We'll have to leave the baby behind," they agree.[19]

Enrique's unyielding drive, so at odds with logic, can be understood within a broad array of damaging psychosocial effects created by the emotional experiences of left-behind children like Pati, Sara, and Teresa's son, Rubén. From confused alliances in young children to teenage rebellion, falling grades and high-risk behavior, these children feel in very tangible ways the presence of their parents' absence. Their caregivers are often stretched thin—aunts with homes and children of their own, older grandparents who lack the stamina to keep the children in line or the education to help them manage schoolwork. Socially, they experience the stigma of a missing parent, no matter how many of their neighbors and classmates are in the same situation.[20]

The result makes for an ironic end for many a parent's migrant hope—plummeting school performance and an understanding of possibility that lies exclusively in the elusive journey north. Even for children like Pati, who grow to make fulfilling lives and whole relationships, the emotional scars run deep enough to spill out onto an October afternoon sofa fifteen years later. No wonder so many of these children are drawn north, led down a parent-paved path that promises knowledge and networks, all the comforts of an immigrant life forged in absence, and the promise of reunion. *Te quiero, mi'ja.* I love you, too, Mamá.

Other children, too, are learning the lessons of the mothercoin. Children like Ellie Stevenson, the five-year-old girl Pati has cared for since birth. During Pati's first pregnancy, Ellie had grown used to the idea of her nanny's baby, kissing Pati's belly, bringing her vitamins and promising to care for little Melanie. Her parents encouraged the idea that Melanie would be a part of their world. Not only did they promise to allow Pati to bring her infant to work with her, they actively prepared the children to help with the baby.

Ellie and her little brother continued their usual routines through the final weeks of Pati's pregnancy, saying goodbye to their nanny in the evenings when she left the house for the new home she now shared with her husband. After a full day with the Stevenson children one Friday in May, Pati greeted Sunday morning with a newborn in her arms. She had only wanted to take a month off, but Mr. Stevenson insisted on longer. "No, that's too short," he had said. "Just rest without worrying about it." So Pati added two more weeks to her planned leave, never suspecting that they would stretch into a year of uncertainty.

"It was my bad luck—and it was a question of bad luck—that the señor found himself out of work just days before I was going to come back to work. The señora told me, 'For right now, he can take care of the kids, but he'll return to work and then we'll need you. You have your job.' A year passed like that, with me waiting for them to call." With these words, Pati's tone becomes charged with a hard-edged nostalgia. "Waiting for them to call," she repeats.

For a year, Pati waited. Newborn to baby to toddler, babysitting here and there for the Stevensons and holding on to the promise of working and mothering without having to choose between the two. The financial strain weighed on Pati's young family, and she turned to Ms. Stevenson for help finding temporary work. "But when you need me," she assured her señora, "I'll be there."

"But she knew," Pati insists. "She would put in her announcements, 'My nanny, *mientras*, for the time being.'" She repeats the word with emphasis, "'*Mientras. For now*, while we don't need her.' So it wasn't easy for someone to contact me."

Pati's voice is harder now, as she narrates the place where power begins to tip and stretch the limits of good intentions. In her accommodating gestures, Ms. Stevenson had come to hold all the cards. The promise to let a nanny bring her child to work with her is everything. The preparation, the conversations with Ellie and her brother. The couple had even given Pati their own minivan during work hours so that she could fit Melanie in the back with the two older children. "Who would do something like that?" Pati asks, still confused by it all, "so that I can go around with my daughter? How could I not wait for them?"

In March, after almost a year of waiting on the Stevensons and with an infant not yet a year old, Pati discovered that she was pregnant again. The day she approached Ms. Stevenson with the news, she was uncertain what the second pregnancy would mean for her job. But she would be showing soon and would have no choice. And then, she understood this kind of honesty to be a natural part of their relationship, "part of the respect, the communication."

"I'm waiting to come back to work with you," she told her señora. "I want to work with you, and I'm willing to do it, even pregnant, just like I did with my other baby. But I understand if you all are uncomfortable with the idea," she went on. "Because I know the pregnancy plus the baby probably makes you uncomfortable. You're free to find someone else if you want to, but if not, I want to work. Your children are safe and happy with me, and I'm going to try to do my best, but it's up to you if you want to hire someone new or you want to stay with me."

"So," Pati says, taking a breath, "I left the decision in her hands. The señora thought for a moment, and then replied, 'No, it's okay. We'll look for someone else.'"

I wait for more explanation. Pati's phone begins to buzz. Throughout our conversation, her story has been interrupted by sounds like this punctuating the stillness of the afternoon—cars revving on the street below, doors and footsteps from the apartment complex, message alerts and the music pushing through the baby monitor. She silences the phone and continues.

"In just a few days, she called me and said that her husband had found work, and that they had found a nanny. From one day to the next, less than a week, I wasn't working for them anymore. I'm a very mature person and I understand how things are. I don't need an explanation. It's logical, it makes sense. They have their two children and they have to look after them. I understand." She pauses to gather her thoughts, shifts on the sofa. "But what was hard for me was that there was a time when I thought that—" emotion strains her voice again, and the rest comes out between deep breaths and trembling shoulders "—that they treated me the way they did because of what *I* had earned. The kind words, the nice things they did for me, I thought it was because they saw how devoted I was to the kids."

"Oh Pati, I'm so sorry."

Words lost to tears, we pause again. I listen to her body tell a story that the language of cause and effect cannot reconcile. Because the mothercoin's logic breaches the limits of such language. Nannies and children grasp the relationship between caring work and emotional bonds intuitively. That these bonds may be violated, that the exchange value of the work could matter more than the wholeness of the relationship, is a lesson that must be learned.

The next part of the story unfolds over the final weeks of July, when Pati agreed to work until the new nanny came. It was Thursday when the girl flew in on a direct flight from Chile. She would be studying in Houston part-time, Pati explains.

"Young?" I ask. "Single? Is she studying at the university?"

Yes, to all. I begin to understand what this young woman can do for the Stevensons that Pati can't offer—an education in class values that goes beyond the day-to-day labor of childcare. It's a common enough transition for many families like the Stevensons. As the children's needs evolve from diapers and playgrounds to homework and piano recitals, some parents seek out caregivers more similar in social position. "No, no," the au pair instructs. "You need to carry the remainder." Or, "Your first finger should be here for the C chord, like this."[21]

When Ms. Stevenson arrived at the house with the new girl in tow—"*Muy bonita*," Pati stresses, "*very* pretty"—the señora told Pati, "If you're not going out with the kids right now, don't go anywhere. Give the girl the car so she can do her shopping."

"So when this girl came," Pati explains, "of course, she lived in the room where I had lived for seven years. They gave her the car they'd bought for me. They gave her the credit card as soon as she got there. They gave her a cell phone, in front of me. And I thought, 'So, it's not what I thought it was. I thought it was a special affection they had for me, but there was never any appreciation or special sense of value for me. It's just that they're good people to anyone.'"

Little by little, clarity came to her. How different things were from what they had seemed. Not personal affection, not earned respect. The Stevensons were simply polite, Pati concluded, with anyone. It was the kind of behavior people in their world practiced and admired, the kind of thing they teach their children.

"The señora called me in the evening. 'Get the kids dressed, please. Help them to dress up nice, because we're going to dinner.' It was a welcome dinner," Pati explains. "They were taking the girl out to eat," her voice wry, a hard edge to her smile.

"Had they ever taken you to dinner?"

"In seven years, they never invited me out to eat."

The next day, little Ellie told her *nana* all about it. "We went to a fancy place," Pati mimics the child's voice, "very pretty, and very expensive." Pati smiles with the memory, all it meant and all that the girl didn't understand. "It didn't matter to me what happened with the nanny," she reflects. "What hurt me was that I wasn't going to be with the children anymore." She breaks down again and cries harder. "What hurt was that I wasn't going to have my job." Her sobs intensify. "It hurt that I needed to work and, pregnant and with a baby, that's not easy."

She sniffs and dabs, pulls herself back into the reason that she relies on. "It's not anyone's fault," she concludes. "It's not the nanny's fault, it's not my bosses' fault that I ended up pregnant. It's not my fault either. This is how things are."

Pati has worked hard to master this language of reconciliation, ever since her mother first said goodbye. But the children she loves have not yet learned the same hard lessons, and on Pati's last day, Ellie insisted on hope:

"Pati, but when your baby is born, the new baby, then when he's big, you can come work with us again. I'm gonna take care of Melanie and you can take care of the baby and of all of us. Because you're our background nanny."

"'Backup'?" I try to clarify.

"No, 'background,'" Pati says. "She would always put us in order: 'You, Pati, you're the first. Then so-and-so, then her, then her. But *you* are the first. We love you the most.'" Pati smiles at the idea. But on that day she knew she needed to help the girl, to remind Ellie that she might love the new nanny just as much, that she had to be a good girl and try. "You need to love her too, because she's going to take care of you." I imagine the two of them there, wrapped up in a relationship without a name—Ellie balancing on Pati's belly perhaps, her fancy dinner dress draped over a chair in the corner, listening carefully as her seven-year nanny still taught her, still loved.

"It's what the children want," Pati concludes, "but these things are a parents' decision. These are just the ideas of a five-year-old little girl."

Before she grows up to take her place in her parents' world, a young child like Ellie must learn a good deal about the way her society values its members. Her first lesson: some nannies are the sort that deserve fancy dinners, others aren't. Her second: only some relationships are worth preserving. Other lessons have been learned among these women and the children they've loved:

A family cannot live on love alone.

Some children never forgive.

Dark-skinned nannies with thick accents do not punish.

Brothers who were born here get to go to college.

Cousins who were born here get to go to the doctor.

Eighteen hundred dangerous miles in the company of a stranger is a risk worth taking.

Some Mexicans are good.

Some Mexicans have too many babies.

When nannies have too many babies, they have to leave.

When mothers can't find good work, they have to leave.

It doesn't matter how much you need her.

In their introduction to *Global Woman*, Arlie Hochschild and Barbara Ehrenreich consider the witness of the children cared for by immigrant nannies and domestics. They write: "In their own living rooms, they are learning vast and tragic global politics. Children see. But they also learn how to disregard what they see. They learn how adults make the visible invisible."[22]

More is made invisible than the work of cleaning and caring and the women who do it. We also learn to ignore the intimate violence experienced by the children who depend on these women. For those who are left behind, the suffering is bound up in their mothers' absence: tensions with caregivers, uneven school performance, increased at-risk behavior. The children who live with their migrant mothers often experience a different kind of pain: more duties at home, fewer opportunities at school, and, in their interaction with their mothers' employers, a profound lesson in the place they and their mothers hold in society.[23] But all of it, the work and the women and the suffering, is real and urgent. To dismiss it takes years of schooling in what is valuable, and what is not.

It may be the idea of value itself that needs examining. In this complicated terrain of love, labor, and the innocence of children, the specter of commodification confuses the nature of value. If a caregiver is hired, if she is paid, then the value she adds must play out by market logic— services rendered, hours calculated, compensation measured, all according to the hard reality of supply and demand. But this work is different, isn't it? Pati knows it when she cries at her mother's love for another. Nicole knows it when she pays off her nanny's house out of guilt. And Ellie Stevenson knows it when she insists that she and Pati are each other's to care for, that they somehow belong the one to the other.

This kind of caring practice carries both an "instrumental" and an "intrinsic" value.[24] It is productive labor that is quantifiable, that can and should be counted in economic models, and it is also something more— the intangible value of human relationship. There is no separating the nanny's work from her love, the mother's love from her work, and there is no imposing the logic of the market on one and the logic of emotion on the other. There is only the logic of relationship.[25] Children know this. To teach them otherwise is its own violence.

In separating home and family from global politics, we have both ignored the economic value of childrearing and homemaking, and also demonized its commodification. Immigrant nannies sort out right and wrong in the space in between, and so do the children they love. There is a direct line from Ellie's quiet lesson to the violent drama at our border. It begins with the relationship she cannot name and ends at the place where desperation meets chain-link cages. These things are worth discussing. These things matter. They are the lessons we teach our children.

CHAPTER 7

LOVE AND LABOR

My friends told me, "Don't love them like you do because from
one day to the next you won't be with them anymore."

PATI

Sara

Last year on Mother's Day, Sara's son Drew made her cry. It happened on a Monday, when she picked him up from school. In her son's elementary school, filled with Hispanic children who share overlapping languages and customs, Mexican Mother's Day becomes everyone's Día de la Madre, and it is celebrated on the tenth of May, no matter what day of the week it falls on, and no matter who has to work.[1] Everybody in Drew's world knows this. But Sara's employers lived far from Drew's world.

"They had a celebration at school and all of the moms went," Sara explains. "I couldn't miss a day from work. So, he waited for me. He expected me there. Later, I pulled up in the car, and asked him, 'How was your day? Did it go okay? What did you have for lunch?'

" 'It was good. But you know something, Mami? All of my friends had their mom there and you never came. I waited for you, and you never came. Why didn't you come?' "

In Sara's retelling, her son's words come across with an added edge, the judgment of an adult in the voice of a child. It is a judgment that resonates. I, too, have felt the shameful certainty that all the other mothers must surely have been there.

"Just right now," she goes on, "I'm in a terrible depression. Because my son, two days ago, he told my brother-in-law that he wishes he could have a mom like Celia's, his cousin. Because her mom doesn't yell, she's not always mad. He says he wants a different mom, because his mom gets mad a lot and isn't ever home and can't ever go to his activities."

Her voice gets louder, frustration and anger pushing through, "I go to work, and the kids I take care of treat me badly and I come home frustrated, asking myself why they treat me that way. All I ever give them is love, I give them all the love they could need. I'm more than nice to them, I never raise my voice. So when I get home, I'm frustrated and out of patience, angry and tired from working eight, ten hours. And then he starts acting up and I don't have any patience."

She pauses and sighs, sorting out the meaning of the child's emotions. "I've given so much of myself to work and not to my kids that I'm losing my children's love. And I understand my mom, because she did the same thing. In order to give us a better life, she left us. The only difference was all that distance."

Sara and I have been talking for a while now, and the children have begun to get restless. A dog barks loudly. Her daughter approaches to ask a mumbled question. "*Mi amor,*" she responds, "we're going to leave real soon." Her son inserts himself. "Just stay right there," she says. "Papito, sweetie, you're coming with me." Her nephew begs. "*Sí, amor,*" she responds. All of them needing and begging and wanting and demanding. Sara remains focused on the telling as she orchestrates her constant responses—*mi amor, papito*—affectionate words that must do the important job of assuring them all that her attention is always with them, no matter the obligations she must tend to, no matter the work at hand.

Somehow, for Sara, it doesn't matter that she tends to these needing creatures with patience as we talk. It doesn't matter that she has financed their home and their shoes and their futures, that her long hours have created their American dream or that each of her work days has ended in a home filled with their dinner-hungry whines and dirty laundry and unfinished homework. For Sara, there is only a child for whom she has not been available enough, not patient or kind or loving enough. Never good enough.

Across cultures and social classes, a mother's mandate to presence and sacrifice persists. Whether she pursues education and a career, is bound to kitchen and apron strings, or is expected to serve her man along with her children. Whether she is free to demand "help" from her partner or freer still to manage the details of domestic outsourcing, a "good mother" must tend to her children's needs with grace, patience, and above all else, constant emotional availability. This, women learn, is how to be good.[2] Sara responds to this lesson when she calms her impatient children and nephew—*ahorita, mi amor; quédate, papito*—even as she works to weave together all the threads of her complicated narrative. But she doesn't recognize these caring habits of hers for what they are, the cultivated gestures of a culturally prescribed good mother stretched thin by the realities of a world that doesn't support her parenting.

It's the same world that left her own mother unsupported, struggling through poverty, social illegitimacy, and an abusive marriage to meet all the needs and all the expectations.

"I identify a little with my mom," Sara confesses, "because she left us behind in order to give us something better. I got a house, thinking I could create a better future for them. But getting a house means that I have to work a lot, because I'm both mother and father for them. But when I got it, I didn't think that I'd have to leave them so much."

Sara has told me before that her own mother had to be "both father and mother" to her and her little sisters. Alike in so many ways. And if Sara has failed to be both breadwinning father and morally good mother, then what is to stop her son, Drew, from feeling the same resentment his Aunt Maribel holds?

"My sister is twenty-one now. Ever since she came here, her job has been to take care of kids in her house. She's never given her kids to anyone to look after them, because she doesn't want her kids to miss her like she did with her mom. My sister can't forgive my mother. She doesn't forgive my mom for leaving her behind. She doesn't forgive her for coming here to the US. She doesn't forgive her for a lot of things."

Sara has been speaking low, her sister just across the playground. The kids continue to break into our conversation. When one cries out to her, she responds, "*vente, vente ya.*" To me she says, "Give me a moment," and moves toward the picnic table on the other side of the park, where daughter, son, sister, niece, and nephew play and need and want and call for her. After a few low-spoken words, she returns to my side and picks up her story, cataloguing all the ways her choices have fallen short of her children's expectations.

"So I'm afraid," she concludes. "I'm afraid, because my son has a very strong character. I don't think he's going to change. He's not like other kids who would say, 'Okay, I get it; Mommy had to work.' Not him. He wants it all."

What a child needs, a mother must give. But need is a slippery creature, nudged this way and that by all we want for them and all we're told they deserve. Easy to say "love, nourishment, safety, education." But the choices Sara has had to make are more complicated than these abstractions—a Mother's Day celebration or a well-paying job, a house to keep them safe or afternoons of play, a fallen toddler on a playground or the chance to explain herself to this larger world that feels set up against her. For a woman like Sara, and so many mothers, the way she determines and responds to her children's needs becomes the fabric of her moral self-concept—that place where identity and values converge.[3] It is a sense of self that is integral to our common humanity, as important as food on the table, safety on the streets, or hope on the migrant trail.

Rosa

When Rosa and her children traded their small house in Chietla for an unfurnished apartment in Houston in 1990, she understood that the price of having her family together at last would be years of hard work.

"When we arrived, there wasn't anything to eat. No place to sit or sleep. We had to start from zero."

In the lean years that followed, Rosa laid the foundation for her American life through frugal living, hard labor, and a lot of hustle. Making ends meet meant finding jobs, and in the world she navigated—driven by casual recommendations among patronas and playground conversations between *nanas*—a worker's reputation was the currency that secured the jobs. Smart, capable, experienced, and, above all, trustworthy. To earn this recommendation from one employer unlocked an entire network.

In time, though, Rosa's reputation came to mean more to her than just a means to an end. Bound up in her identity as worker and woman, the trustworthiness others saw in her became a source of her own self-respect.

Of all the jobs Rosa had as a cleaner and nanny in Houston, the most impactful were the thirteen years she spent working for my brother's family. And though I didn't see it at the time, the casual conversations she and I shared in kitchens and driveways while cousins played would draw me into a network of employers for whom my word became the gold bullion that backed the coin.

Over two decades of deepening relationships and shifting work arrangements, I saw Rosa often and watched my nephews' dependence on her grow along with their parents' trust. As the boys reached school age and schedules changed, Rosa called on me to help her find extra work when she needed it. I'd phone a neighbor or two, send out a message to friends, an unspoken promise implicit in every recommendation: *You can trust her.* I don't think I understood the weight of that endorsement at the time, how hungry the potential employer on the other end of the line might be for reassurance—that her children would be safe, that her home would be protected. It would be years before I came face to face with my own power to affect Rosa's prospects, not until the day she showed up at my front door with red eyes and a heaving chest and demanded I make a phone call.

Before then, before our interviews, Rosa had mostly been a number that occasionally popped up on my screen. She would call to look for a casa to replace a job lost to changing needs or to check in on my nephews after the family moved away. Soon, the boys reached out to her, and she told me with pride about how they called her on her birthday and friended her on Facebook. Tremendous pride, tremendous affection, all of it bound up in the trust she had earned.

As her recommendations multiplied, Rosa eased into a working life in which her reputation, experience, and increased financial security made it possible to choose employers, to negotiate pay, and to demand the respect she felt she deserved. At that point, she was charging up to a hundred dollars a house and only rarely accepting hourly work, and never for less than twenty dollars an hour.[4]

But relationships matter, so when the employer for whom Rosa nannied asked her to clean for a friend as a favor, Rosa took the thirteen-dollar-an-hour a job in good faith. But the disrespect she encountered was too much. "I went to help her, but the family, they sit down to eat, and they can't even offer a bite of their food, not even a glass of water! Nothing. I mean, if you're working, it's right to offer a glass of water or a soda, no? Don't they think the cleaning lady gets hungry?

Don't they think the lady gets thirsty? I only went for one day. I never went back."

The memory of this slight takes her to a reflection on the early years, when work was defined by quantity over quality. "I'm not saying I'm rich now, but before—when I was really screwed, *bien jodida*—I worked too much, and always for so little."

So maybe back when Rosa was really screwed, she had sacrificed respect for cash in hand. Just like she had sacrificed the presence of her husband years before for the sake of her nursing baby, the wholeness of family for the chance to get ahead. These choices don't come easy amid the conflicting ideals she confronts—about immigrants who must work harder than the rest, while caring for their families and learning English and waiting patiently for papers that may never come; about mothers who must always be present and maids who must never be thirsty. Such a tangle of standards can threaten the integrity of a woman's sense of herself.

The deep internal conflicts that emerge are more difficult to narrate than a story about getting fired for being pregnant or being shaken down by a dirty cop at the border. At times in these interviews, the conflicts exceed the bounds of the story the women tell and spill out into moments of narrative dissonance, that movement in which the story comes up against itself and can no longer find the words. In Rosa's case, it started with a knock at my door.

It would have been a year or so after we sat for our formal interview. A weekend afternoon, Saturday or Sunday. My husband and I both heard it, three sharp bangs—*pom, pom, pom.* I opened the door to find Rosa standing firm with her arms crossed at her chest and her face flushed and tear-stained. "Señora Elizabeth, Señora Elizabeth," she began as soon as I opened the door, "Christina accused me. She accused me of stealing. I didn't steal from her, señora. Why would I steal from her?"

"Oh, Rosa, here, sit down." My husband helped her to a plastic chair on our porch and sat to listen quietly. "But who is Christina?" I asked.

"Christina, your friend," she insisted. "The one you recommended me to."

Confused at first, I was able to place the woman after another question or two. She was not my friend, I explained, but someone I had met on a back-to-school errand several months past. We had stood in line together, she was new in town, she asked about the school, about the grocery store, if I knew anyone who cleaned. Christina. Yes.

"She says I stole her earrings. Why would I steal earrings? I have plenty of my own! I don't need her earrings." Rosa sits with her arms still crossed, her speech fast and punctuated by quick rises in pitch. All of her is charged with anger.

I lean against her red SUV, newer and shinier than my own dented minivan, and tell her how sorry I am. "But Rosa," I ask, "what do you want me to do?"

"I want you to call her!" Louder now, indignant, "I want you to tell her I don't steal!"

So I step gently over the border that separates my observations and Rosa's experience, and I dial the woman's number. It's still in my phone, under *Christina, met at uniform store.*

She answers. I reintroduce myself and explain. "I'm here with Rosa. She's very upset."

"Oh," followed by silence. "I see."

I tell her what I know of Rosa, the years she cared for my brother's children, the times she's babysat my own. I tell her about all the people I know who've been pleased with her work, all the complaints I've never received. I tell her how much I trust Rosa. That she's earned my trust and that of my family. After all these years in our homes, unsupervised.

Christina's words are low and even as she explains her case: *The earrings are gone. Rosa had been there. And so . . .* "It breaks my heart," she insists more than once. Emotion breaks through in her voice as she tells me how much they love Rosa, how she's been like family to them. *Like family.* "But at the same time . . ." Well, *the earrings are gone, aren't they?*

In the end, there's nothing for it. We've each made our case: I've known and trusted Rosa for years. Christina discovered that her earrings were missing, and Rosa was there.

We say our goodbyes, and I report our conversation to Rosa. She asks if my brother will call the woman, too, and I promise her I'll ask. Her breath becomes more even, and she tells us again that she has plenty of earrings of her own. The flush in her cheeks subsides, she laughs that if she ever stole something it would be enough to retire and go back to

Mexico for good. The sun falls behind a Texas lilac tree, softening the harsh heat of the afternoon driveway. We fall into the descending action now, nearing resolution. Rosa has made her stand.

Over the years, I've heard many stories of false accusations from women like Rosa. How to defend your word against theirs when the employer holds all the cards? To hear a patrona claim her employee is "like family" is just as common. It's a sentiment that is easy to fall into when one shares the closeness of bathroom floors and bedsheets but hard to sustain over tensions around pay and work expectations. Harder yet to reconcile with suspicions that can't be confirmed. "How much we love her, *but at the same time . . .*" But I'm far closer to this story than I have been to the others. And Christina's voice and words were not cold and cruel and harsh. They were soft and broken and conflicted. Perhaps, she simply could not sustain the competing moral narratives at play—how many times she's heard reference to "the help who is like family," as often as she's heard about the "the maid inclined to theft."

I ask Rosa if she'll be alright financially. She swats her hand and dismisses my concern. She's got plenty of casas. Christina had even said that she wouldn't say anything to a friend who also employs Rosa. References aren't her concern anymore. Finding work isn't what drove her to my front door on a weekend afternoon. It's something deeper that she seeks to restore, a sense of herself that is as vulnerable to the violence of judgment as her finances once were to the whims of employment. It is the intrinsic value of Rosa-in-relationship, Rosa-in-trust.

We each ask after our families and move to say our goodbyes. Before she climbs into the driver's seat of her SUV, Rosa turns to me and asks, "The señor, he's going to call too, right?"

Of course he will, I assure her. After all, Rosa is like family to them.

Pati

When it was time for Pati to say goodbye to the Stevenson family, the kids were at tae kwan do class and there was only her patrona to bid farewell. After the wait and the doubt and the new nanny and the fancy dinner, Pati recounts one final blow.

"She just said, 'Okay, here's your pay for the week. Let us know when your baby is born. We'll be in touch.' And I was like, 'oh, okay, fine.'" She struggles with her emotions, teary-eyed and angry, "Why would I want them to see my baby? When I know there wasn't any relationship? It was all a work relationship for them with me. A relationship based on work. If there's no work, there's no relationship. For me, it was a different kind of relationship. For me, there was a kind of familiarity there. But they didn't see it this way, there was never any kind of recognition at all."

How to understand this complicated terrain? When we have no categories to name a relationship that is both beyond transaction and still so inextricably bound to its context of exchange. Love and money simply feel unmixable, despite the inescapable truth that they mix all the time, from weekly allowance and joint bank accounts to nursing homes and inheritance. We work to qualify the transactions, or to minimize the emotion, because we've learned to perceive the two as irreconcilable—that the exchange of money diminishes the authenticity of the love, that the messiness of emotion compromises the rational logic of transaction.[5]

The contradiction plays out in Pati's sighs and anger. Inside of her story, confronted with her pain, I look for an explanation.

"When they introduced the nanny to you," I ask, "did the woman show any embarrassment or awkwardness?"

"No, no. I mean, it isn't anyone's fault."

"You're very good, you know. Because what they did was disrespectful."

This is how I respond. I can't help it. I break. I want her to hear it. I don't care about the book or my author's persona or the illusion of any observer's distance; I just want her to know—pregnant and crying and still the little left-behind girl she has told me she was—I want her to know that she was done wrong. That she doesn't deserve this, that she's worth more. I want her to know that none of this is fair. That it may make sense, it may be logical, but something is not right here. *Something about all these reasonable, strategic calculations has wounded you, and here is a space to sort out the hows and the whys.*

Here is a space where the logic of the way things are unravels, compelling us toward a more tenacious interrogation of blame. Because if Pati's circumstances really aren't anyone's fault, then her pain must be somehow misplaced, a casualty of this indifferent and anonymous world. But our indifferent world is not anonymous. It emerges from the stories we circulate, the quiet doubts we ignore, and the moments when we wipe our tears, take a deep breath, and swallow the pain as if it is somehow illegitimate. To linger for a moment at the intersection of logical choices and unexplained suffering is to drive a wedge in the gears of the story. It is a stopping place that deserves a voice.

"What frustrates me was something dry in the relationship," Pati considers. "I love the children," she declares in a strong, clear voice. "*Yo amo a los niños.* And I feel a profound respect for the family and a gratitude that I think I'll have forever. But you know, many people told me, 'Here, they're going to use you.' And I said, 'No, or if that happens . . . I mean, I live off of my job, so either they're going to use me or others will. If they're using me, I'm using them, too, because I need work and they need someone to do the job. What matters to me is to be happy in what I'm doing. If something happens someday, well, that's how it goes.'"

Who can say who is being used? When the relationship is so much more complicated than the words available to name it—*nanny, maid, muchacha, help.* A vocabulary too weak to lay claim to the privileges of intimacy in a confusing emotional landscape of relationships that feel bigger than work arrangements, deeper than wages earned. In a moment of limited resources—one woman's time and energy to devote to the Stevensons' children and to Pati's own—there is no language Pati can call on to denounce an envelope in the hand and a casual goodbye. "Here's your check, we'll be in touch."

What Pati feels for the Stevenson children is something else entirely. "For me, taking care of my daughter and taking care of these kids, I treat them the same. Except my daughter is here twenty-four hours a day and I feel complete because she's *my* daughter, she's *mine.* She can call me 'Mamá' and I feel happy. But the love, the admiration that you feel, the happiness watching them grow and starting to talk, beginning to walk or eat on their own, I felt the same joy with them that I do with my daughter. And everyone chastised me and told me not to do it." She looks down and sighs deeply, "Ah."

"I go around with pictures of them in my wallet, not of my daughter," she goes on. "In the beginning, my husband was jealous of the kids, for my daughter. He'd tell me, 'When are you going to change that photo?' But I tell him, 'They're *photos,* photos! If I change a photo, it's not going to change a place in my heart.' I tell him, 'The fact that you love me doesn't mean that you're going to stop loving your mom or your sister. There's enough love for everyone.'

"But now, I think, I don't know if, to keep from getting hurt, I should learn to stop loving them, because they aren't mine. I love them, but it's not healthy to love them the way I do, because I don't have them any-more—" Pati breaks down once more, her body pushing through her resolve, "and I don't think I'll ever have them again."

Again, she is overcome by tears and emotion. Again, I wait. The detail about the photos draws me to the memory of a storybook I used to read to my children, a gift to my oldest daughter when I was pregnant with her little brother. In the story, a stuffed blue kangaroo, beloved by the child who takes it to bed each night, feels replaced as the little girl acquires more and more plush friends. With each birthday party or holiday, her bed becomes more crowded and Blue Kangaroo is pushed further to the edge.

My children loved the book and we read it so often I could recite each word and recall each delicate drawing. But the story's happy ending always puzzled me. Because, although the lesson is sweet—that there is enough love for all—in fact, the Blue Kangaroo is only assured of his place in the little girl's heart when the child retrieves the dejected toy from her baby brother and exchanges him for all the others. "You can have all these," the character cries, "but not Blue Kangaroo."[6]

Is love an unlimited resource? Maybe. Is there enough for all the children and all the mothers and othermothers? We want there to be, so very badly. But for Blue Kangaroo, for the daughter left behind and the "background nanny," pregnant and sent to the end of a long line of others, it takes more than a promise to believe that love expands even while time and money contract. For a transnational child, there must be presence, touch and voice. For a hired nanny, there must be some naming of the special relationship, something beyond "babysitter" that transcends transaction and conveys the privilege of belonging. Otherwise, all the sense of self that is bound up in loving children who are not her own might be reduced to a story she tells about the photos in her wallet.

Pati composes herself and pivots back to logic. "But the other part is the idea that parents are always looking for the best for their kids. It makes sense," she insists again. "If I put myself in this family's place, I'm going to say, 'Okay, a nanny with two kids, she's not going to take as good care of my kids as hers.'"

"But do you think that the kids would have suffered at all for being with you?"

"No! Just the opposite. My priority, of course, is always going to be my daughter, but my responsibility was with those kids. Even those days when I was working, I would feel bad about my baby. I'd put her in the crib while I made the kids breakfast or lunch, and she would cry, 'Mami, Mami, Mami!' And I'd think, 'It's better not to work. I need it, the work, but my daughter also needs attention.'"

"But their mother would have done the same, if it was her third," I laugh, thinking of my own youngest child, so often left to cry herself to sleep while dinner boiled over or tantrums called me away. It's a knowing laugh, a rueful laugh, because I know what Pati knows—that a parent's resources are limited, that children don't always get what they need.

"Yeah, but, that's where the emotional part comes in for me," Pati reflects. "When I think, 'Well, I can't do it. It's true, I can't. *I can't*. I can't do it all.'"

Where my resigned chuckle meets Pati's tearful defeat, a common thread: Despite what we know about what we *can* do, each of us still believes that we *should* be able to do it all. I consider my third in the crib and the ten-year-old manuscript on my desk, and my laugh is dry and resentful and a little bit ashamed. Pati reflects on the difference between priority and responsibility and the way love and conflict infuses them all, and her tears are whole-bodied and full and hastily muted. "*Es lógico*," she says again and again. "It makes sense."

For me and Pati and Ms. Stevenson, circumstances dictate how well we can fulfill our own notions of good mothering, culturally distinct in many ways, yet anchored in a common mandate: to provide for our children, to prepare them for the world they will meet, and to be there for them in a way fathers aren't expected to. This is why Ms. Stevenson felt wounded when Pati suggested that leaving her child to work would be wrong. It's why I felt ashamed of my crying child left too long in her crib, and why Pati's body spills over with emotion in the irreconcilable space between the baby calling *Mami* and the integrity that called her to prepare lunch for the Stevensons. A perfect lunch, attentively prepared.

After all, this is why she was hired—to provide a presence that would honor, for at least one family, a mother's duty be there for the children, unfailingly.

"*No puedo*," Pati repeats. "I can't do it all."

Poet Adrienne Rich writes eloquently of the experience of mothering, its meaning-making and ambivalence, the tenderness and the anger. At the source of her private experiences, she identifies a public conception of motherhood as a social institution—a role defined by a system of beliefs and the obligations and the social demands it engenders. The institution operates on a logic of moral value: One is good if one loves her children before herself at all moments. In her first writing on the subject, Rich recalls, "As my eldest son, now aged twenty-one, remarked . . . : 'You seemed to feel you ought to love us all the time. But there *is* no human relationship where you love the other person at every moment.' Yes, I tried to explain to him, but women—above all, mothers—have been supposed to love that way."[7]

Above all, mothers.

In its uncritical joining of paid labor to the moral expectations of motherhood, the mothercoin brings together two incompatible value systems. One holds that there is enough love to go around, enough space in the wallet for all the photos. The other trades in resources that are limited—time, money, physical energy. When the relative values of the mothercoin are pitted against each other, women like Pati and Rosa and Sara are forced to violate their own moral imperatives. They can't nurture and protect at the same time; they can't love unconditionally within the bounds of conditional employment; they can't provide concrete hope through public labor while giving constant love through private presence.

And yet, the world would tell them that the choice is theirs. The conflicts cut deep for women especially, who are taught from an early age to understand themselves in terms of relationships—daughters, wives, mothers.[8] Deep enough to threaten that wholeness of self we call integrity, a fullness of humanity where desire and morality meet the act of choosing. This is the wellspring of power, the source of voice.

Something of this wholeness may be restored when a woman like Pati tells her story. In personal narrative, her experience is the ultimate authority, an undeniably valuable organizing principle. In telling, she chooses what to relate and what to suppress, what to explain and emphasize or whisper in a one-word answer, forcing the listener's hand, *What happened next?* And though my conversations with these women are bound by the same power structures that shape their work and public lives, the core of the stories yet emerges from the very impulse to fullness that the mothercoin threatens. So that the truth of the telling lies in the voice itself.

A portrait emerges. Complex women—strong and weak and flawed and capable and often pushing back against the limits imposed on them. Women who exercise power even as they suffer the moral harm of the mothercoin. Women who leverage their employers' needs, shape their children's perceptions, and grab tight to freedoms made possible by their own will and faith. So that, in content and form, in all this narrative landscape of damaging choices and suffocating limitations, moments of power and agency persist.

CHAPTER 8

TELLING STORIES

By the grace of God and the USA.

ROSA

Sara

It's almost time to go. The children are getting restless—mine, Sara's. Here at this forced closing, it's important to sort out the meanings in it all. At this time, in this place, what does it mean to choose?

"One last question," I lean in toward Sara and ask, carefully. "Your sister says that it would have been better if you all stayed home, poor but together. What do you say?"

Sara sighs and tells a final story.

"When we came here, our family came apart. It's very sad, because my parents separated. My mom married someone else. The family really came apart; everyone went their separate ways."

"Do you attribute that to the separation? Or to having come to this country?"

"To this country," she responds quickly, forcefully.

"In El Salvador, women are raised to be housewives, to obey their husbands and everything. They come to a different culture, the women are liberal and they have different customs, they're free to make their own decisions without having to ask their husbands' permission first. Imagine someone who comes from the rancho. She's like a baby who was just born and is out in the world. So someone like that who comes to this world here—Wow! you can do anything. And even more if they've had a life with a partner who ..." she pauses, searching for the words, "*maltrato*

179

doméstico, domestic violence. In El Salvador, it's very common. There in El Salvador, the husbands, the majority of the husbands hit their wives and do everything to them and the women can't say anything. Just 'okay' because they're afraid their man is going to leave them. Because they depend on the man economically. So when they come here, everything's different."

In communities like Sara's cantón, the vulnerability of women and girls is palpable. Rural misogyny is more intense than urban, poor more intense than rich, all of it structurally pervasive. The kind of domestic violence that Sara describes emerges at the intersection of historical misogyny, the broad social insecurity that results from regional corruption and criminal activity, and a political system that allows gender-based violence to go unpunished. All of these factors—from the social acceptance of domestic abuse to El Salvador's 5 percent conviction rate for femicide and the institutionalized rape of sisters and daughters as gang vengeance—emerge from social and cultural meaning systems that devalue women.[1] They are sex objects and servants, badges of honor or shame, victims less worthy of justice.

In the US, women like Sara's mother see the possibility of a different way.

"My father wasn't the best husband," Sara goes on, "*no fue el mejor de los esposos.* And when he came here, he tried to be the same and he would hit my mom. He'd beat her and everything. But one day, she said, 'Okay, enough,' and she told him that he couldn't do that here. That here, we women had a lot of support, and that she had decided to leave him."

When Sara's mom made this move, she relied not only on the values she encountered in the US, but also on a newfound economic independence and freedom of movement that would have been impossible in her small Salvadoran cantón.[2] But cultural values, individual experience, and personal desires come together in complicated ways, and when Sara considers her mother's choices, she stops short of celebrating resistance. In fact, when Sara speaks of her mother—as a parent, as a wife—it feels at times as if she is speaking about herself.

Though her own husband has entered very little in our conversation—that twenty-five-year-old man who enticed a fifteen-year-old with the promise of a better life—the words Sara uses to describe him resonate with her mother's story. Other than the fact of her marriage, she has only mentioned the man she married one other time, in response to my inquiry about his role in caring for her son.

"And your husband?" I'd asked.

"My husband," she said in a low voice, "he's not the best husband around, *no es el mejor de los esposos.*"

These words echo a shared experience between mother and daughter. But in the choices Sara makes about how to narrate her own personal history, a different response emerges. Sara expresses a kind of longing for a time before choices like the ones her mother made were possible, and on this day, one moment in Sara's life on an iron bench in Lafayette Park, her longing takes the shape of regret.

"If we had stayed there, my mom and dad would probably be together. It would have been a different life, but I think it would have been better. Because, in the end, it didn't do much for us, because we separated. Over time, you could see how we had a better economic situation, but the emotional side, that went badly for us. Badly. Because . . . Well, look. I have my little sister. I left her when she was a little baby and now she has a baby. She got married really young, *jovencita,*" Sara repeats the word forcefully, the sharp edge in her voice cuts into the diminutive's innocence. "At twelve years old."

Twelve years old. In El Salvador, where a third of all births are to teenage mothers and one in four girls reports that their first sexual experience was non-consensual.[3]

"So, it didn't do much for us, all of this. Because my mom made money and we lived well and all, but . . ."

Sara continues to reach for words, stumbling over stilted beginnings and incomplete thoughts in a manner out of step with the free-flowing rhythm of her narrative so far. It's as if here in this ending place of evaluation and meaning-making, she would like to pull together all the stolen girlhoods and abandoned babies and double-edged freedoms and place them neatly in a sentence or two that could contain them. An ending—happy or unhappy—final enough to illuminate the chain of cause and effect that started long ago in the foothills of the Chaparrastique volcano and ended here on a mild winter afternoon at a neighborhood park in Houston, Texas.

"So that's why, if I could turn back time, I would stay in my country."

"Yeah?"

"Yeah. Definitely. Without thinking twice. Because I think that, if I'd had my kids in my country, I would have been there with them, and they would think better of me."

Only a breath or two ago, Sara told me about the house she got for her kids. She insisted that she had been both the father and the mother that circumstances demanded—the provider of material needs, of shelter and safety and an American future that meant hope for something better. Only a breath or two ago, she spoke of her heroic role in securing an American dream for her family—a house of their own, schools and jobs and plastic bottles of Canola oil like liquid gold on the pantry shelf. She made the journey at fourteen, found the work, saved the money, birthed the babies. She sent remittances home to her grandparents and sisters from her very first check and still does to this day. All of this, Sara has been sure to record.

But there is a pull and tug in her story that demands regret, a moral call to the good mother that can't be fulfilled by houses and shoes and an American future. Her son wants a mother who comes to Mother's Day assemblies and always smiles. Always. He has learned to expect it of her from all the same voices that have taught Sara to expect it from herself. Manly voices that put their feet up at the end of the workday while she moves from job to bus to kitchen. Powerful voices that tell her to be grateful for low wages and insecure work because she crossed a line in the night. *Pueblo chico* voices that whisper "marriage" to a violated twelve-year-old girl. Raw, wounded voices that blame the powerless longing of a left-behind child on a mother's desperate choice. There are so few public voices that might point Sara and her son toward some larger cause. No social services officer explaining the failures of a broken healthcare system or colleagues in the park asserting workplace rights.[4] No voices that trace the lines of her landscape of choice across a vast map of patriarchy and xenophobia and economic policy that ignores the human costs of labor. For Sara, there is just one woman, choosing alone.

By framing her narrative in regret, Sara can respond to these voices and still open up a space for pride in her American dream—the house and the remittances and her children's future paved in concrete and electric light. Within the confines of this park bench conversation, she can be both nurturer and provider, mother and father both. By demonstrating that she is willing to sacrifice all she's gained, she recovers the moral imperative of her mothering identity and gives a name to the mothercoin's damaging paradox: regret. Even so, all the regret in the world isn't enough to quiet the powerful push and pull that compels the mothercoin northward.

"Just now," Sara mentions as we move to say our goodbyes, "an aunt of mine is about to migrate, leaving her four kids in El Salvador. So it's going to be the same as what my mom did."

Rosa

"We bought a house here, by the grace of God and the USA, because here, this country is for making progress, for making something of yourself, not for coming just to sit around. That's why you'll always see me working. First of all, because I like it. And we suffered for a long time. Now that we can, it's fair for us to give ourselves a new life."

"Do you think coming here has served you well?" I ask.

"Yes, yes, yes. So much. Now my kids, one of them owns a house. They all live well. My kids have always been hard workers. Because of my husband, because he taught them to work, to be responsible. My kids, they like to get ahead."

A house, security, a future for the children, Rosa's narrative reads like a regular immigrant success story of old. A tale of moral worth and strength of character, where material comfort is the reward for suffering and hope and endurance, all by the sweat of her brow. But Rosa is older now, and she feels the pull of the rancho and a different way of life. With one foot here and one foot on the other side, she considers the life she made here and stitches together all the pieces of her own Mexican American dream.

"Now, with everything we've done," Rosa reflects, "we're comfortable. We want to retire—to go to Mexico. I'm not interested in staying here. For living, I don't like it here, not for living. For working, yes. But to live without working, I'm going home to Mexico."

In Rosa's familiar words, I hear the echo of a sentiment repeated often among the immigrants I've encountered: *pa' trabajar sí, pa' vivir, no.* The US is a place where dreams can come true because it is a place where there are good wage-earning jobs to be found, but something is missing here. In this country, Rosa has learned, work is plentiful and lucrative, but it's also everything. There's no material comfort without current employment, no illness or old age without economic uncertainty, no dependency of young children without complicated private workarounds. In the end, the work-equals-hope equation that drives the American dream can only take a woman like Rosa so far, and her own retirement dreams are painted in red, white, and green.

But as so many immigrants discover, time has a way of revising our plans in spite of us. And by the spring of 2019, when I meet with Rosa for a follow-up interview, the dangers of Mexico's new reality have made the prospect of a peaceful retirement unlikely for a successful immigrant with diamond earrings and a cherry-red SUV. In 2019, Rosa and Arturo have installed themselves comfortably in their daughter Lila's house in south Houston, where we meet on a warm spring day with my phone's red recording light blinking on the coffee table between us.

In the open living room of Lila's modest two-story home, bright with trinkets and toys and a purple accent wall dotted with framed photos of children, Rosa and I revisit the stories she has told before. New details and familiar plots, the same intonations, some fresh perspectives. Rosa still works off and on, and Arturo too, but only desirable jobs and never so much that they can't spend months at a time in their other home, the rancho down in Puebla. The rancho is where her roots lie, family and community and a place to come home to when it's time to live life fully, instead of living to work. For years, Rosa has returned home for holidays and celebrations, like the quinceañera party where her son, Martín, met his wife, Julieta, for the first time.

Julieta first told me her story in 2016, in the stillness of an autumn afternoon while her infant son napped in a room down the hall. Still and composed on a polished dining room stool, she spoke softly as she recounted the years of separation and risk that had marked her love story with Rosa's son, Martín. Three years' courtship on either side of the border, six more months of separation after the wedding, a border crossing fraught with a midnight car crash and hours lost in the desert. After a year cleaning houses for cash in Houston, the couple took a chance and applied for Julieta's residency only for her to be sent back to Mexico, where she waited almost two years while Martín worked with a lawyer to appeal the denial. In the end, success, reunion, and years of hard work ahead.

Julieta spent the next few years cleaning houses on the weekends and earning fourteen dollars an hour as a full-time nanny-housekeeper during the week. "I worked for four years," she told me with pride, "and from those four years, *gracias a Dios*, we were able to buy this home. It was worth it. It was worth it to work so much. My husband knew that I was working so that we could make something of ourselves."

But somewhere along the way to her own American dream, motherhood complicated Julieta's story. First, the pregnancy compromised the job—when childcare challenges limited Julieta's availability, her four-year patrona was unwilling to compromise, and Julieta was let go. Then, the child diminished the dream of return—"My husband, before we got married, he bought a little piece of land back in Puebla. We plan to build something there, something for a small store, to sell clothes or a convenience store, a little *papelería*.⁵ But I've always known that I would go back alone," her voice breaks, her composure lost. "Because my son, he's from here. He's born here. He's going to want to stay here." Softly, for only a moment, Julieta had cried.

Three years later, when the same woman walks through the door of her sister-in-law's home to join me and Rosa, Julieta's eyes are dry. She arrives in the middle of our conversation, disrupting Rosa's narrative flow with the movement and voices of a front door and footsteps and two young children spilling into their aunt's familiar home. Julieta moves into the room in athletic clothes and tennis shoes, her straight black hair pulled back now as it was then, and greets me hesitantly before falling into the leather couch opposite where I sit. She sighs and listens for a bit. I perceive a familiar weariness in her, the weight of these last few years of need-meeting and body-tending, three meals a day, midnight coughs, and uncertain futures. And all the complicated relationships of extended family.

"When *she* got here," Rosa says, gesturing in her daughter-in-law's direction without taking her eyes off me, "Well, it's not the same kind of suffering we had to go through. She suffered in the crossing, because we all suffer there, but the ones who didn't have enough to eat, who had nowhere to sit, nowhere to sleep, that was us, us and our kids. When we arrived here, we had to start from zero. But with her, thank God, it wasn't like that, because we had already established ourselves. When she got here, I even had a house already."

Julieta remains heavy in her seat with one eye on the children—the five-year-old boy who'd been a sleeping toddler when we last talked, the two-year-old sister who'd followed soon after. I look her way and consider the car crash and the crossing, the years of separation.

"I used to kill myself working," Rosa goes on. "I had two kids at home and I had to work. It was harder then. But look at her," she motions again toward Julieta. "She has the ease of not working. She takes care of the kids. Because we're in another time now." Rosa's words are certain, her face at ease. "Ya estamos en otra época."

"No, but I do work," Julieta sits up and throws her voice into the conversation. "Right now I'm working two or three days a week."

"Yeah, but not the whole week," Rosa talks over her, "not full time. When I had the kids, I did work full time—"

"Well, with the kids," Julieta inserts herself again, "because you have to find someone to take care of them, or send them to a daycare."

Julieta explains that she can work while her son is in school, but she has to find a sitter for the girl. Rosa reminds her that she herself used to take the girl twice a week, that she still watches grandchildren on days she doesn't work.

But Julieta clarifies, "I leave her with a friend."

"Do you pay your friend?" I ask.

"Oh yes, I pa—"

Rosa breaks in, "Here, Elizabeth, they all charge you. Everyone charges you here."

In the years since we talked, Julieta has cobbled together various arrangements to accommodate working motherhood—alternating work schedules with Martín, grandmother care, paid childcare, days at home. Working and saving, the couple has sold the apartment and bought a house. By all accounts, theirs is a story of immigrant success. But I remember the quiet tears from before, when Julieta mourned the separation that her return to Mexico would one day surely create in the family. Three years later, sitting across from her in Rosa's spacious living room, I consider her yoga pants and sneakers, the keys tossed onto the coffee table and talk punctuated by motherspeak—*déjalo, cuídate*. I see the weight of her sunken body, so different than the tight posture she'd maintained at our first meeting, and I am struck by how often we are pushed and ebbed and directed by life, even as we hold on to familiar dreams.

"Some time ago, you both told me that you'd like to go back and live out a future in Mexico. I wonder if you still—"

"Well," Rosa begins before I finish the question. "Since just now I have all my kids here, I don't know if . . ." her voice falls and loses steam in the pause, until she finds the words. "What I like is to go back and forth. But to stay forever, now . . . not really anymore."

Her visits to her home in Mexico are frequent and long, she explains, a month at a time. She tells me about her last trip for a sister-in-law's funeral, and I nod and smile, all the while with one eye on Julieta.

"And you, Julieta? I remember before that you had said you would like to go back at some point. Still?"

"Yes, because, well, I'm aware that my kids are from here, I won't be taking them with me. They'll stay here, so I know that I'll go back alone, *voy a regresar sola*—"

"—No!" Rosa interrupts. "Not alone! With Martín!" The strength in her voice is cut by her own laughter, a look in my direction, a wink.

"No," Julieta quickly agrees, "not alone!" We all laugh, a child screams in play, Julieta explains herself in a voice almost lost in the commotion, "but it's practically being alone, not having a child there, back home."

And so by force of interruptions, winks, laughter, and control of the unfolding story, Rosa's tale prevails: By the grace of God and the US of A, this Mexican family has made something of themselves. No room for loss or regret, just one big family with lives both here and there, *aquí en Houston, allá en el rancho.*

"Describe this 'rancho' to me, because, you know, Mexicans use the word 'rancho' and—"

Rosa laughs and takes the lead, "We call it a 'rancho' because—it's a really small town—"[6]

Julieta jumps in, "There are like—"

"—six houses," Rosa interrupts.

"—Well," Julieta takes over, "*houses*, there are like twelve, but with people living in them—"

"—No," Rosa inserts herself and talks over Julieta so that I never hear how many families actually live on the rancho they describe.

"We're mostly all family there," Rosa sums up. "But it's a shame that there isn't anything to live on over there; the ones who are there survive because of the ones who are here, because they send money. But when it comes to work, there isn't any over there."

Rosa's family's rancho is small, and always the first stop when they visit. Martín's land is there, along with Rosa and Arturo's house. Julieta's hometown, Huehuetlán el Chico, is bigger but still in Puebla, and the image of its easy life feeds Julieta's dreams of retirement.

"My father, he's retired now," she told me back in 2016. "He's comfortable there, *tranquilo*. He's alone in his house, but he can get to the store walking. He'll go to mass on Sundays, then maybe to a game, or a friend will invite him to a party. He's not worried about paying rent or the electric bill. He doesn't have these worries that we do, from month to month, so, he's happier."

Huehuetlán el Chico is about twenty minutes away from Rosa's place by car, so that, when Julieta and Martín and the kids spend their annual weeks at home in Mexico, it's easy to go back and forth.

"In Mexico, these kids are happy!" Rosa shouts, rocking back into her smile and bright eyes.

"Yes," Julieta smiles, "they're happy because—"

"—they go every year!—"

"—they're free, like to go outside. They can play in the countryside and here, lots of times—"

"—Here there isn't any countryside!"

I try to picture the place, children running among wild grasses and old men walking to the market, six modest homes living and breathing beside empty and half-constructed houses that wait for those on the other side to come back and make the place whole. But even as I conjure up the image of a town with eyes constantly looking northward, Julieta's heavy sighs stretch back home, *allá*, to meet that northward gaze. Together, the waiting and the longing form their own sort of wholeness.[7]

"Does everyone in the rancho have someone on the other side?" I ask.

"Generally," Rosa answers, "of all the people who live there, almost everyone has people here."

"And the people who live there, are they mostly older?"

"No, no."

"So what work do they do?"

"There *is* work," Rosa responds, then pauses while she looks for a way to explain her contradicting statements. "There's work because there are people who are okay, they survive. I have an uncle—and not just my uncle but a lot of people—he works with crops, you know? He works in the fields. They grow onions, peanuts. And those same people give work to the other people. Because there is work. It's just not as good as what there is here. But people get by. When we were there, we survived. Poor and all, people get by."

"But it's not a place to set a goal for yourself and reach it?"

"No," says Rosa.

"No," says Julieta. "Over there, it's just for spending some time."

So Mexico is for living, not for working. For getting by, not for getting ahead. For retiring one day, or at least for feeding the dream of going back to a place where, if you have a house, *una pequeña construcción*, and enough in your pocket for the market, life can be peaceful again.

"The people who make it there are the ones who have people here," Rosa goes on, "and they send money to them so that they can build houses. Because everyone has a nice house, because, by the grace of God, we're over here. And the ones who are here send money to the ones back home and they build their houses and their tables and everything.

"Because, there are people with money there," she pauses, filling out the picture. "There are people who have cows and who have land and those guys, yeah they make it. But people who have to work for wages, *gente que está en salario*, no. They don't make it. That's why I say that there's a better life here for the ones who want it. The ones who *want* it, *eh*?"

The picture Rosa and Julieta have painted makes it clear that the better life that awaits an immigrant over here in the land of the working isn't only for the immigrant herself. The rancho they return to for celebration and peace and fellowship, benefits directly from migrant labor, it raises their buildings and furnishes their homes. And in return, the rancho embraces their elders and births their next generations—a wife for Martín, a niece to clean alongside her migrant aunt. This is a transnational community, as whole in its spatial dislocation as it is fragmented in its hometown roots.[8] Like the transnational family, the transnational community is knitted together by a tight weave of collective identity and economic dependence, and, like those divided families, these communities find themselves caring and living on one end and earning and sweating on the other. All those houses, sometimes full, sometimes empty, point toward the strain placed on those who launch themselves into the stress of monthly bills and cars that may break down and jobs that vanish at the first swell of an employee's belly—American fruit of a Mexican womb who will understand home differently.

And those houses at the rancho have twins in the north, the Spanish-tiled two-story homes by Lafayette Park, modern ranch houses and three-two track houses and multilevel apartment buildings, all the pinnacle of an American dream that paints itself across dated images of Rockwell-like families and white picket fences. Still the object of desire, still the place where work and success and the moral mettle of a man—of a woman—come together. Each twin in the north, so many of them built by immigrant labor, so many cleaned and maintained by immigrant hands, laborers who live a double dream—for all the casas a week she secures on this side, a forever house on the other. Back home, *allá*.

In the end, the Mexican American dream that Rosa insists on is a joint project: On one hand, the Mexican dream of using American wages to make something of oneself, to lift up a family and a community. On the other, the American dream of having it all—green lawn, white picket fence, good schools, and a steady stream of cheap labor whose health and retirement is some other community's problem.

If Rosa's version of the Mexican American dream glosses over the double-sided nature of the project, Julieta's relationship to the narrative is ambivalent at best.

"How would the two of you—each of you—" I look at Julieta directly, "how would you describe the American dream?"

"Well, for me," Rosa begins (Rosa always begins), "it's like a future. But it's not about wishful thinking, because here, you have to work to achieve the American dream. A lot of people don't get there because they don't work. They don't come here to work. They just come to survive, to get by. And for me, that's not the American dream." Rosa stops and notices that I'm still looking at Julieta. She laughs a bit. "I don't know about her," waving in her daughter-in-law's direction.

We both turn to her, "And for you, Julieta?"

"For us," she begins, "it's an achievement, achieving something you set out to do. That feels good. To achieve a goal that you set for yourself and that you can reach."

It's a reasonable response, in line with hope and getting ahead, making something of yourself rather than just surviving. But there's something in Julieta's answer, in her whole manner, that seems to be holding on to a dream that has nothing to do with America.

Julieta's ambivalence may signal a more complicated relationship to the immigrant project, to the gamble and the casas and the divided families and transnational longing. But on this afternoon in 2019, in the purple-walled house that Rosa shares with the children and grandchildren whose faces adorn the walls, it's Rosa's story that prevails. She wins because of the narrative agency she exerts—the active self-fashioning in her interruptions and talking over, and the shaping of two stories into one. One home here, another *allá*, money in the bank, and papers guarded safely in a cabinet drawer.

In the end, the narrative is wrapped up neatly by the kind old man who administered to Rosa a simplified citizenship test for older applicants. No English requirement, no written exam, just one last question with a fifty-fifty shot.

"The last question was about a war," Rosa explains. "What year, or what it was, something about a war. And I was like, 'What could it be?' So the señor says, 'I'm going to help you. Was it the first or the second?' 'The second,' I said. 'Bravo!' he said. 'You're now an American citizen!'"

Gracias a Dios y a los Estados Unidos.

Pati

"I've learned this," Pati begins, "things happen for a reason."

Eight years after our first interview, Pati's eyes are bright, her face still round. The words tumble out of her as we settle into a small table on the second floor of a neighborhood library. It is June of 2019, and the soft-spoken and vulnerable woman I remember now radiates energy and movement. Oversized sunglasses perched above her forehead, hair pulled back and brushed with subtle highlights, small gold hoop earrings that bounce when she laughs.

After weeks of texts back and forth, Pati has finally found time to talk—an hour or so between her children's morning activities and their afternoon swim practice. While the kids look for books with their father in the children's stacks below, Pati catches me up on all that's happened since she was let go by the Stevensons eight years earlier—pregnant and distraught and caught between feeling and reason. In the telling, the betrayal she had felt at the dismissal subsides and the events of eight years ago become part of a larger narrative arc, one that is charged with a kind of providential design.

Where eight years ago Pati had moved quickly over the year she spent waiting for her job to return to full time, now she details the feeling of those months. She tells me how exhausted she had become, pregnant and nannying and mothering a toddler. "The first three months were horrible. I would fall asleep on the floor with my baby girl. Between that in the mornings, and then in the afternoons pick up the children and cook and do a little cleaning, it was exhausting." Unable to choose between her health and her income, she had let the señora make the choice for her.

But in the end, the replacement nanny with the fancy dinner invitation and the university studies didn't last the year. Six months in, she quit from one day to the next, leaving the family with no childcare and the bitter memory of a careless employee. Pati heard it all from her friend who still cleaned for the Stevensons—how the new girl didn't comb little Ellie's hair, how she left dirty dishes in the sink and expected the maid to clean her bathroom, how she came down to serve the kids breakfast in her pajamas.

When Ms. Stevenson called Pati on the phone to beg her to return, only months after she'd handed Pati her last paycheck and sent her on her way, Pati understood the sequence of events as a blessing in disguise, a kind of divine intervention to resolve the irreconcilable conflict between work, pregnancy, and mothering young children. "Six months," she affirms, "the three longest and hardest months of pregnancy—me with my daughter and a big belly, stressed out. And then another three months with the baby."

In this revised story, the six months Pati was out of work—without income, without security, and without the recognition of her own value as a nanny—become a trial of patience on the way to her reward. At the end of the test: her old job, a higher hourly wage, and a new respect for her contribution to the family.

"Those six months, they saw how someone truly cares for their children, and how a person looks out for their interests. So, they must have thought, 'What Pati contributes to my family, that counts for more than what I'm going to pay her.' So I say," she concludes, "things happen for a reason."

But the demands of caring for two families soon overwhelmed her.

"It was too stressful. Cook, run here and there, the baby has to sleep, the other needs me, run to pick up the kids, get there late, pray, run after them up and down the stairs of the big house, the two-year-old running around, me upstairs nursing the baby, just too much stress. A year and a half after coming back to work, I was collapsing. I had to take care of two houses. My kids cried. They got sick. I was like, 'That's it, no more.'"

When the Stevensons announced a move abroad, it felt to Pati as if fate had stepped in to decide for her once more. Then, three years later—just as she was on the verge of leaving a stingy employer—the wheel turned in her favor yet again. The family returned and offered Pati her old job. She accepted immediately. To her, it felt like part of a greater design, everybody's needs shifting into alignment in a predestined chain of cause and effect. One, two, three.

From my own vantage point across a hushed library nook, I see another side to Pati's story. I see one single woman who has become the stopping place for all the work that drives the domestic lives of two families. One single woman who reaches her breaking point once and again, with no time to stop and consider the larger forces at play. No narrative legacy of fables and tales to nudge her toward anger or resistance. Only her experience and all she's learned to expect from the way of an indifferent and anonymous world.

These days, Pati and Ms. Stevenson are finding a way to manage it all. "We always make it work. There are also the neighbor ladies who help. We're all moms, and between one mom here and one mom there, we find a way to manage."

Patrona and *niñera*, mother and othermother, a tribe of women all crafting creative solutions to the problem of managing family and home in a world that would render such work invisible.

All the moms.

From Pati's own mother, María, and her 1,800-mile creative solution to the problem of food on the table, to Pati's own loss of wages before the realities of her second pregnancy. From the stress and exhaustion of laboring for two families to the sisters and aunts who couldn't be called on to help, to Ms. Stevenson herself and the neighbor ladies she recruited. All the mamás finding a way to make it work on an unequal playing field defined by the inequalities of region, social class, and race and their infinite intersections with maternity, employment, marriage, and status. Theirs is the work that orders our material lives and forges our interpersonal connections—parent, child, partner, neighbor, communities at the park, in the school parking lot, and up and down the grocery store aisles.

These thousands of interactions form the substance of social organization, yet they are rendered so invisible that even one who has dedicated her life to this work understands traumatic job loss in pregnancy and near collapse under the stress of work and childcare as part of a private story, the personal trials of one individual woman. While Pati has come to understand the circumstances of her life in a way that empowers her to live out the fullness of her own story, I am left staring at the other side of the coin, where the visibility of the work reveals a glaring social failure. We as a society have dismissed our responsibility to raise our children and care for our elderly and infirm. We have feminized this care into triviality, swept it under the rug of visibility, and left the mothers among us with little choice but to struggle and endure—or to outsource the work to marginalized others who must bear our burdens and theirs, alone. One single woman.[9]

As our conversation comes to a close, Pati's daughter leans quietly into her mother's shoulder in the hushed air of the Young Adult section, and I ask a final question.

"How is your mother now?"

"Oh," Pati smiles, "perfect, thank goodness. She's been in her job for thirty-four years, the same garage apartment. The señora is alone now. My mom takes care of the house, she cooks, she prepares her coffee."

This last detail lingers, the image of an aging widow receiving her morning coffee from an aging companion. It is a simple morning ritual that must mean more than the contract between employer and employee, and whose meaning must also be bound within that contract and all the messiness of life it entails. Power and wages, affection, desperation, and a thousand and one interpretations of need—what the children need, what the mothers need, the patronas and the *niñeras*. Despite the injustice, despite the privilege and the carelessness and the broad social failures, there is something in this cup of coffee that is strong and beautiful. There must be, in this story we tell.

"Pain and possibility." Reflecting on the agency these women exert—in the living, in the telling—I am drawn to María Ibarra de la Luz's poetic characterization of the experiences of immigrant nannies.[10] Pain in these stories, to be sure—coerced separation from one's home, from one's children, from the children one has grown to love. The inability to access resources and social protections like healthcare and credit, labor protections for the pregnant and over-worked. Pain in the unacknowledged value of one's labor or the relationships that labor engenders, and in the profound public silence of lives unwitnessed outside the bounds of private expression. And there is pain, certainly, in all the voices I have not heard. Those women who politely declined my requests to interview, the ones I never met, and those whose stories succumbed to deserts or rivers, to an emboldened border or a heavy hand behind closed doors.

But for the women in this book, and for many others, the gamble did pay off in important ways. Herein lies the possibility. The empowerment of a woman who has been raised for dependence and finds herself the wage-earning administrator of her own life and that of her family. The liberation of a woman who has been raised for subservience and finds herself supported by a community that demands she be respected. The impact of a shadow-worker who shapes her occupation through playground conversations, and the potential of the same worker who taps into growing networks of organized resistance.

Pain and possibility. The narrative stuff of these stories stands testimony to the material agency of women who are not victims only, but full and complex human beings. They are women who exercise tremendous power in their choices as storytellers, who call up a singular voice that is theirs alone and capable of shaping reality. When Pati reframes her story of inexplicable betrayal into a tale of unanticipated fortune, she recasts herself as someone who is no longer a vulnerable victim. As the narrative subject, she gives form and feeling to the story and endows her experiences with meaning, flesh on bone. Rosa molds a lifetime of struggles and conflict and ambiguous reward into a story of immigrant success. Sara narrates a double-edged tragedy—a provider's triumph and a mother's failure. Alicia finds the voice to say *mejor no*.

The telling is the thing, the bold act of it. To say, "This is my story," is to say, "See me." There is power in the telling because there is potential in the reach of the tale—two feet across a cool iron park bench or two hundred pages of shared experience. A woman's words, a writer's understanding, a reader's measured breath.

THE BROWN MOTHER
BESIDE ME

Late one weekday evening many years ago, I showed up at a friend's place out of sorts and overwhelmed by the demands of keeping house and caring for young children and the tensions it created with my husband. I don't remember what we had been arguing about—dishes or dinner, maybe, folding the laundry. As I sat on my friend's living room sofa and catalogued my frustrations, her husband half-listened, sitting on a re-cliner across from us with the TV remote in hand. Midway through the conversation, he offered his take on my frustrations. "You just need to hire a maid," he said. "That will take care of it."

At the time neither my friend nor I could find the words to respond, speechless and offended and clutching our chardonnays. Now, on the other side of midnight feedings and domestic negotiations and the nar-rative journeys of a handful of women who have organized their lives around childcare and household work, I understand why outsourcing these tasks to women more desperate than I will never be a real solution. The reasons are practical, they are moral, and they matter to us all.

The price of the mothercoin[1]

The architecture of our contemporary social order rests on a weak foun-dation: the false assumption that our homes and our families are held up by force of love, inexhaustible and economically inconsequential. These stories reveal the cracks in that foundation. Devastated regional economies primed to feed Western demand for labor come up against a language and law of immigration that ignores economic reality for the sake of political advantage. Feminism's advances in the public sphere come up against stagnant gender roles at home and a culture of work that sacrifices family and community for the sake of individual success. Unchecked American individualism and bootstrap ideology come up against the fundamental truth of social organization: We are not a society of individuals. Together, we are responsible for each other, and for our young.

Since that evening at my friend's house, I have taken a seat on other sofas, at kitchen tables and park benches. I've lingered in the bright sunlight on driveways and neighborhood sidewalks, I've read and reflected, all the while listening to stories that, together, reveal what the research doesn't: that the private reach of the public world is not something we know so much as something we feel. It is an experience of value that informs our identity and experience. Our sense of self and our personal histories can't be separated from the choices we're forced to make or from the cultural narratives that penetrate our understanding—stories that so often emerge from the ideological interests of others and nonetheless tell us who we are supposed to be.

These women's stories reveal that the mothercoin is not an industry or an immigration pattern, but an approach to value. The invisibility is what does the harm, the insignificance attributed to the work and to the woman and to the choices she has confronted. When the work is swept under the rug, so are the cultural expectations about a woman's place in the home, on the job. When the woman is little more than a household expense, her landscape of choice succumbs to the cold reality of supply and demand and her humanity is compromised by a hierarchy of value that pits the faces of the mothercoin against each other: presence against protection, labor against love. The deepest damage comes from a language that paints these conflicts as the result of her own choices.

If the mothercoin derives from a public value system in which women and immigrants deserve less, then its greatest violence is its ability to feed that belief system and to reproduce it within us all. Faced with the full humanity of these immigrant nannies, we are called to respond to the moral harm of the mothercoin.[2] The task is daunting. There are systems to dismantle, deep-seated values to uproot, a collective will to muster. Overwhelming. And at the end of a long week of work and balance and worry and tedium and joy, all of this often comes down to just two women, face to face across a kitchen counter.

Here is a place to begin: Listen carefully and choose wisely.

The purchase of empathy[3]

To listen fully to another person's story is to suspend the self for a moment and step into the experience of their lives, embodied and inescapable. When we listen carefully, a certain kind of magic unfolds. At the end of a day at work, when our bodies itch for the feel of our young child who is being cared for by another at home or in a daycare, we will know what it is for an immigrant nanny to be separated from her own child by hundreds of miles and formidable borders. When we experience the panic of securing childcare within the demands of our jobs and budgets, we will feel the economic anxiety of a pregnant domestic worker or the emotional conflict of a nanny who can't be at a school celebration. We will understand, because we feel it, that no one woman can meet such demands, no matter how steady the migrant supply. From this place of empathy, we can choose wisely—as mothers, employers, allies, and voices of influence in our communities.

We may feel powerless to resolve global inequality or regional instability or the inhumanity of draconian immigration policy, but we do have some power to address the American culture of motherhood. Fed by our daily choices around parenting and household work, our culture of intensive mothering sets the stage for what we collectively believe our children need. The impossible expectations that feed this dynamic won't change until we redefine those needs. Resisting the sign-up sheets and the enrichment classes and the elaborate birthdays, letting children struggle through their own projects or whine their way through unscheduled hours, these become political acts capable of resolving the shame in the question many have failed to ask: But what do the nanny's children need?

As employers, we can choose to enact the same kind of contracts and benefits we would expect in our own working lives. We can employ language that acknowledges the responsibilities in our role, shifting from *I need some help* to *I choose to hire an employee, to comply with laws and regulations, and always to remember that the woman who cleans my home and cares for my children has a home and a family of her own.* As allies, we can follow the lead of advocates who work to regulate and legitimize the industry. Organizations like the National Domestic Workers Alliance have empowered domestic workers to educate each other about rights; they've formed alternative cooperative cleaning services, cultivated employer education, and worked to increase the visibility of the women and the industry in the broader public eye.[4]

Beyond employer measures and industry reforms, all of us can give language and voice to the need for a broad social restructuring around the substance and significance of domestic and carework. There are so many avenues of change available—from shared responsibility among partners, to universal pre-K and afterschool programs, to paid parental leave and subsidized childcare. We only lack the collective will. But such will depends on shared values, and when it comes to this more diffuse project of altering the deep meaning systems that inform our structures of work, childcare, and immigration—or to the deeper problem of addressing the global inequity at the root of the mothercoin—there is hope in turning, again, to stories.

Here, I hold tight in faith to a truth articulated for me by a guest speaker in one of my first-year college writing classes. The lecturer, a tenured sociologist of immigration, grew up among migrant farm laborers and went on to earn prestige as a published scholar. He sat on a table in front of the class and explained his motivation in these words: "I wanted to write about these people, because I knew that when you write, no one can deny your existence. And they can't deny the existence of the people you write about, either."[5]

The revolution of value begins with this simple story: *I exist.*

We are all capable of hearing the words. We are all capable of amplifying the voice. It is the truest response I know to the practical and moral harm of the mothercoin. Listen carefully, choose wisely, and seek out the fullness of their humanity. To do so is to learn that the intimate reach of the public world is not exclusive to the woman on the other side of the kitchen table, and that this landscape of policy and practice, choice and narrative, has unacknowledged lessons to teach about our own value as well. Complex truths that, for me, are revealed in a simple second-person pronoun.

The brown mother beside me

When I interviewed Sara under the oak tree in Lafayette Park in 2010, we did not have a preestablished relationship. At our first meeting, I proposed the interview and she agreed immediately. When we sat beside each other a few days later, the words began to tumble out as soon as I opened up a space for her to speak. When she told her story, she wasn't speaking to a sister or a friend or a fellow nanny, not to a social service worker or a consulate representative or a school administrator. She was speaking to me, an Anglo-American woman with a passport and credit cards and a PhD, a sympathetic ear and children who will go to college. A woman who could easily know her employers, whose neighbor may one day hire her. A woman who, despite all of this—or because of it—asked her to share her experiences. Which was another way to ask her who she was.

Shortly into our conversation, I found myself slipping into the familiar *tú* form of address in Spanish, as opposed to the more formal *usted*.[6] *Pero tú, ¿cuándo viniste?* I get confused sometimes, from one interview to the next. I forget with whom I've established a *tú* sort of relationship: Teresa, who at times feels like a friend; Elena, to whom I feel close in age and social class. And those with whom *usted* is the rule: Rosa, who is older; Pati, who is reserved and feels more careful with her words.

With Sara, I'm undecided and the *tú* slips out. ¿Te importa que te tutee? I ask. Is it okay if I use *tú* with you? A bit of nervous laughter, uncertainty. Está bien, she says. "Sure." It's a quick response, almost annoyed at the interruption, like, Why even bother asking? She's right, you know. For the two of us, it's up to me to decide how to address her. So the *tú* slips out. Not because it's my default, but because—I think, now—I felt at ease and unchallenged in our interaction. I found her so eager to talk, so warm and inward-leaning, so very nonthreatening. No matter how many times I invited her to address me in the same way, to her, I remained *usted*.

When I first came to this research, I intended to write a novel that would trace the relationship between a Hispanic nanny and her employer. The driving idea was this: these two women, no matter how well-intentioned or good of heart, can never really be friends. At the time, I understood this dynamic in terms of social class. Too many differences. Social class is a more powerful determiner of worldview than nationality. The distinction between American and Salvadoran is insignificant next to the distinctions between upper-class and working poor, between higher education and minimal schooling, between well-funded 401Ks and one illness away from homelessness. But I was wrong to think that the cultural difference of social class is the obstacle to friendship between a woman like Sara and a woman like me. Because though these differing circumstances and cultures are mighty barriers indeed, they are nothing next to the distance between master and servant. Power is what really divides us. And power is what sits between me and Sara on the bench at Lafayette Park. *¿Te importa el tú?* I ask. *Lo que usted quiera*, she responds. Whatever you like.

After the shared stories and the intimacy, the children's cries, the cool wind blowing, and the afternoon coming to a close, we are left—Sara and I—with the power and the pronouns and the space between us. I will walk away holding onto my understanding of her story, and she will move through her evening with the words and the tone and the tragedy, and continue to live the story. I will listen and transcribe and translate and cut and edit, and she will likely make her family's dinner, wipe down a table and throw her voice across a bedroom door to remind the kids to finish homework, brush their teeth. Perhaps she'll stop for a moment at the threshold of kitchen to den, or before slipping into the bed she shares with a man whose name she never mentioned, and reflect on the two hours she and I spent together. Her story and her voice, her mother's choices and her own. And maybe something of those hours will give new meaning to the self she chooses to fashion. As it has done with me.

It's been over a decade since I began this project. There are reasons. Children to raise, mostly. Diapers and sippy cups and soccer cleats giving way to homecoming mums and college essays. Through it all, teaching my way to a stocked pantry and comfortable home and theatre classes and practice guitars and the cell phones and summer camps we need to reproduce for our children a lifestyle we've come to see as natural. Stacks of student essays and stacks of dirty dishes, snotty tears and slamming doors for which the world must certainly pause. There are reasons it took me over a decade to write this book.

But then, this is not the book I would have written ten years ago, because it's taken this time, and the deep-burrowing intimacy of these conversations within, for me to learn not just to listen, but to hear. Working with these interviews now, I encounter versions of myself that feel quite distant from the person typing these words. There is an impatience in my interruptions, a strain as I wait—neck craning, smile tickling—for the answer I expect, answers that, in some cases, I thought I heard, despite a more profound truth taking shape beneath the words of the woman on the other side.

Somehow, despite all my hoping to hear a voice loud enough to hold up to a blame-hungry world, I have learned in the end to hear the voice they choose to offer—that beautifully metaphorical *voice* that means not only sound and phonemes but also the embodied truth of the witness. To learn this lesson has required two difficult acts: to turn away from the stories I've been trained to expect, and to cede the floor to another.

Last words

"¿Hay algo que te gustaría decir, con la esperanza de que la gente lo leyera en algún momento?"

"Is there anything else you'd like to say, with the hope that people might read it at some time?"

Sara JANUARY 2010

Este país le puede dar a uno muchas cosas. Pero le quita muchas. Le quita más de lo que le da, porque le da una vida económica, pero le quita familia, le quita tiempo que uno comparte con sus hijos. Es muy difícil aquí. Uno tiene que dar a sus hijos a otra persona que uno no sabe ni cómo se lo cuidan, por ir a darle cariño a *otros* niños. Aquí las americanas son bien cuidadosas con sus bebés y todo. Tiene que uno todo hacer. Si ya estamos un poco enojadas, ya nos están mandando a descansar. Ya no nos dejan trabajar. En cambio, los hispanos. Yo voy a pagarle a una hispana de mi mismo lugar; ella sabe que yo no voy a hacer nada si no me trata bien a los niños. Yo no voy a saberlo. Es un bebé. Entonces, yo por eso, si yo puedo volver el tiempo atrás, yo me quedo en mi país. Sin pensarlo dos veces. Porque pienso que si yo hubiera tenido mis hijos en mi país y yo hubiera estado allá ellos hubieran tenido un mejor concepto de mí.

This country can give you a lot of things, but it takes a lot away. It takes away more than it gives, because it gives you an economic life, but it takes away family, it takes away time you spend with your kids. It's very hard here. You have to give your kids to someone else and you don't even know how they take care of them, so you can go and take care of other kids. Here, American women are really careful with their babies and everything. You have to do everything. If we're a little angry, they fire us, they won't let us work anymore. On the other hand, the Hispanics. I'm going to pay a Hispanic woman, who's from my same town. She knows that I'm not going to do anything if she doesn't treat my kids well. I'm not going to know. It's a baby. So, because of all this, if I could turn back time, I would stay in my country. Without thinking twice. Because I think that, if I had had my kids in my country, and I had been there, they would have a better image of me.

Rosa and Julieta APRIL 2019

"Does it feel different today than it did five years ago, or ten?"

Rosa Uno siente contenta y confiada porque tiene uno papeles. Pero referente a la gente que no tienen y están deportando, acá está siendo muy mal. Porque tanta gente que están mandando. Nosotros no nos preocupamos porque tenemos papeles, pero hay gente que no tiene papeles.

You feel confident and happy because you have papers. But when it comes to people who don't have them and who they're deporting, here it's getting really bad. Because there are so many that they're sending back. We don't worry, because we have papers, but there are people who don't have papers.

Julieta Todas las noticias dicen que cambios que va a haber, de las leyes que hacen los de inmigración y que va a haber cambios. Para mí, digo, apenas voy a ser miembro de la ciudadanía. Sí tiene uno la residencia o es ciudadano americano . . . pero otros, no. Ya sean familiares y conocidos, por ellos no se siente uno a gusto. Porque estoy bien yo, pero la otra gente no.

All the news outlets say there are going to be changes, about the laws that Immigration is making and that there are going to be changes. For me, I mean, I'm about to be a citizen. Yeah, you have your residency or you're an American citizen . . . but not others. Whether it's friends and acquaintances, it's because of them that you don't feel comfortable. Because, I'm okay, but others aren't.

Rosa En una palabra, no hay que ser egoísta. Pues, nosotros no tuvimos papeles tampoco. Y pobre gente. He oído que han mandado familias. Y ¿quién sufre? Los niños, los niños.

In a word, you shouldn't be selfish. I mean, we didn't have papers either. And these poor people. I've heard they're sending families back. And who suffers? The children, the children.

Teresa AUGUST 2008

Que se den la oportunidad de conocer a más gente, porque hay gente [que dice,] "O, ¿es blanco? Entonces no le hablo," o "¿Es negro? No hablo." Y no importa el color de la piel. Pienso yo—tal vez mi mente sea pobre o no sé—pero creo que todos somos hijos de Dios y somos iguales.

They should give themselves a chance to get to know more people, because there are people [who will say,] "Oh, they're white? Then, I'm not going to talk to them." Or, "They're Black? I'm not talking." And the color of their skin doesn't matter. I think—maybe I'm not smart or I don't know—but I believe that we're all God's children, and we are equal.

Elena FEBRUARY 2012

Yo tengo otro punto de vista, y es muy crudo. Okey, en tu país no pudiste estudiar. Vienes a este país que tiene muchas oportunidades, ¿por qué no te superas en vez de ponerte a tener hijos? Ayer fui a la misa. Los niñitos, tres, cuatro niñitos y aparte embarazadas. Yo tengo uno y no me doy abasto. Ellos que tienen tres, cuatro niñitos y aparte están embarazados, esa gente, ¿qué no piensa? El hispano es muy trabajador, pero también tiene un problema, que le gusta

hacer muchos niños. "Oye, ¿son gratis? Fregón, hago veinte."
Ese es mi punto de vista. Qué vamos a hacer.

I have another point of view, and it's very crude. Okay, in your coun-
try, you couldn't study. You come to this country that has many oppor-
tunities, so why don't you better yourself instead of just having kids?
Yesterday I went to mass. The little kids, three, four little kids and also
pregnant. I have one and I can't keep up. Those people, who have three,
four little ones and pregnant besides, are they not thinking? Hispanics
are very hard-working, but they also have a problem; they like to have
a lot of kids. "What, they're free? Damn, I'll have twenty!" This is my
point of view, what can you do.

Pati OCTOBER 2011

Es doloroso. Soy una persona madura, pero a la vez, la situación
económica lo hace difícil, muy muy difícil. ¿Cómo yo voy y busco
trabajo? ¿Quién me va a dar trabajo? Por lo que yo hago. Porque soy
niñera. Ahorita es lo que puedo hacer, y es lo que yo quiero hacer.
A lo mejor si yo pudiera trabajar en una oficina, no les importaría
que estaría embarazada, pero casi nadie me daría trabajo sabiendo
que yo estoy embarazada.

Las cosas, yo siempre digo, pasan por algo. Siempre ha sido mi
lema. Las cosas siempre pasan por algo. Así es que, ya veremos qué
pasa luego después. Yo digo, cada quien toma sus decisiones y vivi-
mos en este mundo de que importan más las cosas de uno que las
de otras personas.

It's painful. I'm a mature person, but at the same time, the economic
situation is hard, very very hard. How am I supposed to go and look
for work? Who's going to give me a job? Because of what I do. Because
I'm a nanny. Right now, it's what I can do and it's what I want to do.
Maybe if I could work in an office they wouldn't care that I was preg-
nant. But hardly anyone would give me a job knowing I'm pregnant.
I always say, things happen for a reason. That's always been my
motto. Things always happen for some reason. So, I don't know, we'll
see what happens later on. But I get it, each person makes their own
decisions, and we live in a world where our own concerns matter more
than other people's.

Pati JUNE 2019

"How is your relationship with your mother now?"

¿Con mi familia? Todo perfecto en mi familia. Somos muy unidas.
Mi mamá vive a cinco minutos de acá. Cuando nos podemos ver,
nos vemos. Hacemos reuniones en familia, todo muy bien. Y con
esta otra familia, ¿de mi jefa? todo hacemos funcionar de allí para
acá. Como me dijo, hasta cuando yo iba a entrar al trabajo, me dijo
ella que hasta que los chicos salieran de la high school, que se fueran
para el college. Pero yo ahorita en mi mente, abierta para lo que sea.
Si se termina antes, okey. Si no, también.

With my family? Everything perfect in my family. We're very close.
My mom lives five minutes from here. When we can see each other,
we do. We have family gatherings, everything's great. And with that
other family, my boss's? We make it work somehow. Like she told me
when I was going to start back at work. She told me, "until the kids get
out of high school, until they leave for college." But just now, my mind
is open to whatever. If it ends earlier, okay. If not, that's okay, too.

Magdalena APRIL 2008

Simple y sencillamente que a mí me gustaría que los americanos
pensaran en una forma diferente. Porque, como yo, hay demasiadas mujeres que simple y sencillamente vienen a este país a buscar
un día de trabajo, y luego a regresarnos a nuestras casas y darles de
comer a nuestros hijos, a nuestro esposo, y al siguiente día salir con
la esperanza de que vamos a encontrar otro día de trabajo. Sin la
idea de hacerle daño ni a sus hijos, ni a ellos, ni hacerle daño a este
país. Simple y sencillamente, la esperanza de nosotras es trabajar,
trabajar y trabajar.

Y nosotros los respetamos mucho, y nos gustaría también pues
que nos diera un poquito de valor. Porque respeto todos merece-
mos y todos queremos. Y yo entiendo cuando me faltan el respeto
en inglés, y se lo puedo faltar también en inglés. Igual, los respeto
mucho y los admiro, porque este es un país que tiene demasiadas
oportunidades para nosotros los hispanos. Y no con la idea de
hacerles daño sino con la idea de trabajar y trabajar, y hasta allí.

Just this, that I would like Americans to think differently. Because, like me, there are many, many women who come to this country just for this, to look for one day of work, and then go home to our houses and feed our children, our husband, and the next day leave again with the hope of finding another day of work. Without wanting to do any harm to their kids or to them, without doing harm to this country. Just this, what we want is to work, work, and work.

And we respect you all very much, and we would just like it if you gave us a little value. Because respect is something we all deserve and we all want. I can understand it when people disrespect me in English, and I can disrespect them in English, too. But at the same time, I respect you all very much and I admire you, because this is a country that has many, many opportunities for us Hispanics. And not with the intention of hurting anyone, our idea is just to work and work, and that's it.

Acknowledgments

First and foremost, I would like to acknowledge the women who shared their experiences with me. To talk about your life the way these women have is, I think, quite brave. It exposes a person, but it also empowers. I hope to have honored their courage.

So many have supported this project over the years. I would like to thank my agent, Jessica Papin, for believing in the book and helping to shape it, and my editor, Helene Atwan, whose insight and perceptive eye have inspired my trust. I am truly grateful to Jessica, Helene, and the team at Beacon Press for the talent and integrity with which they usher books they believe in into the world.

Many thanks to the folks at the Program in Writing and Communication at Rice University: Tracy Volz and Jennifer Wilson, who've supported the project with resources and encouragement, and the PWC Writers who've shown up to write, cookies or not.

I'm deeply grateful to Raquel Gaytán for her transcriptions, perspective, and insights into the subtleties of language and culture. A number of tremendously talented writers, readers, and thinkers have given me invaluable feedback on drafts—especially Marcela Salas, Burke Nixon, Katie Garner, Anadeli Bencomo, Eileen Truax, and Tayyba Kanwal. You've all helped to shape this book, in one way or another.

In this book about the ways we mother, I would like to acknowledge the tribe of mothers and othermothers who have informed my own experience—my sisters Lisa, Tricia, Claire, and Elizabeth; my children's caregivers Angélica, Marilú, Londy, and Carmen; my mother-in-law, Carolina, my Tante Marie, and of course, Mom, who I suspect still has much to teach me.

Sofia, Lucas, Amelie—thank you for making room for this project, which took up so much space at times. David, what can I say? Without your storytelling and the tremendous patience you model, I'm not sure if I would have learned to truly listen.

Notes

Introduction

1. By the time of this writing, Lafayette Park had changed—the playground equipment replaced, the oak tree lost to disease. The bench remains, and the children and their caregivers.

2. All names of the nannies, their families, and the families they work for have been changed.

3. The increase in the feminization of migration is a global phenomenon. Women from Asia, North Africa, and South and Central America, as well as Mexico and the Caribbean, migrate to work in wealthier nations within Asia and South America, the Middle East and Gulf States, Europe, and North America. As of 2014, women migrating for carework were the largest occupational group of women migrating globally. Mary Romero, Valerie Preston, and Wenona Giles, "Care Work in a Globalizing World," in *When Care Work Goes Global: Locating the Social Relations of Domestic Work*, ed. Mary Romero, Valerie Preston, and Wenona Giles (Farnham: Ashgate, 2014). Barbara Ehrenreich and Arlie Hochschild, "Introduction," in *Global Woman: Nannies, Maids, and Sex Workers in the New Economy*, ed. Barbara Ehrenreich and Arlie Hochschild (New York: Metropolitan Books, 2003). Smith Silva et al. caution that the term "feminization" of migration "obscures the ways migrant labour has been 'maternalized' and the subsequent effects on mothers and their children." Dorsía Smith Silva, Laila Malik, and Abigail Palko, "Introduction," *Mothers, Mothering, and Globalization* (Toronto: Demeter Press, 2017), 11.

4. Barbara Ehrenreich and Arlie Hochschild, "Introduction," *Global Woman*, 3.

5. Neighborhood parks are important spaces for the creation of community among immigrant workers like the nannies I met; places in which cultural identities are reinforced, value is affirmed, and the unwritten standards of domestic work are negotiated. Tamara Mose Brown, *Raising Brooklyn: Nannies, Childcare, and Caribbeans Creating Community* (New York: New York University Press, 2011).

6. Elena Poniatowska, *La noche de Tlatelolco: Testimonios de historia oral* (México: Ediciones Era, 1971), and John Beverley, *Testimonio: On the Politics of Truth* (Minneapolis: University of Minnesota Press, 2004). Rigoberta Menchú is an indigenous Guatemalan woman and 1992 Nobel Peace Prize recipient whose mediated testimonial, *I, Rigoberta Menchu: An Indian Woman in Guatemala* (London: Verso, 1984), became a source of tremendous controversy around the role of facts, truth,

and discourse in the testimonial genre. Gayatri Chakravorty Spivak, "Can the Subaltern Speak?" in *Marxism and the Interpretation of Culture*, ed. Cary Nelson and Larry Grossberg (Urbana: University of Illinois Press, 1988), 271–313.

7. Conversations about motherhood often fail to acknowledge an unspoken assumption inherent in the woman–mother connection: that women are defined by biological sex, that biological sex comprises an uncomplicated and fixed duality, and that both social gender and biological sex lend themselves to a certain kind of parenting, such that "mothering" is inextricable from "woman." Such essentialism, which understands identity categories as reflective of a person's biological essence, is a major obstacle to resolving persistent injustices in women's experience in the home and family.

8. Evelyn Nakano Glenn, "From Servitude to Service Work: Historical Continuities in the Racial Division of Paid Reproductive Labor," *Signs* 18, no. 1 (1992): 1–43; Denise Segura, "Working at Motherhood: Chicana and Mexicana Immigrant Mothers and Employment," in *Women and Migration in the U.S.–Mexico Borderlands: A Reader*, ed. Denise Segura and Patricia Zevella (Durham, NC: Duke University Press, 2007); and Michelle Walks and Naomi McPherson, "Introduction," *An Anthropology of Mothering* (Bradford, Ontario: Demeter Press, 2011). These terms are bound up in what Adrienne Rich first identified as the "social institution of motherhood"—the practices, policies, laws, and cultural meanings that come together to define the role of mothers in society. Adrienne Rich, *Of Woman Born: Motherhood as Experience and Institution* (New York: Norton, 1976).

Part I A Toss of the Coin

1. Francisco Cantú, *The Line Becomes a River: Dispatches from the Border* (New York: Riverhead Books, 2018), 222.

2. Despite the sometimes awkward inconsistencies of these labels, I use the terms "global south" and "global north" to refer to regions of lesser and greater economic growth respectively. See Eliot Dickinson, "Introduction," *Globalization and Migration: A World in Motion* (Lanham, MD: Rowman and Littlefield, 2017); Barbara Ehrenreich and Arlie Hochschild, eds., *Global Woman: Nannies, Maids, and Sex Workers in the New Economy* (New York: Metropolitan Books, 2003).

3. On these broad economic and social changes, see Pierrette Hondagneu-Sotelo, *Gendered Transitions: Mexican Experiences of Immigration* (Berkeley: University of California Press, 1994); Denise Segura and Patricia Zavella, "Introduction," *Women and Migration in the US–Mexico Borderlands: A Reader*, ed. Denise Segura and Patricia Zevella (Durham, NC: Duke University Press, 2007). On the maquila industry, José Vargas, "Impacto de las maquiladoras centroamericanas en el crecimiento económico y el empleo," *Aldea Mundo Revista sobre Fronteras e Integración* 14, no. 28 (2009): 19–27. On regional crime, see Steven Dudley, "Transnational Crime in Mexico and Central America: Its Evolution and Role in International Migration," Migration Policy Institute, November 2012, https://www.migrationpolicy.org/research/RMSG-CentAm-transnational-crime.

4. D'Vera Cohn, Jeffrey S. Passel, and Kristen Bialik, "Many Immigrants with Temporary Protected Status Face Uncertain Future in U.S.," Pew Research Center, November 27, 2019, https://www.pewresearch.org/fact-tank/2019/11/27/immigrants -temporary-protected-status-in-us. "Temporary Protected Status," US Citizen and Immigration Services, https://www.uscis.gov/humanitarian/temporary-protected-status, accessed April 1, 2021.

5. The growth of the service sector in globalization has given a new face to a long history of domestic servitude. Saskia Sassen observes, "The image of the immigrant woman serving the white middle-class professional woman has replaced that of the black female servant working for the white master in centuries past." "Global Cities and Survival Circuits," in Ehrenreich and Hochschild, *Global Woman*, 262.

Chapter 1 **Motherland**

1. The Cold War era conflicts in Guatemala and El Salvador in the 1980s emerged from a complicated intersection of local oppression and geopolitical ideology that left tens of thousands of civilians dead. Responding to the threat of Western-hemisphere communism, both the Carter and Reagan administrations supported the countries' oppressive military regimes, a strategic position that made it impossible to grant asylum to those who fled their governments' brutality. William Leogrande, *Our Own Backyard: The United States in Central America, 1977–1992* (Chapel Hill: University of North Carolina Press, 1998); "Mass Atrocity Endings," World Peace Foundation, August 7, 2015, https://sites.tufts.edu/atrocityendings/2015/08/07/el-salvador.

2. In the workplace raids and mass deportations of the 1990s, many children of Central American refugees were deported. Those who had been a part of the emerging MS-13 and Barrio 18 maintained their LA connections. The result was a ready-made transnational network prepared to move drugs and people through the illicit jungle corridors used by the guerrilleros of the 1980s. Dudley, "Transnational Crime in Mexico and Central America." Alma Guillermoprieto, "The New Ganglands of El Salvador," *New York Review of Books*, October 10, 2011, https://www .nybooks.com/articles/2011/11/10/new-gangland-el-salvador.

3. On women's migration for domestic work as a family survival strategy, see Sassen, "Global Cities and Survival Circuits."

4. The word *coyote*, commonly used in Mexico and Central America, refers to a paid guide, hired to facilitate unauthorized migration into the US. The term—like the figure it refers to—carries dynamic and culturally nuanced meanings. David Spener, *Clandestine Crossings: Migrants and Coyotes on the Texas–Mexico Border* (Ithaca, NY: Cornell University Press, 2009).

5. Crossing the desert means risking death for unauthorized immigrants, and groups like Border Angels in San Diego and Humane Borders along the Sonoran desert section of the border are just two of several migrant aid organizations that have formalized since the last decade of the twentieth century.

6. Spener, *Clandestine Crossings*; Hondagneu-Sotelo, *Gendered Transitions*.

7. The term "transnational family" refers to families who maintain their family-based relationships and identities across national borders. Joanna Dreby demonstrates the strategies such families employ to maintain a sense of unity in *Divided by Borders: Mexican Migrants and Their Children* (Berkeley: University of California Press, 2010). See also Ernestine Ávila and Pierrette Hondagneu-Sotelo, "'I'm Here, but I'm There': The Meanings of Latina Transnational Motherhood," in *Women and Migration in the U.S.–Mexico Borderlands: A Reader*, ed. Denise Segura and Patricia Zevella (Durham, NC: Duke University Press, 2007); Rhacel Salazar Parreñas, *Children of Global Migration: Transnational Families and Gendered Woes* (Stanford, CA: Stanford University Press, 2005); Arlie Hochschild, "Love and Gold," in Ehrenreich and Hochschild, *Global Woman*; and Leah Schmalzbauer, "Searching for Wages and Mothering from Afar: The Case of Honduran Transnational Families," *Journal of Marriage and Family* 66 (2004): 1317–31.

8. In the 1970s, the Mexican government responded to a weakened economy by supporting large-scale agriculture at the expense of small-scale and subsistence farming, contributing to a broad social transformation in late-twentieth-century Mexico toward an increasingly urban industrial landscape and great legions of internal and external migrants. Hondagneu-Sotelo, *Gendered Transitions*; Segura and Zavella, "Introduction," *Women and Migration*.

9. The Catholic Church was deeply involved in Salvadoran, Guatemalan, and Nicaraguan conflicts in the 1980s, resulting in targeted violence. In March of 1980, Archbishop Oscar Romero was assassinated while saying mass. In December of that same year, four American churchwomen—three nuns from the Maryknoll order and one missionary—were kidnapped by the Salvadoran National Guard, raped, murdered, and abandoned just outside of the airport. The 1989 execution of six Jesuit priests in San Salvador, along with their housekeeper and her daughter, prompted the international community to intervene, resulting in the 1992 Chapultepec Peace Accords. "Archbishop Oscar Romero," Kellogg Institute for International Studies, https://kellogg.nd.edu/archbishop-oscar-romero#tab-1491.

10. The *maquila* industry can be understood as a stopgap solution to the deep and complex problem of regional poverty in a global economy. The industry emerged in the 1970s as a regional response to economic crisis. After the North American Free Trade Agreement came into effect in 1994, the industry spread from Central America to Mexico. With its singular focus on cheap labor, the *maquila* pays notoriously low wages, as low as fifty dollars a month in the 2000s. Vargas, "Impacto de las maquiladoras."

11. Barbara Ehrenreich and Arlie Hochschild, "Introduction"; Mary Romero, Valerie Preston, and Wenona Giles, "Care Work in a Globalizing World," in *When Care Work Goes Global: Locating the Social Relations of Domestic Work*, ed. Mary Romero, Valerie Preston, and Wenona Giles (Farnham: Ashgate, 2014); Dorsía Smith Silva, Laila Malik, and Abigail Palko, "Introduction," *Mothers, Mothering, and Globalization* (Toronto: Demeter Press, 2017).

12. Barbara Ehrenreich and Arlie Hochschild refer to this survival strategy as "the female underside of globalization," "Introduction," 3. On "the feminization of survival," see Sassen, "Global Cities and Survival Routes."

Chapter 2 Crossing Over

1. David Spener identifies a culture of *coyotaje* among border-crossers, a set of practices that negotiate changing border enforcement policies from within social relationships based on trust and familiarity. *Clandestine Crossings.*

2. IRCA called for increased employer accountability, a path to legal citizenship for 2.6 million unauthorized immigrants, and a substantial increase in appropriations and staffing for immigration enforcement. The act resulted in an increase of 750 percent in border security spending, from $1 billion to $4.9 billion by 2002, and increased the border enforcement staff from under 10,000 in the 1970s to over 40,000 by 2003. Muzaffar Chishti, Doris Meissner, and Claire Bergeron, "At Its 25th Anniversary, IRCA's Legacy Lives On," Migration Policy Institute, November 16, 2011, https://www.migrationpolicy.org/article/its-25th-anniversary-ircas-legacy -lives; David Dixon and Julia Gelatt, "Immigration Enforcement Spending Since IRCA," Migration Policy Institute, November 2005, https://www.migrationpolicy .org/research/immigration-enforcement-spending-irca; Melissa del Bosque, "Checkpoint Nation," *Texas Observer*, October 8, 2018, https://www.texasobserver.org/check point-nation.

3. The term "operation" was used as far back as 1954, when the Immigration and Naturalization Service (INS) executed the infamous Operation Wetback, in which they deported at least 300,000 people, American citizens among them. The operations of the 1990s created a 24/7 "wall" of border agents along the most heavily trafficked areas of the border. Hondagneu-Sotelo, *Gendered Transitions.*

4. When Sara crossed the border, a typical sum for a coyote-assisted migration from El Salvador to the United States would have been a few thousand dollars. By 2017, the rate had climbed to eight thousand. Juan Carlos Rivera, "Coyotes les cobran hasta $8,000 a los 'mojados,'" *La Prensa*, January 23, 2017, https://www.laprensa.hn /honduras/1037863-410/coyotes-les-cobran-hasta-8000-a-los-mojados. "*Pisos*" are a kind of commission, usually per head, that smugglers pay to criminal organizations encountered on the migrant trail. Dudley, "Transnational Crime in Mexico and Central America."

5. The Trump administration's 2018 "zero tolerance" policy, within the constraints of a Supreme Court ruling governing treatment of undocumented minors, resulted in the systematic separation of children and parents who arrived at the border as families. "The Trump Administration's 'Zero Tolerance' Immigration Enforcement Policy" Congressional Research Service, February 2, 2021, https://fas.org/sgp/crs /homesec/R45266.pdf.

6. Lina Newton traces the emergence of this narrative in the rhetoric of immi-

gration reform in the late 1980s and 1990s. She identifies a shift toward the construction of illegal immigrants as "an essentially deviant group of people" and the border as a "lawless land." *Illegal, Alien, or Immigrant: The Politics of Immigration Reform* (New York: New York University Press, 2008). A similar dynamic of association happened in 2003, when the newly created Department of Homeland Security took charge of immigration and customs activity, creating a structural link between immigration and security, such that the association between immigrants and criminals appeared natural. Episode 1 of *Homeland Insecurity*, RAICES, May 27, 2020, https://www.raicestexas.org/arts-and-culture/homeland-insecurity. In fact, the Marshall Project's detailed examination of the intersection of crime and immigration found no link between the two. Anna Flagg, "The Myth of the Criminal Immigrant," Marshall Project, March 30, 2018, https://www.themarshallproject.org/2018/03/30/the-myth-of-the-criminal-immigrant.

7. At the turn of the century, nearly half of all unauthorized immigrants—from Mexico, Central America, and the Caribbean, to Southeast Asia, the Philippines, and Africa—were visa overstayers. Legally, their crime is the same as those who cross the border in hiding, a misdemeanor offense prosecuted in civil court. "Modes of Entry for the Unauthorized Migrant Population," Pew Research Center, May 22, 2006, https://www.pewresearch.org/hispanic/2006/05/22/modes-of-entry-for-the-unauthorized-migrant-population. Laura Jarrett, "Are Undocumented Immigrants Committing a Crime? Not Necessarily," CNN, February 24, 2017, https://www.cnn.com/2017/02/24/politics/undocumented-immigrants-not-necessarily-criminal.

8. Mexico's economic crisis of the 1980s, beginning with a peso devaluation crisis in 1976, coincided with increased demand for low-wage construction and service work in the US, resulting in a dramatic increase in migration; this increase spurred the immigration reforms that would fortify the border in the 1990s.

9. Hondagneu-Sotelo, *Gendered Transitions*.

10. Rosa knows how to turn a phrase. Her original, "*Los más fregones, los más rateros.*"

11. The federal judicial police, *los judiciales*, were eliminated in 2002.

12. Américo Paredes, a mid-twentieth century South Texas folklorist, first studied the spirit of resistance inherent to the corrido—a poetic form born of the conflicts of a violent border imposed in the mid-nineteenth century across the heart of a culturally contiguous community. Américo Paredes, *With His Pistol in His Hand: A Border Ballad and Its Hero* (Austin: University of Texas Press, 1958).

13. "*Lo que sufrí lo he recuperado con creces / A los mojados les dedico mi canción.*" Los Tigres del Norte, "Tres veces mojado." My translation.

14. Though not technically a desert, the land around the South Texas–Tamaulipas border is rough terrain, populated with thorny mesquite and prickly pear and huisache, thirsty in dry seasons, and scorching in summer, with temperatures over 100 degrees. Spener, *Clandestine Crossings*, 70.

15. Christiane Harzig affirms that, in any migration system, "Stories of success outnumbering stories of failure and personal contacts are as vital to the maintenance of a migration system as are state policies and recruitment agencies that

facilitate movement." "Domestics of the World (Unite?): Labor Migration Systems and Personal Trajectories of Household Workers in Historical and Global Perspective," *Journal of American Ethnic History* 25, no. 2/3 (2006): 48–73, 50.

16. Luis Alberto Urrea, *The Devil's Highway* (New York: Bay Back Books, 2004).

17. Dudley, "Transnational Crime in Mexico and Central America"; Jacobo García, "La masacre de 72 migrantes que conmovió a Centroamérica, impune siete años después," *El País*, August 24, 2017, https://elpais.com/internacional/2017/08/23/mexico /1503503716_558953.html.

18. On preemptive birth control, see Guillermoprieto, "The New Ganglands"; Rebecca Cammisa, dir., *Which Way Home*, Documentress Films, 2009. On border patrol agent assaults, see Manny Fernández, "They Were Stopped at the Texas Border. Their Nightmare Had Only Just Begun," *New York Times*, November 12, 2018, https://www.nytimes.com/2018/11/12/us/rape-texas-border-immigrants-esteban -manzanares.html; Manny Fernández, "'You Have to Pay with Your Body': The Hidden Nightmare of Sexual Violence on the Border," *New York Times*, March 3, 2019, https://www.nytimes.com/2019/03/03/us/border-rapes-migrant-women.html; Chris Boyette and Emanuella Grinberg, "US Border Patrol Agent Accused of Sexual Assault," CNN.com, May 22, 2019, https://www.cnn.com/2019/05/22/us/arizona-border -patrol-agent-sexual-assault/index.html.

19. "Deaths by Border Patrol," Southern Border Communities Coalition, last updated March 10, 2021, https://www.southernborder.org/deaths_by_border_patrol. In addition to these reports of physical violence, the corruption within the US Customs and Border Protection agency is well documented since the department's inception in 2003. Experts say the situation is enabled by unorthodox background screening and a lack of structural accountability and historically worsens during hiring surges. Mia Steinle, "13 CBP Employees Arrested for Corruption this Administration," Project on Government Oversight, April 23, 2018, https://www.pogo.org/investigation /2018/04/13-cbp-employees-arrested-for-corruption-this-administration.

20. In this passage, former border patrol agent Francisco Cantú presents this violence within its complicated context, describing the strategy and ultimate mercy that motivates it. "But still," he writes, "I have nightmares." *The Line Becomes a River*, 33–34.

21. Urrea, *The Devil's Highway*, 16.

22. Jay Root and Todd Wiseman, *Beyond the Wall: A Texas Tribune Documentary on Immigration and Border Security*, *Texas Tribune*, March 29, 2017, https://www .texastribune.org/2017/03/29/beyond-wall-texas-tribune-documentary, 10:34–10:46.

23. Though her brother had gone before, all Pati's pronouns are feminine, in keeping with the unique vulnerability of women on the migrant trail.

24. The expanded "border zone" is a hundred-mile-wide strip of land that stretches along the northern side of the US–Mexico dividing line, within which Customs and Border Patrol operates official checkpoints that are exempt from the bounds of warrants or consent. Del Bosque, "Checkpoint Nation"; "The Constitution in the 100-Mile Border Zone," American Civil Liberties Union, https://www.aclu .org/other/constitution-100-mile-border-zone.

Part II: **The Flip Side**

1. ire'ne lara silva, "Cortando las nubes, or, Death Came on Horses," *Flesh to Bone* (San Francisco: Aunt Lute Books, 2013), 51.

2. Arlie Hochschild defines the global care chain as a "series of personal links between people across the globe, based on the paid or unpaid work of caring." In her 2001 piece, "Love and Gold," she writes of the ways in which this global chain of care becomes a "care drain" as the quality and quantity of care is diminished at each link in the global chain. Arlie Hochschild "Global Care Chains and Emotional Surplus Value," in *On the Edge: Living with Global Capitalism*, ed. Will Hutton and Anthony Giddens (London: Jonathan Cape, 2000), 130–46.

3. Wendy Chavkin observes a fragmentation of mothering in this period, in which carework and reproduction has become increasingly outsourced to the third world in the form of nannies, surrogates, and adopted children. As a result of this shift, the social role of mother is elevated in value while the biological and caretaking functions of motherhood are devalued. Wendy Chavkin "The Globalization of Motherhood," in *The Globalization of Motherhood: Deconstructions and Reconstructions of Biology and Care*, ed. Wendy Chavkin and Jane Maree Maher (New York: Routledge, 2010), 3–15.

4. For a fuller discussion of the phenomenon of the global care deficit, see Chavkin, "Globalization"; Hochschild and Ehrenreich, "Introduction"; and Salazar Parreñas, *Children of Globalization*.

Chapter 3 **The Nature of the Job**

1. US-granted Temporary Protected Status began when Hurricane Mitch struck Central America in October 1998, prompting an international response that included a stay of deportation for many Honduran and Nicaraguan immigrants living in the US. TPS was granted to Salvadorans in 2001 following a series of earthquakes and other weather events and to Haitians in the aftermath of a devastating 2010 earthquake. As of this writing, the TPS status of immigrants from Nicaragua, Honduras, and El Salvador is uncertain. Cohn et al., "Many Immigrants"; "Temporary Protected Status"; Gabriel Lesser and Jeanne Batalova, "Central American Immigrants in the United States," Migration Policy Institute, August 15, 2019, https://www.migrationpolicy.org/article/central-american-immigrants-united-states-2017; Jill H. Wilson, "Temporary Protected Status and Deferred Enforced Departure" Congressional Research Service, last updated August 9, 2021, https://sgp.fas.org/crs/homesec/RS20844.pdf.

2. The Nicaraguan Adjustment and Central American Relief Act (NACARA), passed on November 19, 1997, suspended deportation for approved immigrants from Guatemala, El Salvador, and some former Soviet-bloc countries who had entered the country before 1990. "Nicaraguan Adjustment and Central American Relief Act," *Immigration History*, University of Texas at Austin, 2019, https://immigrationhistory

.org/item/nicaraguan-adjustment-and-central-american-relief-act. Sarah Gammage, "El Salvador: Despite End to Civil War, Emigration Continues," Migration Policy Institute, July 26, 2007, https://www.migrationpolicy.org/article/el-salvador-despite-end-civil-war-emigration-continues.

3. Outside of the US, in places like the UAE and Taiwan, the line between poor working conditions and outright abuse often dissolves on an institutional level, leaving the welfare of vulnerable women up to the will and whims of an employer. Rhacel Salazar Parreñas, "Labor Regimes of Indenture: A Global Perspective on Migrant Domestic Work," lecture, Rice University Chao Center for Asian Studies, April 10, 2019; Joy M. Zarembka, "America's Dirty Work: Migrant Maids and Modern-Day Slavery," in Ehrenreich and Hochschild, *Global Woman*, 142–53.

4. An extensive survey conducted by the National Domestic Workers Alliance documented abuses ranging from verbal to physical and sexual. The most common reasons given for avoiding explicit resistance were the fear of jeopardizing current and future job opportunities and the fear that results from immigration status. National Domestic Workers Alliance, *Home Economics: The Invisible and Unregulated World of Domestic Work* (NDWA, 2012), 33–34, https://www.domesticworkers.org/wp-content/uploads/2021/06/HomeEconomicsReport.pdf.

5. In 2018, 234,000 cases of labor trafficking were reported in Texas alone, "Houston, We Have a Problem: The Scourge of Human Trafficking," Texas Medical Center, December 17, 2019, https://www.tmc.edu/news/2019/12/houston-we-have-a-problem-the-scourge-of-human-trafficking. For an overview of the problem of labor trafficking in the US, "Labor Trafficking of Domestic Workers at a Glance," Polaris Project, 2011, https://humantraffickinghotline.org/sites/default/files/Labor%20Trafficking%20of%20Domestic%20Workers%20-%20At-A-Glance.pdf. Joy Zarembka studies the prevalence of labor trafficking among foreign-born domestics brought in on diplomatic and other visas as imported household servants, "America's Dirty Work." Globally, estimates of victims of forced labor run as high as 12.3 million, 2.5 million as a result of trafficking, Romero et al., "Care Work in a Globalizing World," 12–13.

6. *Muchacha* is a common term for girls or young women. Its use as a familiar Latin American term for the domestic servant parallels the practice of calling African American and West Indian housekeepers "girl" regardless of their age.

7. Options can be more limited outside of the US where structured migrant worker programs limit a worker's mobility by linking her legal migration status exclusively to her employer, as is the case in the UAE, or setting a standard period during which the domestic must work for her employers before applying for residency, as is the case within Canada. On the "Wild West," see interview with Ai-jen Poo, "'You're Mostly Isolated and Alone': Why Some Domestic Workers Are Vulnerable to Exploitation," *PBS Newshour Weekend*, August 12, 2018, https://www.pbs.org/newshour/nation/ai-jen-poo-domestic-workers-exploitation.

8. Pierrette Hondagneu-Sotelo, *Doméstica: Immigrant Workers Cleaning and Caring in the Shadows of Affluence* (Berkeley: University of California Press, 2001).

Mary Romero's 1992 study of Chicana domestics in Denver reveals a marked preference for day work. *Maid in the USA* (New York: Routledge, 1992). Among West Indian nannies in the northeast, the same live-in to live-out trajectory exists, but a path to legal residency and different backgrounds allow many women eventually to move out of carework altogether. Shellee Colen, "'Just a Little Respect': West Indian Domestic Workers in New York City," in *Muchachas No More: Household Workers in Latin America and the Caribbean*, ed. Elsa Chaney and Mary García Castro (Philadelphia: Temple University Press, 1989); Tamara Mose Brown, *Raising Brooklyn: Nannies, Childcare, and Caribbeans Creating Community* (New York: New York University Press, 2011).

9. In Sara's home country of El Salvador, the teenage pregnancy rate is nearly twice that of the US, and very young pregnancies are common enough to merit their own statistic: in 2015, three out of every thousand births were to girls aged fourteen or younger, *Mapa de embarazos en niñas y adolescentes en El Salvador 2015*, Fondo de Población de las Naciones Unidas (FPNU) El Salvador, July 2016, https://issuu.com /lpglaprensagrafica/docs/mapa_embarazos2015_4web-1/2. Particularly in rural areas, poverty, limited education, and extremely patriarchal conservative values combine to make very early pregnancy and child brides common; activists and human rights organizations cite the familiar case of a child as young as twelve being forced to marry her rapist by families driven by poverty and the social weight of family honor. Anastasia Moloney, "In El Salvador, Girls Under 12 Most at Risk of Getting Pregnant by Rape: U.N. Study," Reuters, November 24, 2016, https://www.reuters.com/article /us-el-salvador-girls-rape/in-el-salvador-girls-under-12-most-at-risk-of-getting -pregnant-by-rape-u-n-study-idUSKBN13J1RJ.

10. Judith Rollins describes the traditional maternalism of the mistress–maid relationship in her 1985 study of African American domestic workers, *Between Women: Domestics and Their Employers* (Philadelphia: Temple University Press, 1985). Romero advocates for a strictly business-like relationship in her study of Chicanas, *Maid in the USA*. Hondagneu-Sotelo's work with Latina domestics in Los Angeles, however, finds a marked desire for a kind of personal relationship that avoids the patronizing and deference implicit in maternalism. Hondagneu-Sotelo, *Doméstica*. Colen finds that the West Indian caregivers she interviews in New York are most concerned with social demonstrations of respect, an important part of their cultures. Colen, "'Just a Little Respect.'"

11. An important part of this legacy is the damaging mammy stereotype associated with African American women in the US. On this and other maternal stereotypes associated with black women, see Patricia Hill Collins, "The Meaning of Motherhood in Black Culture and Mother–Daughter Relationships," in *Maternal Theory: Essential Readings*, ed. Andrea O'Reilly (Toronto: Demeter Press, 2007), 274–89. See also Rollins, *Between Women*; and Brown, *Raising Brooklyn*.

12. The experience of the mistress–maid relationship as a kind of "love affair" isn't unique to Sara. In her work exploring contemporary motherhood, Katie B. Garner has found that employers, too, often describe their relationships with their domestic

worker employees in these terms: "So many women I talked to framed their relationship with the nannies who worked for them in terms of a romantic relationship." Personal correspondence, June 2019. See also Katie B. Garner, "Mirroring a Mother's Love: A Chodorowian Analysis of the Complicated Relationship Between Mothers and Nannies," in *Nancy Chodorow and the Reproduction of Mothering*, ed. Petra Bueskens (London: Palgrave Macmillan, 2021).

13. The anxiety of the period found an equally fertile mark in the demonization of black mothers, using the image of the undeserving "welfare mom" to cast judgment on all but a certain kind of mother—white, middle-class, heterosexual, and married. Molly Ladd-Taylor, "Mother-Worship/Mother-Blame: Politics and Welfare in an Uncertain Age," in *Maternal Theory: Essential Readings*, ed. Andrea O'Reilly (Toronto: Demeter Press, 2007), 660–67.

14. Francisco Ayala, *Oppenheimer* (Mexico: Fondo de Cultura Económica, 1942).

15. Global migrants are rarely the poorest of the poor. It takes resources to arrange migration, both authorized and unauthorized. Scholars have traced the phenomenon among Filipina careworkers and West Indian nannies and domestics. Both of these groups are characterized by women with middle-class and professional backgrounds, pulled to migrate by domestic service wages that surpass professional pay at home. Rhacel Salazar Parreñas, *Servants of Globalization: Women, Migration and Domestic Work* (Stanford, CA: Stanford University Press, 2001); Colen, "'Just a Little Respect'"; Brown, *Raising Brooklyn*.

16. Immigrant church networks offer more than job references. Increasingly, Mexican and Central American immigrants have turned toward evangelical communities to address a broad range of needs, spiritual and material, another survival strategy in response to life in the shadows. "The Shifting Religious Identity of Latinos in the United States," Pew Research Center, May 7, 2014, https://www.pewforum.org/2014/05/07/the-shifting-religious-identity-of-latinos-in-the-united-states.

17. On the role of employer and employee networks, see Romero, *Maid in the USA*, Romero et al., "Care Work in a Globalizing World," Hondagneau-Sotelo, *Doméstica*, and Brown, *Raising Brooklyn*. Some employers report experiencing significant pushback for offering benefits like paid vacations or paying more than the going rate, Hondagneu-Sotelo, *Doméstica*, 84. In the twenty-first-century shift to the gig economy, nanny broker services like Care.com have become important sources of industry regulation as well.

18. The wage theft Elena is referring to is as common among nannies and domestics as it is among day laborers and construction workers, and many advocacy groups work on behalf of unauthorized workers to recover back pay for wage theft. Houston's own Fe y Justicia workers' rights collective works to inform these men and others about the legal options for recovering lost wages. Tamara Rose Brown describes strategies used by the Domestic Workers Union (now the National Domestic Workers Alliance) in chapter 7 of *Raising Brooklyn*.

19. On the racialized domestic worker class in the United States, see Evelyn Nakano Glenn, "From Servitude to Service Work: Historical Continuities in the Racial

Division of Paid Reproductive Labor," *Signs* 18, no. 1 (1992): 1–43. On the role of government welfare policies in maintaining a class of women of color assigned to serve the needs of white middle- and upper-class women, see Grace Chang, "Undocumented Latinas: The New Employable Mother," in *Mothering: Ideology, Experience, and Agency*, ed. Evelyn Nakano Glenn and Grace Chang (New York: Routledge, 1994).

20. Class mobility, which can be understood as the relationship between earnings of parents and offspring, is higher in developed regions than in developing ones. However, according to an ongoing study by the Economic Policy Institute, the US ranks below several of its economic peers in actual opportunity for economic advancement from one generation to the next, especially among the poor and working class. Elise Gould, "US Lags Behind Peer Countries in Mobility," Economic Policy Institute, October 10, 2012, https://www.epi.org/publication/usa-lags-peer-countries -mobility.

21. These associations emerge from a tandem development of the nineteenth century "cult of domesticity" and a new domestic economy of consumption. Romero, *Maid in the USA*. On the language of consumption, see Hondagneu-Sotelo, *Dómestica*, xi, 12.

22. For a discussion of the economic pressures facing the American middle class, especially in terms of housing and childcare, see Alissa Quart, *Squeezed: Why Our Families Can't Afford America* (New York: Ecco, 2018).

23. The US Department of Health and Human Services considers childcare affordable if it costs 10 percent of a family's income or less. According to a 2016 report from the Organization for Economic Cooperation and Development, families in the US spend an average of 25.6 percent of the income for two-parent families, and 52.7 percent of a single parent's income. "The Cost of Childcare in Texas," Economic Policy Institute, last updated October 2020, https://www.epi.org/child-care-costs -in-the-united-states/#/TX; Jacqueline Howard, "The Costs of Childcare Around the World," CNN, April 25, 2018, https://www.cnn.com/2018/04/25/health/child-care -parenting-explainer-intl/index.html.

24. Of the thirty-four countries in the Organization for Economic Cooperation and Development, the US ranks near the bottom in early childhood education and is the only advanced economy that does not guarantee maternity leave for working mothers. Sara Mead, "Child Care Laggard," *U.S. News and World Report*, February 23, 2017, https://www.usnews.com/opinion/knowledge-bank/articles/2017-02-23/the-us -is-a-laggard-on-child-care.

25. The average workweek in the US extended considerably in the late twentieth century. Social structures that would support working parents, like subsidized childcare and paid family and medical leave, have failed to address this change. Ehrenreich and Hochschild, "Introduction," 8–9.

26. Despite these challenges, labor organizers have had increasing success among domestic workers. Most notably, the National Domestic Workers Alliance has been an important advocate and political voice for these women. In Houston, the Fe y Justicia Worker Center has worked specifically with domestic workers to inform local women of their rights and create a community of workers to advocate for themselves.

Brown details some of the success and the significant challenges to organizing among West Indian workers in New York, *Raising Brooklyn*.

27. This sentiment is echoed by others, like Sara, who laments "taking care of an American child is really hard. They're so careful about everything. Right now I work with a woman who is so careful that, I take the child to the park and he can't even get a scratch or she'll scream to high heaven."

28. The nanny's relationships with her charges and with her own children are shaped by the reciprocal influence of social class and cultural perceptions of childhood needs. Julia Wrigley discusses the importance of social class reproduction in the shifting nanny–employer dynamics of school-age children in *Other People's Children* (New York: Basic Books, 1995). Mary Romero notes that the children of domestic workers—like most working-class children—experience a shorter period of dependency than the children their mothers care for, in *The Maid's Daughter* (New York: New York University Press, 2011).

29. Domestic workers report negotiating for control over the work process and express an explicit preference for employers who avoid micromanaging. Romero, *Maid in the USA*; Hondagneu-Sotelo, *Doméstica*.

30. The term *machismo* (*machista* is the adjective) from the Spanish *macho*, for male, refers to a system of cultural values that elevates the masculine to the point of what may be understood as hypermasculinity. Machismo, like any cultural phenomenon, is as complex and varied as the individuals and communities it influences. For a variety of perspectives, see *Muy Macho: Latino Men Confront Their Manhood*, ed. Ray González (New York: Anchor Books, 1996). Octavio Paz explains the emergence of the mid-twentieth-century Mexican mentality in terms of its relationship to the indigenous mother, Malintzín/Malinche, a historical and mythologized figure who had been traditionally construed alternatively as a passive victim or a blameworthy traitor within the Madonna–whore paradigm, in his influential essay "Los hijos de la Malinche," *El laberinto de la soledad* (Mexico City: Cuadernos Americanos, 1947). This construction has since been revised by feminists; see for example Margo Glantz's feminist reading "Las hijas de la Malinche," *Debate Feminista* 3, no. 6 (1992): 161–79.

31. Confronted with the mothercoin's subordination of relationship to transaction, these nannies debate the relative benefit of moving away from authentic emotion and toward the performed feelings of emotional labor. Arlie Hochschild's theory of emotion management accounts for the effects and implications of unacknowledged emotional labor—an experience of inauthenticity capable of damaging a person's sense of self. *The Managed Heart: Commercialization of Human Feeling* (Berkeley: University of California Press, 1983).

32. The metaphor of the "global heart transplant" as one facet of the global care drain was coined by Arlie Hochschild, "Love and Gold." Sociologists have dedicated some careful attention to the left-behind children of transnational mothers, finding that experiences vary by age and community but that the status is broadly imbued with a sense of loss that is rarely fully recovered. Salazar Parreñas, *Children of Globalization*; Dreby, *Divided by Borders*.

33. Joan C. Tronto, "The 'Nanny' Question in Feminism," *Hypatia*, 17, no. 2, special issue: "Feminist Philosophies of Love and Work" (2002): 34–51. In her study of the intermingling of economic transaction and intimacy, Viviana Zelizer emphasizes the trust that informs intimate relationships like the ones between immigrant nannies and the families they work for. *The Purchase of Intimacy* (Princeton, NJ: Princeton University Press, 2005).

34. Hand in Hand, Domestic Employers Network, an initiative of NDWA, offers a wealth of resources for employers, including sample contracts and information about existing labor laws that apply to domestic workers, https://domesticemployers.org. For a discussion of measures that can be taken to improve the experience of domestic workers, see Hondagneu-Sotelo's *Doméstica*, "Inside the Job."

35. "Wages and the Fair Labor Standards Act," US Department of Labor, https://www.dol.gov/agencies/whd/flsa; Hondagneu-Sotelo, *Doméstica*, 212–15. Domestic workers were excluded from the first iteration of the FLSA in 1938, only gaining a right to standard wages and overtime pay in 1974. The occupation is still excluded from workplace safety protections under OSHA, as well as maternity and other family benefits promised by the Family and Medical Leave Act. Globally, only 10 percent of domestic workers have the same rights as other workers, and almost 30 percent are excluded from all labor code protections. Romero et al., "Care Work in a Globalizing World." On the distinction between independent contract labor and domestic employment, see "Nanny: Independent Contractor or Employee?" HomeWork Solutions, https://www.homeworksolutions.com/knowledge-center/nanny-independent-contractor. As of 2021, domestic workers earning at least $2,300 per year are classified as employees.

Chapter 4 Pregnant Complications

1. Sara would be referring to the Texas Health and Human Services office, which manages access to Medicaid and the Children's Health Insurance Program (CHIP).

2. In the context of abstract and descriptive colors, the Spanish word for *black* is *negro*; but when categorizing groups of people, *moreno* is more commonly used to refer to those of African descent. However, while social divisions along racial lines are ubiquitous in the Spanish-speaking world, for many Hispanics, the linguistic construct of white, Black, Latinx, etc., is a uniquely North American distinction.

3. Policy is very clear on this: only the child's immigration status is relevant to a child's application for CHIP. Despite this safeguard, the healthcare and legal systems are so labyrinthine and changing that misinformation and abuse abound, often compromising access for those who do have a right to state-funded health insurance under the law. This is particularly challenging for the million-plus children born in Texas to noncitizen parents. In fact, despite the CHIP program and others like it, citizen children with immigrant parents are far more likely to be uninsured in the US, and proposed changes to public-charge policies would decrease access significantly. Samantha Artiga and Anthony Damico, "Nearly 20 Million Children Live in

Immigrant Families That Could Be Affected by Evolving Immigration Policies," Kaiser Family Foundation, April 18, 2018, https://www.kff.org/disparities-policy/issue-brief /nearly-20-million-children-live-in-immigrant-families-that-could-be-affected -by-evolving-immigration-policies/; Anne Dunkelberg, *Immigrants' Access to Healthcare in Texas: An Updated Landscape* (Center for Public Policy Priorities, October 2016), https://everytexan.org/images/HW_2016_ImmigrantsAccess_FullReport.pdf.

4. Severance pay is included among legal protections in some Latin American countries and is a target of organizing in others. Merike Blofield, "Feudal Enclaves and Political Reforms: Domestic Workers in Latin America," *Latin American Research Review* 44, no. 1 (2009): 158–90.

5. Alissa Quart discusses contemporary pregnancy discrimination in the American workplace and demonstrates the interpretive limits that have diminished the power of the 1978 Pregnancy Discrimination Act. Quart, *Squeezed*, 15–17, 28–29.

6. Rosa sometimes contradicts herself—ages of children, timing of crossings. Still, it's her story I try to tell.

7. Alicia is from San Nicolás, a town in the state of Hidalgo near the city of Pachuca.

8. In all likelihood, these arrangements were worked out between the employers and the brothers, who would have addressed any of these kinds of questions. Thanks to Raquel Gaytán for this observation.

9. The *pulga*, or flea market, is a common source for the false documents some unauthorized workers use to procure a job. "They never check it," Alicia assures me.

10. Adrienne Rich devotes a good deal of space to maternal ambivalence in her groundbreaking contemplation of motherhood, *Of Woman Born*, a book-length analysis of all that is assumed to be natural of mothers.

11. Marla V. Anderson and M. D. Rutherford, "Evidence of a Nesting Psychology During Human Pregnancy," *Evolution and Human Behavior* 34, no. 6 (2013): 390–97, https://www.sciencedirect.com/science/article/pii/S1090513813000706.

12. Arlie Hochschild, *The Managed Heart*, 7; "Emotion Work, Feeling Rules, and Social Status," *American Journal of Sociology* 85, no. 3 (1979): 551–75. On the emotional labor required of the servant-as-confidante, see Rollins, *Between Women*. On the range of emotional labor performed among domestics, see Romero, *Maid in the USA* and *The Maid's Daughter*; and María de la Luz Ibarra, "Mexican Immigrant Women and the New Domestic Labor." Recently, the term "emotional labor" has been used to refer to the broader work that women often do, both to fulfill domestic and caring "women's work," as well as to fulfill their socially imposed gendered expectation to please—boss, children, partner, neighbor. Gemma Hartley, *Fed Up: Emotional Labor, Women, and the Way Forward* (New York: Harper One, 2018).

13. The concept of social reproduction emerges from a Marxist materialist framework and is sometimes extended beyond birthing and childrearing to education, healthcare, and other civil services. See Nakano Glenn, "From Servitude." Others have expanded the concept. Mary Romero's work demonstrates the process by which the children of employees and employers are socialized into society's hierarchies of

class, race, gender, and citizenship, thereby reproducing inequality and injustice. Viviana Zelizer perceives more than just "instrumental" value in social reproduction, identifying an "intrinsic" value in carework's ability to cultivate deeper understandings of culture, society, and morality. See Zelizer, *The Purchase of Intimacy*, 32.

14. Marilyn Waring, *Counting for Nothing: What Men Value and What Women Are Worth*, 2nd ed. (Toronto: University of Toronto Press, 1999); Nancy Folbre, *The Invisible Heart: Economics and Family Values* (New York: New Press, 2001).

Chapter 5   *Las Patronas*

1. Throughout Latin America in the late twentieth century, "one-fifth to one-third of the female labor force [was] occupied in domestic service," Elsa Chaney and Maria Garcia Castro, "Introduction," *Muchachas No More: Household Workers in Latin American and the Caribbean*, ed. Elsa Chaney and Maria Garcia Castro (Philadelphia: Temple University Press, 1989), 3. Magdalena León considers the Colombian "*empleada*" of the late twentieth century to be working "with the very same ideology of service to others" as the *ama de casa*, or housewife. See León, "Domestic Labor and Domestic Service in Colombia," in *Muchachas No More*, 324–49. See Alfonso Cuarón's 2018 film *Roma* for an elegant portrayal of the life of a domestic servant in a middle-class neighborhood in Mexico City.

2. In Houston, the average cost of living in 2019 was $1,918.94 a month, making Diana's salary enough to live modestly in the city. Tim Gallen and Olivia Pulsinelli, "How Houston's Cost of Living Compares to the Biggest US Cities," *Houston Business Journal*, August 27, 2019, https://www.bizjournals.com/houston/news/2019/08/27/how-houstons-cost-of-living-compares-to-the.html; Move.org, https://www.move.org/lowest-cost-of-living-by-us-city. By comparison, the Houston Independent School District offered a starting salary of almost $55,000 to first-year teachers in 2019.

3. Ann Crittenden traces the story of the American housewife's erasure from the public economy in *The Price of Motherhood: Why the Most Important Job in the World Is Still the Least Valued* (New York: Metropolitan Books, 2001). Mary Romero also describes the evolution of the housewife's role, noting the moves from producer to consumer to supervisor, a trajectory that transformed domestic service from skilled, task-based work into unskilled labor, diffuse and paid by the hour. See Romero, *Maid in the USA*.

4. Ann Crittenden, *The Price of Motherhood*, chapters 3 and 4, "How Mother's Work Was Disappeared," and "The Truly Invisible Hand."

5. Ann Crittenden, *The Price of Motherhood*, 63.

6. Prominent economists have developed models that include unpaid labor in the measurement of an economy's health. See Folbre, *Invisible Heart*, and Marylin Waring's foundational study of the economic value of labor and resources that are not counted among goods bought and sold, *Counting for Nothing*.

7. On discrimination of mothers in the workplace, Claire Cain Miller notes, "college-educated women make about 90 percent as much as men at age 25 and about

55 percent as much at age 45." Cain Miller, "The Gender Pay Gap Is Largely Because of Motherhood," *New York Times*, May 13, 2017, https://www.nytimes.com/2017/05/13/upshot/the-gender-pay-gap-is-largely-because-of-motherhood.html. On the use of welfare and immigration policy to maintain a servant class, see Romero, *The Maid's Daughter*, and Grace Chang, *Disposable Domestics: Immigrant Women Workers in the Global Economy* (Cambridge, MA: South End Press, 2000).

8. Jenny's school district allows employers no more than ten days of paid leave per year for all needs—illness, family emergencies, dentist appointments, or the demands of an infant and a postpartum body. The federal Family and Medical Leave Act of 1993 provides for protection from firing for up to twelve weeks after the birth or adoption of a child, but it fails to stipulate any continued pay. "Family and Medical Leave Act," US Department of Labor, https://www.dol.gov/agencies/whd/fmla.

9. On the role of trust in hiring practices among employers of domestic and careworkers, see Hondagneu-Sotelo, *Doméstica*, chapter 3.

10. On the dual problems of quality and affordability in the US childcare system, see Quartz, *Squeezed*. On the relative cost of childcare in the US, see "The Cost of Childcare in Texas," and Howard, "The Costs of Childcare." For an excellent discussion of the US childcare system, see Gloria Riviera's 2021 podcast *No One Is Coming to Save Us* (Lemonada Media).

11. Mead, "The US Is a Laggard on Child Care."

12. Nonetheless, women and their advocates in the US have long challenged patriarchal control of their sexuality beyond the contexts of just abortion and birth control. From protests against the racist and ableist forced sterilization of women, to contemporary advocacy for accessible pap smears and breastfeeding friendly workplaces and public spaces, women understand that reproductive rights encompass a spectrum of experiences. On the pitfalls of "choice" as a discursive strategy for reproductive rights, See Rickie Solinger, *Beggars and Choosers: How the Politics of Choice Shapes Adoption, Abortion, and Welfare in the United States* (New York: Hill and Wang, 2001); and Ladd-Taylor, "Mother-Worship/Mother-Blame."

13. On forced sterilization, see Lisa Ko, "Unwanted Sterilization and Eugenics Programs in the United States," PBS.org, January 29, 2016, https://www.pbs.org/independentlens/blog/unwanted-sterilization-and-eugenics-programs-in-the-united-states/; and Rich, *Of Woman Born*, "Introduction."

14. Black women's relationship to welfare in this country is the story of two extremes: on one end, a reality of discrimination and barred access and on the other, the hateful rhetoric of indolent "welfare queens." On the welfare rights movement of the 1970s, see Premilla Nadasen, *Rethinking The Welfare Rights Movement* (New York: Routledge, 2012). On the dynamic that secures poor women of color for domestic and service work, see Chang, "Undocumented Latinas." On the discursive and institutional construction of the "good" mother as class and race-based, see Ladd-Taylor, "Mother-Worship/Mother-Blame."

15. While feminism has generally relegated motherhood to an aside, a substantial tradition of writing on the topic provides a robust framework for thinking about

maternity. On the scholarly field of motherhood studies, see Samira Kawash, "New Directions in Motherhood Studies," *Signs* 36, no. 4 (2011): 969–1003. See also work done by Andrea O'Reilly at Demeter Press and its partners, the *Journal of the Motherhood Initiative* and IAMAS—International Association of Maternal Action and Scholarship. In popular culture, a constant stream of books, including the recent *All the Rage: Mothers, Fathers, and the Myth of Equal Partnership* by Darcy Lockman (New York: Harper Collins, 2019), sound the call for more support for mothers. Joan Blades and Kristin Rowe-Finkbeiner's *The Motherhood Manifesto: What America's Moms Want—And What to Do About It* (New York: Nation Books, 2006) has moved from book to documentary to movement; https://www.momsrising.org.

16. Cynthia Hess, Tanima Ahmed, and Jeff Hayes, "Providing Unpaid Household and Care Work in the United States: Uncovering Inequality," Institute for Women's Policy Research, January 2020, https://iwpr.org/wp-content/uploads/2020/01/IWPR-Providing-Unpaid-Household-and-Care-Work-in-the-United-States-Uncovering-Inequality.pdf; Romero et al., "Care Work in a Globalizing World."

17. Sharon Hays develops the concept of "intensive mothering" in *The Cultural Contradictions of Motherhood* (New Haven, CT: Yale University Press, 1996), in which she describes a parenting style that is child-centered and emotionally, physically, and financially draining. Judith Warner's best-selling *Perfect Madness: Motherhood in an Age of Anxiety* (New York: Riverhead Books, 2005) also addresses the phenomenon. See also Anna Kuroczycka Schultes, "Mothering Woes: 'Mothering' and the Mother–Au Pair Relationship," in *An Anthropology of Mothering*, ed. Michelle Walks and Naomi McPherson (Toronto: Demeter Press, 2011), 266–77.

18. Others have noted the particular irony in hiring domestic and careworkers for the sake of a woman's freedom: the maintenance of patriarchal power structure is recreated within the work relationships. Romero, *The Maid's Daughter*; Tronto, "The Nanny Question."

Part III **Value Proposition**

1. Gloria Anzaldúa, *Borderlands/La Frontera: The New Mestiza* (San Francisco: Aunt Lute Books, 1987), 108.

2. The history of African American women in domestic service includes a legacy of slavery in the south, post-emancipation recruitment in the north, and a late mid-century decline such that the one third of all African American women in the industry in the 1920s had dropped to only 5 percent by 1980. In the southwest, Chicana girls were tracked into domestic service by school training and government work programs that framed their labor as a valuable education in American values. Romero, *Maid in the USA*. For a historical overview of race and domestic service in the US, see Nakano Glenn, "From Servitude."

3. On "employable mothers," see Chang, "Undocumented Latinas." On "welfare queens," see Ladd-Taylor, "Mother-Worship." On "anchor babies," see Newton, *Illegal*.

4. Hill Collins describes an African American mothering ideal organized around a community of *othermothers*—"women who assist bloodmothers by sharing mothering responsibilities" and who take collective responsibility for social reproduction. "The Meaning of Motherhood," 278. See also Dani McClain, *We Live for the We: The Political Power of Black Motherhood* (New York: Bold Type Books, 2019). Denise Segura finds that Mexican immigrant women bring with them a sense of pride in their breadwinning roles as mothers, a value that only turns to ambivalence when it is filtered through American cultural values in their American-born daughters. Segura, "Working at Motherhood." See also *Latina/Chicana Mothering*, ed. Dorsía Smith Silva (Toronto: Demeter Press, 2011).

Chapter 6: *Los Niños*

1. According to girlsnotbrides.org, 26 percent of girls in El Salvador are married before eighteen, 6 percent under fifteen. "El Salvador," Girls Not Brides, https://atlas .girlsnotbrides.org/map/el-salvador, accessed April 1, 2021.

2. The Immigration Reform and Control Act (IRCA) passed in 1986; the Nicaraguan Adjustment and Central American Relief Act (NACARA) passed in 1997.

3. "*Mojado*," meaning "wetback," is a pejorative term that refers to those who cross the border through the waters of the Rio Grande.

4. Care ethics is a moral philosophy in which the moral nature of caring practices is understood via "nuanced narratives" that acknowledge principles of rights and justice while prioritizing relationship. Its implications are not limited to close, personal relationships, but extend to broader social structures and global contexts. Virginia Held, *The Ethics of Care: Personal, Political, and Global* (Oxford: Oxford University Press, 2006); Tronto, "The Nanny Question." Eva Feder Kittay translates these ideas eloquently to the language of human rights in "The Moral Harm of Migrant Carework: Realizing a Global Right to Care," *Philosophical Topics* 37, no. 2 (Fall 2009): 53–73.

5. Interactions like these perpetuate a social system structured around the relative privileges of gender, race, social class, and citizenship. To learn that the Hispanic maid can be disrespected without serious consequence is to learn about one's place relative to all poor Hispanic women. Mary Romero reveals the mechanisms of this kind of social reproduction among the children of employers and domestic employees, with particular emphasis on rituals of deference that serve to reinforce a child's perception of everyone's place in society, in *The Maid's Daughter*.

6. Since the DREAM Act was first proposed in 2001, the changing political landscape around immigration reform has resulted in several versions of the bill, the most recent being a 2019 proposal reinvigorated in the wake of the tumultuous back-and-forth over Obama's 2012 DACA order that Trump tried to end and Biden has tried to protect. These measures seek to lend legitimacy to children brought to the country illegally, allowing them the chance to study, work, or serve in the armed forces, and to pursue a path to citizenship. The Migration Policy Institute estimates

that this legislation would affect up to 2.3 million people. "The DREAM Act, DACA, and Other Policies Designed to Protect Dreamers," American Immigration Council, September 3, 2019, https://www.americanimmigrationcouncil.org/research/drea m-act-daca-and-other-policies-designed-protect-dreamers. For a personal narrative, see Jose Antonio Vargas, *Dear America: Notes of an Undocumented Citizen* (New York: Harper Collins, 2018).

7. Studies have documented negative effects of immigration-related fear on the health and development of children in immigrant communities. Samantha Artiga and Petry Ubri, "Living in an Immigrant Family in America: How Fear and Toxic Stress Are Affecting Daily Life, Well-Being, and Health," Kaiser Family Foundation, December 13, 2017, https://www.kff.org/disparities-policy/issue-brief/living-in-an -immigrant-family-in-america-how-fear-and-toxic-stress-are-affecting-daily-life -well-being-health; Wendy Cervantes, Rebecca Ullrich, and Hannah Matthews, "Our Children's Fear: Immigration Policy's Effects on Young Children," Center for Law and Social Policy (CLASP), March 2018, https://eric.ed.gov/?id=ED582818; Artiga and Damico, "Nearly 20 Million Children." In addition to the damage done by the emotion itself, fear of apprehension can keep immigrant families from schools and hospitals, as it did in the wake of Trump's 2017 policy changes and posturing. Monica Rhor, "Trump's Immigrant Crackdown Brings 'Blanket of Fear' to Houston Schools," *Houston Chronicle*, December 21, 2017, https://www.houstonchronicle.com /news/houston-texas/houston/article/Trump-s-immigrant-crackdown-brings -blanket-of-12442229.php.

8. Workplace raids have historically been the blunt instrument of US immigration enforcement. Researchers have found direct links between fear of deportation and the physical and emotional health of immigrant communities, both documented and undocumented. Karen Hacker et al., "The Impact of Immigration and Customs Enforcement on Immigrant Health: Perceptions of Immigrants in Everett, Massachusetts, USA," *Social Science & Medicine* 73, no. 4 (2011): 586–94, https://www .sciencedirect.com/science/article/pii/S0277953611003522?via%3Dihub. Jorge Ramos details the costs in resources and fear caused by immigration raids in "The Invisibles," the first chapter of his *A Country for All: An Immigrant Manifesto* (New York: Vintage Books, 2010). During the Trump administration, raids were one of many strategies to ratchet up a kind of pervasive fear designed to be its own blunt instrument of deterrence. Michelle Mittelstad, "Shaping a Narrative of 'Crisis' at Border, Trump Administration Takes Muscular Action," Migration Policy Institute, December 19, 2018, https://www.migrationpolicy.org/article/top-10-2018-issue-3-border-crisis -narrative-trump-administration-action. Ruben Vives, "'I Left My Tacos on the Table and Took Off Running': Immigrants Remember the Workplace Raids of the 1980s," *Los Angeles Times*, January 9, 2017, https://www.latimes.com/local/california/la-me -immigration-trump-fears-20170109-story.html.

9. Rather than increase deportations, the Obama administration shifted strategy to narrowly focused priorities: formal removal for recent border crossers and targeted removal of unauthorized immigrants with a criminal record. As a result,

border apprehensions and removals increased while deportations of noncitizens already living in the US dropped sharply. Muzaffar Chishti, Sarah Pierce, and Jessica Bolter, "The Obama Record on Deportations: Deporter in Chief or Not?," Migration Policy Institute, January 26, 2017, https://www.migrationpolicy.org/article/obama-record-deportations-deporter-chief-or-not.

10. Sarah Pierce, "Immigration-Related Policy Changes in the First Two Years of the Trump Administration," Migration Policy Institute, May 2019, https://www.migrationpolicy.org/research/immigration-policy-changes-two-years-trump-administration. Mittelstad, "Shaping a Narrative of 'Crisis.'"

11. Under the Department of Homeland Security (DHS), created in 2002, Immigration and Customs Enforcement (ICE) enforces immigration policies in the interior while US Customs and Border Protection (CBP) patrols the border.

12. Policy analysts confirm that this activity emerges from an "explicit, targeted policy" designed to elicit generalized anxiety in immigrant communities. Randy Capps, Muzaffar Chishti, Julia Gelatt, Jessica Bolter, and Ariel G. Ruiz Soto, "Revving Up the Deportation Machinery: Enforcement under Trump and the Pushback," Migration Policy Institute, May 2018, https://www.migrationpolicy.org/research/revving-deportation-machinery-under-trump-and-pushback.

13. A teacher in a 2018 study remembers a four-year-old girl in her class who was afraid that Trump would send her mother back to Mexico. The teacher explains, "Her mother is not even from Mexico." Cervantes et al., "Our Children's Fear." Monica Rhor tells stories of children gripped in fear at the start of Trump's presidency: a seventh-grader sits motionless, terrified that ICE agents will pull him out of his classroom; a fifth-grader, fearful of her parents' deportation, asks her teacher for a shovel to dig up savings in the backyard. Rhor, "Trump's Immigrant Crackdown."

14. A February 2017 memorandum from the Secretary of the DHS to authorities in CPB, ICE, and Office of Refugee Resettlement (ORR), drafted in response to Trump's January 17 executive order, outlines this new policy, "Memorandum," US Department of Homeland Security, February 20, 2017, https://www.dhs.gov/sites/default/files/publications/17_0220_S1_Implementing-the-Presidents-Border-Security-Immigration-Enforcement-Improvement-Policies.pdf. The memo responds to Trump's January 2017 executive order, "Presidential Executive Order 13767: Border Security and Immigration Enforcement Improvements," US Department of Homeland Security, January 25, 2017, https://www.dhs.gov/publication/executive-order-13767.

15. The Flores Agreement of 1997 resulted from the case of a fifteen-year-old girl held indefinitely in unsafe conditions in a San Diego detention center. The agreement required that immigrant children detained at the border be held no longer than twenty days; that they be released into the custody of a parent, relative, or suitable guardian; and that the conditions of their detention fulfill basic requirements of child welfare. In 2015, amid a sustained surge in the numbers of unaccompanied minors arriving at the border, the Obama administration petitioned unsuccessfully for an exemption from the time constraints of the agreement. During the Trump administration, the agreement became the target of sustained administrative attacks in the

wake of the administration's zero tolerance policy. "The History of the Flores Settlement and Its Effects on Immigration," National Public Radio, June 22, 2018, https://www.npr.org/2018/06/22/622678753/the-history-of-the-flores-settlement-and-its-effects-on-immigration.

16. Investigations into these holding centers and long-term shelters have revealed cases of neglect and abuse. The long-term health consequences of the system manifest regardless. Medical and sociological researchers have published ample evidence that indefinite detention and separation result in increased depression, anxiety, and suicidal thoughts among mothers and children as well as significant psychological and developmental harm. Michael Garcia Bochenek, "Trump's Order Changes One Harmful Approach for Another," Human Rights Watch, June 21, 2018, https://www.hrw.org/news/2018/06/21/trumps-order-changes-one-harmful-approach-another; Rachel Kronick, Cécile Rousseau, and Janet Cleveland, "Asylum-Seeking Children's Experiences of Detention in Canada: A Qualitative Study," American Journal of Orthopsychiatry 85, no. 3, May 2015, https://doi.org/10.1037/ort0000061; Sara Mares, "Fifteen Years of Detaining Children Who Seek Asylum in Australia—Evidence and Consequences," Australasian Psychiatry, December 8, 2015, https://doi.org/10.1177/1039856215620029.

17. Former USCIS mission statement: "USCIS secures America's promise as a nation of immigrants by providing accurate and useful information to our customers, granting immigration and citizenship benefits, promoting an awareness and understanding of citizenship, and ensuring the integrity of our immigration system." Current USCIS mission statement, as of February 2018: "U.S. Citizenship and Immigration Services administers the nation's lawful immigration system, safeguarding its integrity and promise by efficiently and fairly adjudicating requests for immigration benefits while protecting Americans, securing the homeland, and honoring our values" (https://www.uscis.gov/about-us).

18. "Family Separation by the Numbers," ACLU, https://www.aclu.org/issues/immigrants-rights/immigrants-rights-and-detention/family-separation, accessed June 6, 2020; Miriam Jordan and Caitlin Dickerson, "More Than 450 Migrant Parents May Have Been Deported Without Their Children," New York Times, July 24, 2018, https://www.nytimes.com/2018/07/24/us/migrant-parents-deported-children.html. As of November 2018, the ORR held over 14,000 migrant children. Tal Kopan, "More Than 14,000 Immigrant Children Are in U.S. Custody, an All-Time High," San Francisco Chronicle, November 16, 2018, https://www.sfchronicle.com/nation/article/More-than-14-000-immigrant-children-are-in-U-S-13399510.php.

19. Sonia Nazario, Enrique's Journey: A Six-Part Times Series, Los Angeles Times, 2002, "Chapter Two: Badly Beaten, a Boy Seeks Mercy in a Rail-Side Town," September 30, 2002, https://www.latimes.com/nation/immigration/la-fg-enriques-journey-chapter-two-mainbar-story.html; "Chapter 6: At Journey's End, a Dark River, Perhaps a New Life," October 7, 2003, https://www.latimes.com/nation/immigration/la-fg-enriques-journey-chapter-six-mainbar-story.html. Nazario also published a

book-length version of the story, *Enrique's Journey: The Story of a Boy's Dangerous Odyssey to Reunite with his Mother* (New York: Random House, 2006).

20. Joanna Dreby, "Children and Power in Mexican Transnational Families," *Journal of Marriage and Family* 69, no. 4 (2007): 1050–64; Salazar Parreñas, *Children of Global Migration*.

21. Julia Wrigley discusses the deliberations parents make regarding the relative advantages of hiring childcare providers with social class backgrounds more similar to their own in *Other People's Children*.

22. Barbara Ehrenreich and Arlie Hochschild, *Global Woman*, "Introduction," 12. Mary Romero's research with the children of domestic workers reveals the profound lessons in value that these children learn—that care is a commodity to be consumed, and that certain kinds of parenting are the privilege of certain kinds of people in *The Maid's Daughter*.

23. Joanna Dreby, *Divided* and "Children and Power in Mexican Transnational Families," Salazar Parreñas, *Children of Globalization*; Romero, *The Maid's Daughter*.

24. Held, *The Ethics of Care*, 108–9.

25. Viviana Zelizer argues that the inevitable intermingling of intimacy and transaction in our "connected lives" generates constant relational work designed to draw moral boundaries around the meeting place of love and money in *The Purchase of Intimacy*.

Chapter 7 **Love and Labor**

1. Drew's elementary school reflected a broader Hispanic community in Houston that has in some ways converged with a Mexican identity cut off from its affiliation with nation, associated over time with a working-class, racialized identity, such that "Mexican" has less to do with nationality than with a particular social experience in the US.

2. Rhacel Salazar Parreñas studies gender in transnational families, tracing the tension between women's increased freedom to redefine gender roles and the strong pushback they receive from communities who try to keep them in their traditional roles. She finds that all members of transnational families and communities—including the mothers themselves—believe that a mother's obligation to manage the emotional and logistical needs of their children's daily lives follows her in migration, drawing her emotionally and psychologically back, even as the away-father carries only the responsibility to send remittances home. See Salazar Parreñas, *Children of Globalization*.

3. Our "moral personhood" is firmly rooted in our relationships, regardless of the autonomy with which we enter into them. Held, *The Ethics of Care*, 45. Diana Tietjens Meyers, "Narrative and Moral Life," in *Setting the Moral Compass*, ed. Cheshire Calhoun (London: Oxford University Press, 2004), 288–305.

4. The going rate for housecleaning in Houston at the time was about $75/house, City-Data forum, May 2009, http://www.city-data.com/forum/houston/660009 -average-rate-house-cleaning.html. The difference between pay for a task and pay by

the hour has been important over the history of domestic work in America, joining the distinction between live-in and day work as one of the most significant factors in an employee's relative power. Romero identifies the distinction as time-based "labor power" versus skill-based "labor services," the latter allowing a worker to control her time and methods, in *Maid in the USA*.

5. Zelizer, *The Purchase of Intimacy*.

6. Emma Chichester Clark, *I Love You, Blue Kangaroo!* (New York: Doubleday Books for Young Readers, 1999).

7. Rich, *Of Woman Born*, 23.

8. Feder Kittay, "The Moral Harm of Migrant Carework."

Chapter 8 Telling Stories

1. A 2017 report of the UN's committee on the Elimination of Discrimination against Women reveals the social and legal causes of gender-based violence in El Salvador: social norms that enable a culture of violence, accept sexual relationships and marriage between young girls and older men, and expect wives to submit to husbands; low rates of investigation and conviction for domestic abuse, sex assault, and femicide; a lack of protection strategies for rampant gender-based violence and trafficking of girls by criminal gangs; legal recognition of pregnancy as a legitimate reason for marriage before the age of 18; and the absolute criminalization of abortion. See "Concluding Observations on the Combined Eighth and Ninth Periodic Reports of El Salvador," UN Committee on the Elimination of Discrimination Against Women, March 3, 2017, https://digitallibrary.un.org/record/863872?ln=en. Impunity for gender-based violence is pervasive in the region. Globally, in 2015, El Salvador ranked third for highest rate of violent deaths of women, Honduras fifth. Jeffrey Hallock, Ariel G. Ruiz Soto, and Michael Fix, "In Search of Safety, Growing Numbers of Women Flee Central America," Migration Policy Institute, May 30, 2018, https://www.migrationpolicy.org/article/search-safety-growing-numbers-women-flee-central-america.

2. The experience of migration has been shown to change migrant women's relationship to marriage, as they respond to increased power and autonomy, as well as challenges to cultural identity. Jennifer Hirsch, "'En el norte la mujer manda': Gender, Generation, and Geography in a Mexican Transnational Community," in *Women and Migration in the U.S.–Mexico Borderlands: A Reader*, ed. Denise Segura and Patricia Zevella (Durham, NC: Duke University Press, 2007), 438–55.

3. "Concluding Observations on the Combined Eighth and Ninth Periodic Reports of El Salvador"; Moloney, "In El Salvador, Girls Under 12 Most at Risk of Getting Pregnant by Rape: U.N. Study."

4. Though Sara hasn't encountered organizers, organizations like the NDWA take exactly this approach—talking with women in the local park and other gathering places to garner support for collective action.

5. In the margins of this interview's transcription, the transcriber who worked

with Julieta's interview has written *Classic dream of the Mexican immigrant; my little town is filled with these buildings.* Empty now, as life unfolds on the other side of migrant hope.

6. The Dictionary of Mexican Spanish gives familiar definitions of *rancho*—a large expanse of land for agriculture and raising animals; a home on this land, empty or inhabited—https://dem.colmex.mx/Ver/rancho. Rosa offers her colloquial definition: "We say it's a rancho because it's a town, a really small town, but in Mexico we also say 'rancho' for the people who have cows and horses and everything."

7. The pull of *allá*, back there, is familiar in literature and poetry of exiles and emigrants—that commonplace of migrant nostalgia for a sense of home that has become both space and time at once, a certain past in a certain place that is, in memory, as right and ideal as the habits and mismatched values of a foreign home are wrong.

8. On transnationalism as a pattern of migration, see Nina Glick Schiller, Linda Basch, and Cristina Szanton Blanc, "From Immigrant to Transmigrant: Theorizing Transnational Migration," *Anthropological Quarterly* 68 (1999): 48–63.

9. This dynamic is disrupted by cultural forms of Black motherhood in the US, which have developed a strong tradition of community-based mothering and hold transformative potential for all of us. See McClain, *We Live for the We.*

10. In her study of late-twentieth-century domestic labor, Ibarra identifies the "pain and possibility" engendered by a shadow industry defined by immigration, racial hierarchy, and opportunities for empowerment. Ibarra's sophisticated understanding of agency in what she calls the New Domestic Labor, focuses on a refined understanding of "the parameters of choice" that these women encounter. María Ibarra de la Luz, "Mexican Immigrant Women." For a discussion of the many layers of economic agency among Mexican and West Indian immigrant nannies, see Romero, *The Maid's Daughter,* and Brown, *Raising Brooklyn.*

Conclusion

1. The title of this section is a conscious allusion to Ann Crittenden's *The Price of Motherhood,* which lays out the financial price women pay as a result of their motherhood, relative to fathers.

2. Scholars have offered eloquent elaborations of the moral harm inherent in women's global migration for domestic work. Of note: Eva Feder Kittay, "The Moral Harm in Migrant Carework," and Joan Tronto, "The 'Nanny' Question." The ethics of care offers a framework to understand and address the moral dimensions of this harmful dynamic because it conceives of our personhood in the context of our relationships. In its relational focus, it differs fundamentally from Kantian and utilitarian moral philosophies that perceive only autonomous, self-interested individuals. The change in orientation has transformational potential.

3. The title of this section is a conscious allusion to Viviana Zelizer's *The Purchase of Intimacy,* which explores the intermingling of intimate relationships and economic transactions.

4. The National Domestic Workers Alliance is actively working along with other advocates toward state-by-state implementation of a National Domestic Workers' Bill of Rights that would ensure these regulations are enforced and do even more to professionalize domestic work. At the global level, the International Labour Organization adopted a convention in 2011 detailing a broad set of protections for workers, an accomplishment achieved largely through efforts of domestic worker organization. As of this writing, thirty countries—excluding the US—have ratified the convention, the most recent being Mexico. Ratifications of C189–Domestic Workers Convention, 2011, International Labour Organization, https://www.ilo.org/dyn/normlex /en/f?p=NORMLEXPUB:11300:0::NO::P11300_INSTRUMENT_ID:2551460, accessed April 1, 2021. Locally, organizations like the California Domestic Workers Coalition and Houston's own Fe y Justicia Worker Center have been working steadily to support their members.

5. Many thanks to Sergio Chávez, who has more than once shared his experiences, enthusiasm, and humor with my students.

6. Spanish, like most Romance languages, uses two forms of direct address, sometimes three, with a lot of variation among them. Though the rules of usage vary across region and social class, at its most basic, *tú* is for close friends and peers and *usted* is for strangers and elders, a signal of respect and social distance.

Index